COUNTY CORK, IRELAND

I0027696

A COLLECTION
OF
1851 CENSUS RECORDS

JOSEPHINE MASTERSON

CLEARFIELD

Printed with permission of
Dr. David V. Craig
Director of the National Archives
Dublin, Ireland

Printed for
Clearfield Company, Inc. by
Genealogical Publishing Co., Inc.
Baltimore, Maryland
1994

Reprinted for
Clearfield Company, Inc. by
Genealogical Publishing Co., Inc.
Baltimore, Maryland
1996, 1999, 2004

International Standard Book Number: 0-8063-4610-8

Made in the United States of America

TABLE OF CONTENTS

These are the townlands and respective parishes included in this
transcription:

Ballinacarriga	KC	Gurtone	KC
Ballinaparka N	LE	Kielbeg	LE
Ballinaparka S	LE	Kilally E	KW
Ballinglanna N	KC	Kilally W	KW
Ballinglanna S	KC	Kilclogh	MA
Ballinrush Lr	KC	Kilmurry N	LE
Ballinrush Up	KW	Kilmurry S	LE
Ballinvoher	KW	Kilworth	KW
Ballydarown Glebe	KC	Knockanabohelly	KC
Ballyderown	KC	Knockanohill	KW
Ballyhenden	KC	Knockaskehane	LE
Ballylackan	LE	Leitrim	LE
Ballyvoskillikin	KC	Loughnahilly	KC
Boherdeveroge	KC	Macroney Lr	MA
Castlecooke	MA	Macroney Up	MA
Coolalisheen	LE	Maryville	KW
Downing N	KC	Monedrisane	KW
Downing S	KC	Moorpark	KW
Glanseskin	KW	Sharroclure	MA
Glenwood	KC	Toor	KW
Graig	KW	Whitebog	KW

iii

1851 Census Records of Four Parishes of County Cork, Ireland
(The Union of Kilworth)

This transcription and index was done from a xeroxed copy of document
M4685 obtained from the National Archives in Dublin, Ireland, who hold a
photostatic copy of the original handwritten transcription. The location
of the original is not known by the National Archives. A transcript of
the original transcript (999/643), accessioned separately and at a different date, is also in their possession. It lists persons living (also some
absent from the household) in March of 1851. As far as I know this information is not available at this time (1992) in the United States on
film from the Family History Centers of The Church of Jesus Christ of
Latter-day Saints (LDS). The reason for this work was to make it available to genealogical researchers in the U. S. interested in Irish records.

The title County Cork Ireland, a Collection of 1851 Census Records is
used for brevity and library indexing purposes. The census records are
those of two parishes of County Cork (Kilcrumper and Kilworth) and parts
of two (Leitrim and Macroney), which make up the Union of Kilworth.

While working on this material it was noted that one page is missing
from the records for Downing North Townland, Kilcrumper Parish, consisting
of records 78 through 107, although the material obtained from Dublin
showed no consecutively numbered page or pages missing. This left two
children listed on page 24, numbers 108 and 109, without the rest of the
family. However, the missing information (see Appendix) was obtained from
the National Archives from their Manuscript 999/643 which is a duplicate
transcription done by another hand, accessioned separately at a different
date. It is believed that the Manuscript M4685 transcription was done by
Rev. Francis Brady whose name and family listing appear first in the

When looking over the manuscript in general it appears that the four
parishes are in the Barony of Condons and Clongibbon because this is the
only barony noted in some of the columns after the parish name. Another
omission which caused some confusion was that the name of the parish in
which the Townland of Loughnahilly is located, Kilcrumper, was not
indicated in the parish column. In the process of identifying the parish
for this townland it was noted that the townlands in the Parish of
Kilcrumper may be in the Barony of Condons and Clongibbon or in the Barony
of Fermoy. The original transcriber evidently did not bother to go into
detail on this subject, omitting both the parish (Kilcrumper) and the
barony (Fermoy) for the Townland of Loughnahilly. Approximately half of
the Parish of Kilcrumper is in one barony (Condons and Clongibbon) and the
other half is in another barony (Fermoy). This may be of interest to a
researcher trying to locate a townland in which his ancestors lived.

The Parishes of Kilcrumper and Kilworth appear to be complete except
for the one page missing from Kilcrumper Parish noted above which has been
added at the end as an Appendix, on the last page. The Parish of Leitrim
appears to have the Townlands of Ballynamuddagh, Cronohill, Knockatrasnane
and Propoge missing. The Parish of Macroney, consisting of about 16
townlands, has only five townlands represented: Castlecooke, Kilclogh,
Macroney Upper and Lower and Sharroclure. The explanation for this is
that the parishes included constituted the Union of Kilworth, a Church of
Ireland unit of administration established in the year 1692.

Variations in the spelling of the townlands make it difficult to account for those represented and those missing. Some variations are:

-Condons and Clongibbon Barony is sometimes spelled Condons and Clangibbon.

-Ballinacarriga Townland, listed in Kilcrumper Parish in Griffith's Valuation (1851-1853), is not found in that parish in the Census of Ireland, 1871, Alphabetical Index to the Townlands and Towns of Ireland. Lisnasallagh is found in Kilcrumper Parish, Barony of Fermoy, County Cork, in 1871 but not in 1851.

-Ballydarown Glebe is alphabetized before Ballyderown

-Ballyhenden may be found as Ballyhinden or Ballyhindon.

-Ballyvoskillikin was also found as Ballyvoskilleekeer.

-Boherdeveroge may be spelled Boherderroge.

-Graig was also found as Graigue.

-Gurtone, listed in Griffith's Valuation, was not found in the Index for 1871.

-Both Knockanabohelly and the spelling Knockanabohelee are found in Manuscript M4685 but Griffith's and the Index use Knockanenabohilly.

-Monedrisane was found also as Monadrishane.

It is not the purpose of this work to be definitive on this subject but the possiblity of variations should be mentioned so that the researcher has some idea of the problems he or she may encounter in locating the townlands.

A Guide to the columns and abbreviations in the transcription:

The census listings had household numbers starting with No. 1 for each townland. Instead of this number a computer number appears in the first column in order to sort by family groupings. The families are listed in the order in which they appear in the townland. For indexing purposes it was thought that listing by townland, in alphabetical order, was better than sorting by parish. The parish name is represented by abbreviations in a right hand column: KC for Kilcrumper, KW for Kilworth, LE for Leitrim and MA for Macroney.

Most of the abbreviations should be easily interpreted such as na for not available, hk for housekeeper, lab for laborer. Capital letters were used for D/L (daughter-in-law) and M/L (mother-in-law) because the small letter "l" may be confused with the number one.

The number in the extreme right hand column headed "page" refers to the page number where the listing is found on the photostatic copy should one want to consult this in Dublin at the National Archives.

NUM	SURNAME	GIVEN NAME	AGE	REL	OCCUP	REMARKS	TOWNLAND	PARISH	PAGE
001	SULLIVAN	Ellen	38	head		wife to John in Amer	Ballinacarriga	KC	08
001	SULLIVAN	David	13	son			Ballinacarriga	KC	08
001	SULLIVAN	Johanna	7	dau			Ballinacarriga	KC	08
001	SULLIVAN	Margaret	6	dau			Ballinacarriga	KC	08
001	SULLIVAN	Stephen	3	son			Ballinacarriga	KC	08
002	DOWNEY	Edmond	50	head	caretaker	widower	Ballinacarriga	KC	01
002	DOWNEY	Edmond	16	son			Ballinacarriga	KC	08
002	DOWNEY	William	14	son			Ballinacarriga	KC	08
002	DOWNEY	Jeremiah	12	son			Ballinacarriga	KC	08
002	DOWNEY	Cornelius	9	son			Ballinacarriga	KC	08
002	DOWNEY	James	7	son			Ballinacarriga	KC	08
002	HEFFERNON	Bridget	60	serv	hk		Ballinacarriga	KC	08
003	STEELE	John	60	head	lab		Ballinacarriga	KC	08
003	STEELE	Ellen	60	wife			Ballinacarriga	KC	08
004	FINN	Bartholomew	40	head	lab		Ballinacarriga	KC	08
004	FINN	Ellen	25	wife			Ballinacarriga	KC	08
004	FINN	Mary	2	dau			Ballinacarriga	KC	08
005	BOWEN	Catherine	30	head		widow	Ballinacarriga	KC	08
005	BOWEN	John	7	son			Ballinacarriga	KC	08
005	BOWEN	Bridget	2	dau			Ballinacarriga	KC	08
006	EGAN	Michael	35	head	lab		Ballinacarriga	KC	08
006	EGAN	Ellen	30	wife			Ballinacarriga	KC	08
006	EGAN	Eliza	5	dau			Ballinacarriga	KC	08
006	EGAN	James	3	son			Ballinacarriga	KC	08
006	EGAN	John	2	son			Ballinacarriga	KC	08
006	EGAN	Mary	30	sist			Ballinacarriga	KC	08
006	EGAN	Ellen	22	sist			Ballinacarriga	KC	08
006	SULLIVAN	Ann	20	lodg			Ballinacarriga	KC	08
007	WILKINSON	Michael	40	head	carpenter		Ballinacarriga	KC	09
007	WILKINSON	Mary	36	wife			Ballinacarriga	KC	09
007	WILKINSON	Catherine	16	dau			Ballinacarriga	KC	09
007	WILKINSON	William	9	son			Ballinacarriga	KC	09
007	WILKINSON	Bridget	7	dau			Ballinacarriga	KC	09
007	WILKINSON	Edmond	5	son			Ballinacarriga	KC	09
007	WILKINSON	Michael	3	son			Ballinacarriga	KC	09
008	BOWEN	James	36	head	lab		Ballinacarriga	KC	09
008	BOWEN	Ellen	28	wife			Ballinacarriga	KC	09
008	BOWEN	James	5	son			Ballinacarriga	KC	09
008	BOWEN	Bridget	2	dau			Ballinacarriga	KC	09
008	CROTTY	Mary	36	S/L			Ballinacarriga	KC	09
009	BOWEN	John	45	head	lab		Ballinacarriga	KC	09
009	BOWEN	Johanna	60	wife			Ballinacarriga	KC	09

009 BOWEN	Elizabeth	12	dau			Ballinacarriga	KC	09
012 RICE	Edmond	41	head	farmer		Ballinacarriga	KC	10
012 RICE	Eliza	40	wife			Ballinacarriga	KC	10
012 RICE	Mary	16	dau			Ballinacarriga	KC	10
012 RICE	William	14	son			Ballinacarriga	KC	10
012 RICE	Ellen	10	dau			Ballinacarriga	KC	10
012 RICE	Jane	8	dau			Ballinacarriga	KC	10
012 RICE	Edward	6	son			Ballinacarriga	KC	10
012 RICE	Richard	5	son			Ballinacarriga	KC	10
012 RICE	James	3	son			Ballinacarriga	KC	10
012 BOWEN	Anthony	32	serv	lab		Ballinacarriga	KC	10
012 HOSKIN	George	30	serv	lab		Ballinacarriga	KC	10
012 HEALY	John	40	serv	cow herd		Ballinacarriga	KC	10
012 DEVINE	William	18	serv	lab		Ballinacarriga	KC	10
012 PILLON	Mary	40	serv			Ballinacarriga	KC	10
012 DONOGHUE	Ellen	25	serv			Ballinacarriga	KC	10
012 LUBY	Ellen	24	serv			Ballinacarriga	KC	10
013 WOODS	Mary	60	head		widow	Ballinacarriga	KC	10
013 WOODS	Patrick	24	son	lab		Ballinacarriga	KC	10
013 WOODS	William	22	na	lab		Ballinacarriga	KC	10
013 WOODS	Maurice	18	son	lab		Ballinacarriga	KC	10
013 WOODS	Johanna	15	dau			Ballinacarriga	KC	10
013 WOODS	Ann	12	dau			Ballinacarriga	KC	10
013 WOODS	Margaret	10	dau			Ballinacarriga	KC	10
014 HENNESY	Ellen	40	wife		hus.Denis in America	Ballinacarriga	KC	10
014 HENNESY	James	7	son			Ballinacarriga	KC	10
014 HENNESY	Mary	4	dau			Ballinacarriga	KC	10
014 HENNESY	Catherine	18m	dau			Ballinacarriga	KC	10
014 DRAKE	Johanna	50	lodg			Ballinacarriga	KC	10
539 FLYNN	Edmond	56	head	carpenter		Ballinaparka N	LE	13
539 FLYNN	John	27	son	carpenter		Ballinaparka N	LE	13
539 FLYNN	Edmond	18	son	lab		Ballinaparka N	LE	13
540 BALDWIN	Cornelius	30	head	ploughman		Ballinaparka N	LE	13
540 BALDWIN	Mary	25	wife			Ballinaparka N	LE	13
540 BALDWIN	Johanna	7	dau			Ballinaparka N	LE	13
540 BALDWIN	Edmond	4	son			Ballinaparka N	LE	13
540 BALDWIN	Eliza	9 m	dau		(age unclear)	Ballinaparka N	LE	13
541 MYLES	Catherine	56	head	farmer	widow	Ballinaparka N	LE	13
541 MYLES	James	28	son	blacksmith		Ballinaparka N	LE	13
541 MYLES	Patrick	26	son	farmer		Ballinaparka N	LE	13
541 MYLES	Catherine	24	dau			Ballinaparka N	LE	13
541 MYLES	Daniel	20	son			Ballinaparka N	LE	13
541 MYLES	Edmond	16	son			Ballinaparka N	LE	13
542 DALY	James	38	head	schoolmaster		Ballinaparka N	LE	13
542 DALY	Honora	30	wife			Ballinaparka N	LE	13
542 DALY	John	5	son			Ballinaparka N	LE	13
542 DALY	David	6 m	son			Ballinaparka N	LE	13

542	SHEELY	Ellen	20	S/L		Ballinaparka N	LE	13
543	RICE	Richard	75	head farmer		Ballinaparka N	LE	13
543	RICE	Catherine	67	wife		Ballinaparka N	LE	13
543	RICE	Thomas	42	son farmer		Ballinaparka N	LE	13
543	RICE	John	38	son lab		Ballinaparka N	LE	13
543	RICE	Ellen	5	gr/d		Ballinaparka N	LE	13
543	BRIEN	John	15	serv		Ballinaparka N	LE	13
543	STANTON	Mary	40	visi		Ballinaparka N	LE	13
544	FLYNN	Thomas	46	head lab		Ballinaparka N	LE	13
544	FLYNN	Johanna	40	wife		Ballinaparka N	LE	13
544	FLYNN	Elen	16	dau		Ballinaparka N	LE	13
544	FLYNN	Mary	14	dau		Ballinaparka N	LE	13
544	FLYNN	Catherine	12	dau		Ballinaparka N	LE	13
544	FLYNN	Anne	10	dau		Ballinaparka N	LE	13
544	FLYNN	James	7	son		Ballinaparka N	LE	13
544	FLYNN	Thomas	5	son		Ballinaparka N	LE	13
544	FLYNN	John	3	son		Ballinaparka N	LE	13
545	BROUDER	John	40	head lab		Ballinaparka N	LE	13
545	BROUDER	Alice	32	wife		Ballinaparka N	LE	13
545	BROUDER	Patrick	9	son		Ballinaparka N	LE	13
545	BROUDER	Honora	5	dau	dau to John	Ballinaparka N	LE	14
545	BROUDER	Catherine	3	dau		Ballinaparka N	LE	14
546	COLBERT	Edmond	60	head lab		Ballinaparka N	LE	14
546	COLBERT	Ellen	16	dau		Ballinaparka N	LE	14
546	COLBERT	Bridget	14	dau		Ballinaparka N	LE	14
547	LINEHAN	Catherine	52	head	widow	Ballinaparka N	LE	14
547	McNAMARA	Ellen	40	sist		Ballinaparka N	LE	14
548	DORAN	Owen	30	head caretaker	to Mr. Campion	Ballinaparka N	LE	14
548	DORAN	Jane	26	wife		Ballinaparka N	LE	14
548	DORAN	Jane	5	dau		Ballinaparka N	LE	14
548	DORAN	Jeremiah	2	son		Ballinaparka N	LE	14
548	DORAN	Catherine	1 m	dau		Ballinaparka N	LE	14
548	DORAN	William	25	brot		Ballinaparka N	LE	14
548	BRIEN	John	5	Br/L		Ballinaparka N	LE	14
549	HEGARTY	Anne	50	head	widow, liv. alone	Ballinaparka S	LE	14
550	DORAN	Edward	46	head lab		Ballinaparka S	LE	14
550	DORAN	Mary	16	dau		Ballinaparka S	LE	14
550	DORAN	Margaret	9	dau		Ballinaparka S	LE	14
550	DORAN	Bridget	8	dau		Ballinaparka S	LE	14
010	KENRICK	William	60	head farmer		Ballinglanna N	KC	09
010	KENRICK	Catherine	60	wife		Ballinglanna N	KC	09
010	KENRICK	Mary	28	dau		Ballinglanna N	KC	09
010	KENRICK	Thomas	25	S/L lab		Ballinglanna N	KC	09
010	KENRICK	Catherine	18	dau		Ballinglanna N	KC	09
010	KENRICK	Hannah	14	dau		Ballinglanna N	KC	09

010 KENRICK	Michael	26	neph			Ballinglanna N	KC	09
011 MURPHY	Maurice	50	head farmer			Ballinglanna N	KC	09
011 MURPHY	Hannora	36	wife			Ballinglanna N	KC	09
011 MURPHY	Mary	13	dau			Ballinglanna N	KC	09
011 MURPHY	Hannah	11	dau			Ballinglanna N	KC	09
011 MURPHY	Thomas	9	son	son to Maurice		Ballinglanna N	KC	10
011 MURPHY	Daniel	6	son			Ballinglanna N	KC	10
011 MURPHY	Patrick	2	son			Ballinglanna N	KC	10
011 MURPHY	Patrick	56	brot lab			Ballinglanna N	KC	10
011 MURPHY	William	20	neph lab			Ballinglanna N	KC	10
011 MURPHY	Mary	23	niec			Ballinglanna N	KC	10
011 MURPHY	Hannah	18	niec			Ballinglanna N	KC	10
011 MURPHY	Ellen	15	niec			Ballinglanna N	KC	10
011 MURPHY	Thomas	10	neph			Ballinglanna N	KC	10
016 SULLIVAN	James	40	head farmer			Ballinglanna N	KC	10
016 SULLIVAN	Hannora	40	wife			Ballinglanna N	KC	10
016 SULLIVAN	Mary	60	moth			Ballinglanna N	KC	10
016 SULLIVAN	Ellen	30	sist			Ballinglanna N	KC	10
016 SULLIVAN	John	24	brot			Ballinglanna N	KC	10
016 SULLIVAN	Catherine	18	sist			Ballinglanna N	KC	10
016 TOOHILL	David	3	neph			Ballinglanna N	KC	10
017 TOOHILL	Edmond	46	head farmer			Ballinglanna N	KC	10
017 TOOHILL	Hannah	39	wife			Ballinglanna N	KC	10
017 TOOHILL	Edmond	18	son lab			Ballinglanna N	KC	10
017 TOOHILL	Catherine	11	dau			Ballinglanna N	KC	10
017 TOOHILL	James	9	son			Ballinglanna N	KC	10
017 TOOHILL	Patrick	7	son			Ballinglanna N	KC	10
017 TOOHILL	Elenor	5	dau			Ballinglanna N	KC	10
017 TOOHILL	John	3	son			Ballinglanna N	KC	10
017 TOOHILL	David	15m	son			Ballinglanna N	KC	10
017 TOOHILL	Edmond	20	neph			Ballinglanna N	KC	10
017 TOOHILL	James	47	cous			Ballinglanna N	KC	10
017 TOOHILL	Ellen	21	niec			Ballinglanna N	KC	10
017 COURTNEY	John	23	serv lab			Ballinglanna N	KC	10
018 TOOHILL	Edward	55	head farmer			Ballinglanna N	KC	10
018 TOOHILL	Julia	53	wife			Ballinglanna N	KC	10
018 TOOHILL	Bridget	17	dau			Ballinglanna N	KC	10
019 TOOHILL	Edmond	68	head farmer			Ballinglanna N	KC	11
019 TOOHILL	Eliza	52	wife			Ballinglanna N	KC	11
019 TOOHILL	Patrick	26	son farmer			Ballinglanna N	KC	11
019 TOOHILL	James	24	son lab			Ballinglanna N	KC	11
019 TOOHILL	John	22	son lab			Ballinglanna N	KC	11
019 TOOHILL	Edmond	15	son lab			Ballinglanna N	KC	11
019 TOOHILL	Maurice	13	son			Ballinglanna N	KC	11
019 TOOHILL	David	10	son			Ballinglanna N	KC	11
019 TOOHILL	Eliza	20	dau			Ballinglanna N	KC	11
019 TOOHILL	Johanna	18	dau			Ballinglanna N	KC	11
019 TOOHILL	Susan	11	dau			Ballinglanna N	KC	11

020 O'NEIL	Cornelius	30	head lab		Ballinglanna N	KC	11
020 O'NEIL	Mary	25	wife		Ballinglanna N	KC	11
020 O'NEIL	Michael	5	son		Ballinglanna N	KC	11
020 O'NEIL	Patrick	3	son		Ballinglanna N	KC	11
021 MEAGHER	John	60	head farmer		Ballinglanna N	KC	11
021 MEAGHER	Honora	58	wife		Ballinglanna N	KC	11
021 MEAGHER	Margaret	21	dau		Ballinglanna N	KC	11
021 MEAGHER	Terence	19	son		Ballinglanna N	KC	11
021 MEAGHER	Honora	17	dau		Ballinglanna N	KC	11
021 REGAN	Edmond	30	st/s		Ballinglanna N	KC	11
021 REGAN	Margaret	27	wife	wife to Edmond	Ballinglanna N	KC	11
022 DIVINE	James	60	head farmer		Ballinglanna N	KC	11
022 DIVINE	Ellen	56	wife		Ballinglanna N	KC	11
022 DIVINE	John	30	son lab		Ballinglanna N	KC	11
022 DIVINE	James	8	son		Ballinglanna N	KC	11
022 WHITE	Catherine	18	serv		Ballinglanna N	KC	11
023 DIVINE	James	52	head farmer		Ballinglanna N	KC	11
023 DIVINE	Catherine	35	wife		Ballinglanna N	KC	11
023 DIVINE	Edmond	19	son lab		Ballinglanna N	KC	11
023 DIVINE	James	17	son lab		Ballinglanna N	KC	11
023 DIVINE	Michael	10	son		Ballinglanna N	KC	11
023 DIVINE	Mary	8	dau		Ballinglanna N	KC	11
024 DIVINE	Thomas	52	head farmer		Ballinglanna N	KC	11
024 DIVINE	Catherine	45	wife		Ballinglanna N	KC	11
024 DIVINE	William	23	son		Ballinglanna N	KC	11
024 DIVINE	Thomas	10	son		Ballinglanna N	KC	11
024 DIVINE	James	8	son		Ballinglanna N	KC	11
024 DIVINE	Daniel	4	son		Ballinglanna N	KC	11
024 DIVINE	Mary	1 m	dau		Ballinglanna N	KC	11
024 CURTIN	Daniel	48	brot		Ballinglanna N	KC	11
024 CURTIN	Denis	14	neph		Ballinglanna N	KC	11
025 McNAMARA	Michael	50	head farmer		Ballinglanna S	KC	11
025 McNAMARA	Elizabeth	40	wife		Ballinglanna S	KC	11
025 McNAMARA	Cornelius	19	son lab		Ballinglanna S	KC	11
025 McNAMARA	Maurice	18	son lab		Ballinglanna S	KC	11
025 McNAMARA	Mary	16	dau		Ballinglanna S	KC	11
025 McNAMARA	Daniel	14	son		Ballinglanna S	KC	11
025 McNAMARA	Michael	12	son		Ballinglanna S	KC	11
025 McNAMARA	Edward	10	son		Ballinglanna S	KC	11
025 McNAMARA	Ellen	8	dau		Ballinglanna S	KC	11
025 McNAMARA	Catherine	6	dau		Ballinglanna S	KC	11
025 McNAMARA	John	4	son		Ballinglanna S	KC	11
025 McNAMARA	James	10m	son		Ballinglanna S	KC	11
026 CONDON	Ellen	80	head	widow	Ballinglanna S	KC	11
026 CONDON	Michael	35	son farmer		Ballinglanna S	KC	11
026 CONDON	Patrick	30	son farmer		Ballinglanna S	KC	11
026 CONDON	Bridget	10	gr/d		Ballinglanna S	KC	11
026 GEARY	Catherine	25	visi		Ballinglanna S	KC	11

027 NUNAN	Johanna	74	head	widow	Ballinglanna S	KC	11
027 NUNAN	John	37	son farmer		Ballinglanna S	KC	11
027 NUNAN	William	35	son farmer		Ballinglanna S	KC	12
027 NUNAN	Ellen	33	D/L		Ballinglanna S	KC	12
027 NUNAN	Patrick	2	gr/s		Ballinglanna S	KC	12
027 NUNAN	Honora	11m	gr/d		Ballinglanna S	KC	12
027 DALTON	Honora	18	serv		Ballinglanna S	KC	12
028 NUNAN	Mary	70	head	widow	Ballinglanna S	KC	12
028 NUNAN	John	43	son farmer		Ballinglanna S	KC	12
028 NUNAN	Honora	34	D/L	wife to John	Ballinglanna S	KC	12
028 NUNAN	Ellen	12	gr/d	dau to John	Ballinglanna S	KC	12
028 NUNAN	Mary	10	gr/d		Ballinglanna S	KC	12
028 NUNAN	Catherine	8	gr/d		Ballinglanna S	KC	12
028 NUNAN	Maurice	6	gr/s		Ballinglanna S	KC	12
028 NUNAN	Edmond	4	gr/s		Ballinglanna S	KC	12
028 NUNAN	Honora	3	gr/d		Ballinglanna S	KC	12
028 NUNAN	Michael	1 m	gr/s		Ballinglanna S	KC	12
028 NUNAN	Patrick	28	serv	(same surname)	Ballinglanna S	KC	12
028 RICE	Bridget	20	serv		Ballinglanna S	KC	12
029 SULLIVAN	John	27	head farmer		Ballinglanna S	KC	12
029 SULLIVAN	Patrick	24	brot lab		Ballinglanna S	KC	12
029 SULLIVAN	Honora	25	sist		Ballinglanna S	KC	12
030 GERAN	Daniel	45	head coroner&farm Esq.		Ballinrush Lr	KC	04
030 GERAN	Maryann	38	wife		Ballinrush Lr	KC	04
030 GERAN	Allice	8	dau		Ballinrush Lr	KC	04
030 GERAN	Anthony	7	son		Ballinrush Lr	KC	04
030 GERAN	Edward	6	son		Ballinrush Lr	KC	04
030 GERAN	Mary	4	dau		Ballinrush Lr	KC	04
030 GERAN	Daniel	3	son		Ballinrush Lr	KC	04
030 CRONAN	Mary	42	serv		Ballinrush Lr	KC	04
030 DWYER	Mary	18	serv		Ballinrush Lr	KC	04
030 BRADY	Margaret	60	serv hk		Ballinrush Lr	KC	04
030 TWOMY	Mary	40	serv milkmaid		Ballinrush Lr	KC	04
030 ROCHE	Mary	74	visi		Ballinrush Lr	KC	04
030 SHEEHAN	David	60	serv steward		Ballinrush Lr	KC	04
030 BROUDER	Richard	16	serv		Ballinrush Lr	KC	04
030 CASEY	Mary	15	serv milkmaid		Ballinrush Lr	KC	04
030 ROCHE	Mary	40	serv milk woman		Ballinrush Lr	KC	04
030 ROCHE	Margaret	16	serv milkmaid		Ballinrush Lr	KC	04
031 PINE	Walter	52	head lab	employer Mr. GERAN	Ballinrush Lr	KC	04
031 PINE	Johanna	43	wife		Ballinrush Lr	KC	04
031 PINE	David	28	son lab		Ballinrush Lr	KC	04
031 PINE	John	23	son lab		Ballinrush Lr	KC	04
031 PINE	Edward	21	son lab		Ballinrush Lr	KC	04
031 PINE	Walter	18	son lab		Ballinrush Lr	KC	04
031 PINE	Patrick	12	son		Ballinrush Lr	KC	04
031 PINE	Catherine	10	dau		Ballinrush Lr	KC	04
032 HURLY	John	45	head ploughman	employer Mr. GERAN	Ballinrush Lr	KC	04
032 HURLY	Bridget	37	wife		Ballinrush Lr	KC	04

032 HURLY	Timothy	45	son	(age s/b 15? sic)	Ballinrush Lr	KC	04
032 HURLY	Eliza	13	dau		Ballinrush Lr	KC	04
032 HURLY	Mary	11	dau		Ballinrush Lr	KC	04
032 HURLY	Norry	9	dau		Ballinrush Lr	KC	04
032 HURLY	Patrick	7	son		Ballinrush Lr	KC	05
032 HURLY	Maurice	5	son		Ballinrush Lr	KC	05
032 HURLY	Bridget	3	dau		Ballinrush Lr	KC	05
033 LEHANE	Johanna	48	head	widow	Ballinrush Lr	KC	05
033 LEHANE	Daniel	23	son lab		Ballinrush Lr	KC	05
033 LEHANE	Denis	19	son lab		Ballinrush Lr	KC	05
033 LEHANE	Cornelius	10	son		Ballinrush Lr	KC	05
034 CONDON	John	52	head wood ranger	empl. E. McCASHEL	Ballinrush Lr	KC	05
034 CONDON	Eliza	78	moth		Ballinrush Lr	KC	05
034 CONDON	William	14	son		Ballinrush Lr	KC	05
034 CONDON	Eliza	10	dau		Ballinrush Lr	KC	05
034 CONDON	Mary	8	dau		Ballinrush Lr	KC	05
034 CONDON	Maurice	7	son		Ballinrush Lr	KC	05
034 McCRAITH	Jeremiah	24	serv lab		Ballinrush Lr	KC	05
034 MEARA	Mary	48	serv		Ballinrush Lr	KC	05
035 COURTNEY	Edward	36	head farmer		Ballinrush Lr	KC	05
035 COURTNEY	Margaret	28	wife		Ballinrush Lr	KC	05
035 COURTNEY	Mary	24	sist		Ballinrush Lr	KC	05
035 COURTNEY	John	40	serv lab		Ballinrush Lr	KC	05
035 COURTNEY	Catherine	18	serv		Ballinrush Lr	KC	05
036 CALLAGHAN	Timothy	64	head farmer		Ballinrush Lr	KC	05
036 CALLAGHAN	Mary	52	wife		Ballinrush Lr	KC	05
036 CALLAGHAN	Thomas	26	son lab		Ballinrush Lr	KC	05
036 CALLAGHAN	Maurice	18	son lab		Ballinrush Lr	KC	05
036 CALLAGHAN	Mary	14	dau		Ballinrush Lr	KC	05
037 CASEY	John	40	head farmer	and road contractor	Ballinrush Lr	KC	05
037 CASEY	Margaret	33	wife		Ballinrush Lr	KC	05
037 CASEY	William	12	son		Ballinrush Lr	KC	05
037 CASEY	Catherine	8	dau		Ballinrush Lr	KC	05
037 CASEY	Margaret	6	dau		Ballinrush Lr	KC	05
037 CASEY	John	4	son		Ballinrush Lr	KC	05
037 CASEY	Patrick	1	son	age 1 yr 10 mo	Ballinrush Lr	KC	05
037 O'BRIEN	Eliza	22	serv		Ballinrush Lr	KC	05
038 McCRAITH	Redmond	42	head lab		Ballinrush Lr	KC	05
038 McCRAITH	Bridget	10	dau		Ballinrush Lr	KC	05
038 McCRAITH	Daniel	5	son		Ballinrush Lr	KC	05
038 McDONNELL	Johanna	25	serv		Ballinrush Lr	KC	05
039 DRAKE	Thomas	30	head farmer		Ballinrush Lr	KC	05
039 DRAKE	Margaret	30	wife		Ballinrush Lr	KC	05
039 DRAKE	William	45	brot		Ballinrush Lr	KC	05
039 DRAKE	John	3	son		Ballinrush Lr	KC	05
039 NUNAN	David	35	serv		Ballinrush Lr	KC	05

040 DIVINE	James	60	head farmer		Ballinrush Lr	KC	05
040 DIVINE	Catherine	35	wife		Ballinrush Lr	KC	05
040 DIVINE	Ellen	27	dau		Ballinrush Lr	KC	05
040 DIVINE	Michael	16	son lab		Ballinrush Lr	KC	05
040 DIVINE	Catherine	14	dau		Ballinrush Lr	KC	05
040 DIVINE	Ann	9	dau		Ballinrush Lr	KC	05
040 DIVINE	Johanna	7	dau		Ballinrush Lr	KC	05
041 McCRAITH	David	48	head farmer		Ballinrush Lr	KC	05
041 McCRAITH	Catherine	48	wife farmer		Ballinrush Lr	KC	05
042 RIORDAN	Mary	56	head	widow	Ballinrush Lr	KC	05
042 RIORDAN	Margaret	19	dau		Ballinrush Lr	KC	05
042 RIORDAN	John	15	son		Ballinrush Lr	KC	05
043 HANLON	Patrick	52	head lab		Ballinrush Lr	KC	06
043 HANLON	Johanna	54	wife		Ballinrush Lr	KC	06
043 HANLON	Maurice	17	son lab		Ballinrush Lr	KC	06
043 HANLON	Catherine	23	dau		Ballinrush Lr	KC	06
043 HANLON	John	14	son		Ballinrush Lr	KC	06
044 RIORDAN	William	70	head farmer		Ballinrush Lr	KC	06
044 RIORDAN	Michael	26	son lab		Ballinrush Lr	KC	06
044 RIORDAN	Bridget	16	dau		Ballinrush Lr	KC	06
045 SULLIVAN	John	58	head lab		Ballinrush Lr	KC	06
045 SULLIVAN	Catherine	50	wife		Ballinrush Lr	KC	06
045 SULLIVAN	William	13	son		Ballinrush Lr	KC	06
045 SULLIVAN	John	9	son		Ballinrush Lr	KC	06
045 SULLIVAN	Ellen	6	dau		Ballinrush Lr	KC	06
131 MAHONY	John	50	head farmer		Ballinrush Up	KW	06
131 MAHONY	Catherine	38	wife		Ballinrush Up	KW	06
131 MAHONY	Thomas	17	son		Ballinrush Up	KW	06
131 MAHONY	Mary	15	dau		Ballinrush Up	KW	06
131 MAHONY	John	11	son		Ballinrush Up	KW	06
131 MAHONY	Honora	9	dau		Ballinrush Up	KW	06
131 MAHONY	Edward	6	son		Ballinrush Up	KW	06
132 KEEFFE	Ellen	52	head	widow	Ballinrush Up	KW	06
132 CORMICK	James	21	son		Ballinrush Up	KW	06
132 DIVINE	Mary	50	visi		Ballinrush Up	KW	06
132 COURTNEY	Susan	50	visi		Ballinrush Up	KW	06
132 COURTNEY	Michael	18	visi		Ballinrush Up	KW	06
133 COURTNEY	Honora	65	head farmer	widow	Ballinrush Up	KW	06
133 COURTNEY	Edmond	42	son lab		Ballinrush Up	KW	06
133 COURTNEY	Thomas	28	son lab		Ballinrush Up	KW	06
133 COURTNEY	Mary	23	dau		Ballinrush Up	KW	06
133 COURTNEY	Patrick	13	serv	(same surname)	Ballinrush Up	KW	06
134 CONDON	Martin	40	head farmer		Ballinrush Up	KW	06
134 CONDON	Mary	38	wife		Ballinrush Up	KW	06
134 CONDON	Thomas	7	son		Ballinrush Up	KW	06

134	CONDON	David	5	son		Ballinrush Up	KW	06
134	CONDON	Catherine	3	dau		Ballinrush Up	KW	06
134	CONDON	Honora	4 m	dau		Ballinrush Up	KW	06
134	CAHILL	John	15	serv		Ballinrush Up	KW	06
135	COURTNEY	John	60	head farmer		Ballinrush Up	KW	06
135	COURTNEY	Ellen	55	wife		Ballinrush Up	KW	06
135	COURTNEY	Mary	18	dau		Ballinrush Up	KW	06
136	CLEARY	Denis	40	head lab		Ballinrush Up	KW	06
136	CLEARY	Margaret	30	wife		Ballinrush Up	KW	06
136	CLEARY	John	11	son		Ballinrush Up	KW	06
136	CLEARY	Daniel	5	son		Ballinrush Up	KW	06
137	HOWARD	William	60	head lab		Ballinrush Up	KW	06
137	HOWARD	Catherine	36	wife		Ballinrush Up	KW	06
137	HOWARD	George	17	son lab		Ballinrush Up	KW	06
137	HOWARD	Michael	15	son		Ballinrush Up	KW	06
138	JOYCE	Michael	40	head lab		Ballinrush Up	KW	06
138	JOYCE	Mary	30	wife		Ballinrush Up	KW	06
139	FING	William	50	head lab		Ballinrush Up	KW	06
139	FING	Johanna	60	wife		Ballinrush Up	KW	06
139	FING	James	13	son		Ballinrush Up	KW	06
139	FING	Margaret	8	dau		Ballinrush Up	KW	06
140	COURTNEY	David	50	head lab		Ballinrush Up	KW	07
140	COURTNEY	Mary	40	wife		Ballinrush Up	KW	07
140	COURTNEY	Thomas	13	son		Ballinrush Up	KW	07
140	COURTNEY	Edmond	9	son		Ballinrush Up	KW	07
140	COURTNEY	Margaret	40	visi	(same surname)	Ballinrush Up	KW	07
141	NEIL	Margaret	57	head farmer	widow	Ballinrush Up	KW	07
141	NEIL	Stephen	22	son farmer		Ballinrush Up	KW	07
141	NEIL	Catherine	23	dau		Ballinrush Up	KW	07
141	NEIL	Ellen	20	dau		Ballinrush Up	KW	07
141	NEIL	John	19	son		Ballinrush Up	KW	07
142	NEIL	Margaret	42	head farmer	widow	Ballinrush Up	KW	07
142	NEIL	Mary	24	dau		Ballinrush Up	KW	07
142	NEIL	Michael	22	son farmer		Ballinrush Up	KW	07
142	NEIL	Thomas	19	son lab		Ballinrush Up	KW	07
142	NEIL	Ellen	16	dau		Ballinrush Up	KW	07
142	NEIL	John	14	son		Ballinrush Up	KW	07
142	NEIL	Myles	12	son		Ballinrush Up	KW	07
142	MURPHY	Catherine	3	gr/d		Ballinrush Up	KW	07
142	MURPHY	Margaret	2	gr/d		Ballinrush Up	KW	07
143	SULLIVAN	Patrick	45	head weaver		Ballinrush Up	KW	07
143	SULLIVAN	Bridget	41	wife		Ballinrush Up	KW	07
143	SULLIVAN	Patrick	17	son		Ballinrush Up	KW	07
143	SULLIVAN	Denis	13	son		Ballinrush Up	KW	07
143	SULLIVAN	Mary	10	dau		Ballinrush Up	KW	07

143 SULLIVAN	John	5	son		Ballinrush Up	KW	07
144 RYAN	Margaret	65	head farmer	widow	Ballinrush Up	KW	07
144 RYAN	Michael	20	son		Ballinrush Up	KW	07
144 RYAN	Ellen	18	dau		Ballinrush Up	KW	07
144 RYAN	Patrick	16	son		Ballinrush Up	KW	07
144 ROCHE	John	3	rel.	relative	Ballinrush Up	KW	07
145 RYAN	Michael	55	head farmer		Ballinrush Up	KW	07
145 RYAN	Catherine	43	wife		Ballinrush Up	KW	07
145 RYAN	Margaret	19	dau		Ballinrush Up	KW	07
145 RYAN	John	17	son		Ballinrush Up	KW	07
145 RYAN	Rodger	14	son		Ballinrush Up	KW	07
145 RYAN	Michael	12	son		Ballinrush Up	KW	07
145 RYAN	Honora	9	dau		Ballinrush Up	KW	07
145 RYAN	Mary	7	dau		Ballinrush Up	KW	07
145 RYAN	Catherine	2	dau		Ballinrush Up	KW	07
145 BERMINGHAM	John	14	visi		Ballinrush Up	KW	07
145 CONROY	Ellen	14	visi		Ballinrush Up	KW	07
146 McDONALD	Mary	38	head	widow	Ballinrush Up	KW	07
146 McDONALD	Michael	14	son		Ballinrush Up	KW	07
146 McDONALD	Thomas	14	son		Ballinrush Up	KW	07
146 CONDON	Ellen	50	lodg	widow	Ballinrush Up	KW	07
146 CONDON	Thomas	12	son	son to Ellen	Ballinrush Up	KW	07
146 CONDON	Patrick	8	son	son to Ellen	Ballinrush Up	KW	07
147 LEAHY	Jeremiah	54	head lab		Ballinrush Up	KW	07
147 LEAHY	Mary	17	dau		Ballinrush Up	KW	07
147 LEAHY	Catherine	13	dau		Ballinrush Up	KW	07
148 CROTTY	James	45	head lab		Ballinrush Up	KW	07
148 CROTTY	Johanna	35	wife		Ballinrush Up	KW	07
148 CROTTY	John	12	son		Ballinrush Up	KW	07
148 CROTTY	Mary	10	dau		Ballinrush Up	KW	07
148 CROTTY	James	8	son		Ballinrush Up	KW	07
148 CROTTY	Jeremiah	6	son		Ballinrush Up	KW	07
148 CROTTY	Bridget	2	dau	age 2 yrs 9 mo	Ballinrush Up	KW	07
149 RYAN	Patrick	41	head farmer		Ballinrush Up	KW	08
149 RYAN	Mary	35	wife		Ballinrush Up	KW	08
149 RYAN	Michael	14	son		Ballinrush Up	KW	08
149 RYAN	Bridget	13	dau		Ballinrush Up	KW	08
149 RYAN	John	10	son		Ballinrush Up	KW	08
149 RYAN	Patrick	8	son		Ballinrush Up	KW	08
149 RYAN	Margaret	4	dau		Ballinrush Up	KW	08
150 CARROLL	Maurice	80	head farmer		Ballinrush Up	KW	08
150 CARROLL	Patrick	33	son farmer		Ballinrush Up	KW	08
150 CARROLL	Mary	30	D/L		Ballinrush Up	KW	08
150 CARROLL	Ellen	12	gr/d		Ballinrush Up	KW	08
150 CARROLL	Timothy	11	gr/s		Ballinrush Up	KW	08
150 CARROLL	Johanna	9	gr/d		Ballinrush Up	KW	08
150 CARROLL	Maurice	7	gr/s		Ballinrush Up	KW	08

150	CARROLL	John	4	gr/s		Ballinrush Up	KW	08
150	CARROLL	Patrick	2	gr/s		Ballinrush Up	KW	08
150	RYALL	Bartholomew	18	serv lab		Ballinrush Up	KW	08
151	O'DONNELL	Michael	40	head farmer		Ballinrush Up	KW	08
151	O'DONNELL	Johanna	35	wife		Ballinrush Up	KW	08
151	O'DONNELL	Rodger	12	son		Ballinrush Up	KW	08
151	O'DONNELL	Eliza	9	dau		Ballinrush Up	KW	09
151	O'DONNELL	Catherine	7	dau		Ballinrush Up	KW	08
151	O'DONNELL	Bridget	5	dau		Ballinrush Up	KW	08
151	O'DONNELL	Michael	2	son		Ballinrush Up	KW	08
151	O'DONNELL	Elizabeth	70	rel.	relative	Ballinrush Up	KW	08
152	DALY	Owen	65	head farmer		Ballinrush Up	KW	08
152	DALY	Margaret	70	wife		Ballinrush Up	KW	08
152	DALY	Patrick	31	son		Ballinrush Up	KW	08
152	DALY	Mary	28	D/L		Ballinrush Up	KW	08
152	DALY	Johanna	4	gr/d		Ballinrush Up	KW	08
152	DALY	Michael	2	son	(grandson?)	Ballinrush Up	KW	08
153	COLBERT	John	40	head lab		Ballinrush Up	KW	09
153	COLBERT	Ellen	36	wife		Ballinrush Up	KW	09
153	COLBERT	Edmond	14	son		Ballinrush Up	KW	09
153	COLBERT	David	11	son		Ballinrush Up	KW	09
153	COLBERT	Michael	4	son		Ballinrush Up	KW	09
153	COLBERT	Mary	2	dau		Ballinrush Up	KW	09
154	ROCHE	David	52	head farmer		Ballinrush Up	KW	09
154	ROCHE	Johanna	53	wife		Ballinrush Up	KW	09
154	ROCHE	Bridget	22	dau		Ballinrush Up	KW	09
154	ROCHE	Catherine	20	dau		Ballinrush Up	KW	09
154	ROCHE	Johanna	17	dau		Ballinrush Up	KW	09
154	ROCHE	Mary	13	dau		Ballinrush Up	KW	09
155	CLIFFORD	John	53	head farmer		Ballinrush Up	KW	09
155	CLIFFORD	Margaret	50	wife		Ballinrush Up	KW	09
155	CLIFFORD	John	19	son lab		Ballinrush Up	KW	09
155	CLIFFORD	Michael	17	son lab		Ballinrush Up	KW	09
155	CLIFFORD	Patrick	15	son lab		Ballinrush Up	KW	09
155	CLIFFORD	James	10	son		Ballinrush Up	KW	09
155	CLIFFORD	William	6	son		Ballinrush Up	KW	09
155	PINCHON	Michael	30	S/L		Ballinrush Up	KW	09
155	PINCHON	Elizabeth	24	D/L	(daughter?)	Ballinrush Up	KW	09
156	KENNEDY	Michael	40	head lab		Ballinrush Up	KW	09
156	KENNEDY	Margaret	33	wife		Ballinrush Up	KW	09
156	KENNEDY	John	10	son		Ballinrush Up	KW	09
156	KENNEDY	Bridget	8	dau		Ballinrush Up	KW	09
156	KENNEDY	Catherine	6	dau		Ballinrush Up	KW	09
156	KENNEDY	Mary	9 m	dau		Ballinrush Up	KW	09
157	ROCHE	Honora	67	head farmer	widow	Ballinvoher	KW	14
157	DAWSON	Catherine	65	sist		Ballinvoher	KW	14
157	DAWSON	John	30	neph		Ballinvoher	KW	14

157 DAWSON	Catherine	24	niec		Ballinvoher	KW	14
158 DAWSON	Michael	40	head lab		Ballinvoher	KW	14
158 BRIEN	Mary	20	niec		Ballinvoher	KW	14
159 RUSSELL	Michael	48	head farmer		Ballinvoher	KW	14
159 RUSSELL	Mary	37	wife		Ballinvoher	KW	14
159 RUSSELL	Catherine	17	dau		Ballinvoher	KW	14
159 RUSSELL	Margaret	15	dau		Ballinvoher	KW	14
159 RUSSELL	Mary	13	dau		Ballinvoher	KW	14
159 RUSSELL	Johanna	11	dau		Ballinvoher	KW	14
159 RUSSELL	Bridget	9	dau		Ballinvoher	KW	14
159 RUSSELL	Ellen	7	dau		Ballinvoher	KW	14
159 RUSSELL	Ann	5	dau		Ballinvoher	KW	14
159 RUSSELL	Honnora	2	dau		Ballinvoher	KW	14
159 RUSSELL	Eliza	1 m	dau		Ballinvoher	KW	14
159 MOLOWPHY	Maurice	36	serv lab		Ballinvoher	KW	14
159 MOLOWPHY	Maurice	14	serv		Ballinvoher	KW	14
160 RYALL	Bartholomew	38	head lab		Ballinvoher	KW	14
160 RYALL	Catherine	40	wife		Ballinvoher	KW	14
160 RYALL	James	15	cous		Ballinvoher	KW	14
161 SULLIVAN	Florence	45	head farmer	(male)	Ballinvoher	KW	14
161 SULLIVAN	Mary	50	wife		Ballinvoher	KW	14
161 SULLIVAN	Ellen	15	dau		Ballinvoher	KW	14
161 SULLIVAN	Elizabeth	12	dau		Ballinvoher	KW	14
161 SULLIVAN	Michael	7	son		Ballinvoher	KW	14
161 HOWE	Martin	21	serv lab		Ballinvoher	KW	14
162 COSKERAN	Margaret	62	head	widow	Ballinvoher	KW	14
162 COSKERAN	Edmond	22	son		Ballinvoher	KW	14
163 MOLOWPHY	Bridget	60	head	widow	Ballinvoher	KW	14
163 MOLOWPHY	James	23	son lab		Ballinvoher	KW	14
163 MOLOWPHY	Bridget	16	dau		Ballinvoher	KW	14
163 MOLOWPHY	James	40	B/L		Ballinvoher	KW	14
163 MOLOWPHY	Catherine	22	niec		Ballinvoher	KW	14
163 KELEHER	Margaret	4	gr/d		Ballinvoher	KW	14
163 JOYCE	Ellen	80	sist		Ballinvoher	KW	14
164 BRIEN	Thomas	40	head farmer		Ballinvoher	KW	15
164 BRIEN	Johanna	30	wife		Ballinvoher	KW	15
164 BRIEN	Catherine	8	dau		Ballinvoher	KW	15
164 BRIEN	Patrick	5	son		Ballinvoher	KW	15
164 BRIEN	Mary	4	dau		Ballinvoher	KW	15
164 BRIEN	John	8 m	son		Ballinvoher	KW	15
164 BRIEN	John	37	brot		Ballinvoher	KW	15
165 SCANLON	John	35	head lab		Ballinvoher	KW	15
165 SCANLON	Mary	28	wife		Ballinvoher	KW	15
166 KEEFFE	John	43	head lab		Ballinvoher	KW	15
166 KEEFFE	Johanna	45	wife		Ballinvoher	KW	15

166 KEEFFE	Patrick	16	son	lab		Ballinvoher	KW	15
166 KEEFFE	Daniel	14	son			Ballinvoher	KW	15
166 KEEFFE	Michael	10	son			Ballinvoher	KW	15
166 KEEFFE	Ellen	8	dau			Ballinvoher	KW	15
166 KEEFFE	Jeremiah	4	son			Ballinvoher	KW	15
167 BRIEN	William	30	head	farmer		Ballinvoher	KW	15
167 BRIEN	Honora	25	wife			Ballinvoher	KW	15
167 BRIEN	Catherine	6	dau			Ballinvoher	KW	15
168 FLANAGAN	James	51	head	farmer		Ballinvoher	KW	15
168 FLANAGAN	Bridget	43	wife			Ballinvoher	KW	15
168 FLANAGAN	Catherine	9	dau			Ballinvoher	KW	15
168 FLANAGAN	David	7	son			Ballinvoher	KW	15
168 FLANAGAN	Jeremiah	5	son			Ballinvoher	KW	15
168 FLANAGAN	Bridget	1	dau			Ballinvoher	KW	15
168 CLEARY	Thomas	16	serv	lab		Ballinvoher	KW	15
169 FLANAGAN	Arthur	46	head	farmer		Ballinvoher	KW	15
169 FLANAGAN	Margaret	36	wife			Ballinvoher	KW	15
169 FLANAGAN	Michael	6	son			Ballinvoher	KW	15
169 FLANAGAN	Margaret	3	dau			Ballinvoher	KW	15
170 CASEY	Johanna	47	head	farmer	widow	Ballinvoher	KW	15
170 CASEY	Ellen	22	dau			Ballinvoher	KW	15
170 CASEY	Julia	20	dau			Ballinvoher	KW	15
170 CASEY	Mary	18	dau			Ballinvoher	KW	15
170 CASEY	Michael	16	son			Ballinvoher	KW	15
170 CASEY	Johanna	12	dau			Ballinvoher	KW	15
170 CASEY	Nancy	11	dau			Ballinvoher	KW	15
170 CASEY	John	9	son			Ballinvoher	KW	15
170 CASEY	Thomas	7	son			Ballinvoher	KW	15
170 CASEY	Patrick	40	rel.		relative	Ballinvoher	KW	15
170 ENGLISH	Phillip	30	serv			Ballinvoher	KW	15
171 SCANLON	James	32	head	lab		Ballinvoher	KW	15
171 SCANLON	Mary	18	wife			Ballinvoher	KW	15
171 MOHER	James	10	B/L			Ballinvoher	KW	15
172 BRIEN	Judith	30	head		widow	Ballinvoher	KW	15
172 BRIEN	Michael	10	son			Ballinvoher	KW	15
172 BRIEN	William	8	son			Ballinvoher	KW	15
172 CLEARY	Ellen	40	visi			Ballinvoher	KW	15
173 MOHER	Ellen	40	head		widow	Ballinvoher	KW	15
173 MOHER	Patrick	14	son			Ballinvoher	KW	15
173 MOHER	Thomas	11	son			Ballinvoher	KW	15
174 CLEARY	Thomas	50	head	farmer		Ballinvoher	KW	16
174 CLEARY	Bridget	40	wife			Ballinvoher	KW	16
174 CLEARY	Michael	23	son			Ballinvoher	KW	16
174 CLEARY	John	21	son			Ballinvoher	KW	16
174 CLEARY	Thomas	17	son			Ballinvoher	KW	16
174 CLEARY	James	12	son			Ballinvoher	KW	16

174 CLEARY	William	10	son		Ballinvoher	KW	16
175 MOHER	David	40	head lab	listed living alone	Ballinvoher	KW	16
176 AHERN	Patrick	35	head carpenter		Ballinvoher	KW	16
176 AHERN	Ellen	25	wife		Ballinvoher	KW	16
177 WALSH	Johanna	44	head	widow	Ballinvoher	KW	16
177 WALSH	John	17	son		Ballinvoher	KW	16
177 WALSH	Mary	15	dau		Ballinvoher	KW	16
178 MOHER	Thomas	70	head farmer		Ballinvoher	KW	16
178 MOHER	Mary	50	wife		Ballinvoher	KW	16
178 CONNORS	Thomas	29	neph		Ballinvoher	KW	16
178 SHEEHAN	Michael	16	neph		Ballinvoher	KW	16
179 CASEY	William	65	head farmer		Ballinvoher	KW	16
179 CASEY	Catherine	50	wife		Ballinvoher	KW	16
179 CASEY	Catherine	21	dau		Ballinvoher	KW	16
179 CASEY	Ann	19	dau		Ballinvoher	KW	16
179 CASEY	Michael	17	son lab		Ballinvoher	KW	16
179 CASEY	Ellen	15	dau		Ballinvoher	KW	16
179 CASEY	Bartholomew	13	son		Ballinvoher	KW	16
179 CASEY	Elizabeth	11	dau		Ballinvoher	KW	16
179 CASEY	Bridget	7	dau		Ballinvoher	KW	16
179 CASEY	William	5	son		Ballinvoher	KW	16
180 PIGOTT	Edmond	40	head lab		Ballinvoher	KW	16
180 PIGOTT	Margaret	38	wife		Ballinvoher	KW	16
180 PIGOTT	Ellen	16	dau		Ballinvoher	KW	16
180 PIGOTT	Michael	6	son		Ballinvoher	KW	16
181 TOBIN	Patrick	40	head farmer		Ballinvoher	KW	16
181 TOBIN	Bridget	35	wife		Ballinvoher	KW	16
181 TOBIN	Mary	8	dau		Ballinvoher	KW	16
181 TOBIN	Ellen	7	dau		Ballinvoher	KW	16
181 TOBIN	Johanna	7	dau		Ballinvoher	KW	16
182 DOWNEY	Samuel	40	head farmer		Ballinvoher	KW	16
182 DOWNEY	Catherine	50	wife		Ballinvoher	KW	16
182 BEARY	Mary	19	rel.	relative	Ballinvoher	KW	16
183 MOLOWPY	Bridget	50	head	widow	Ballinvoher	KW	16
183 MOLOWPY	John	20	son lab		Ballinvoher	KW	16
183 MOLOWPY	Maurice	12	son		Ballinvoher	KW	16
183 MOLOWPY	Elizabeth	11	dau		Ballinvoher	KW	16
183 MOLOWPY	Mary	9	dau		Ballinvoher	KW	16
184 MOLOWPY	Ellen	40	head	widow	Ballinvoher	KW	16
184 MOLOWPY	Thomas	8	son		Ballinvoher	KW	26
184 MOLOWPY	Edward	5	son		Ballinvoher	KW	16
046 BRADY	Francis, Rev.	43	head C.E.clergy	(note "a" in spelling	Ballydarown Glebe	KC	01
046 BRADY	Fanny S.	30	wife	of townland)	Ballydarown Glebe	KC	01

046 BRADY	Susan T.	10	dau		Ballydarown Glebe	KC	01
046 BRADY	Charlotte E.	8	dau		Ballydarown Glebe	KC	01
046 BRADY	Horace N.	7	son		Ballydarown Glebe	KC	01
046 BRADY	Letitia D.	6	dau		Ballydarown Glebe	KC	01
046 BRADY	Ann F.	5	dau		Ballydarown Glebe	KC	01
046 BRADY	Harriet	3	dau		Ballydarown Glebe	KC	01
046 BRADY	T. T. H.	1	son		Ballydarown Glebe	KC	01
046 NORMAN	John	70	F/L	Esq.	Ballydarown Glebe	KC	01
046 NORMAN	Susan M.	60	M/L		Ballydarown Glebe	KC	01
046 NORMAN	Susan M.	20	S/L		Ballydarown Glebe	KC	01
046 HEFFERNON	Edward H.	14	visi		Ballydarown Glebe	KC	01
046 BASSETT	Maryann	30	serv		Ballydarown Glebe	KC	01
046 BASSETT	Catherine	10	dau	dau to Maryann B.	Ballydarown Glebe	KC	01
046 MILTON	Maria	17	serv		Ballydarown Glebe	KC	01
046 WALSH	Mary	36	serv		Ballydarown Glebe	KC	01
046 WARNER	Henry	21	serv		Ballydarown Glebe	KC	01
047 BOLSTER	Richard	33	serv steward	employer Rev.BRADY	Ballydarown Glebe	KC	01
047 BOLSTER	Angelina	28	wife		Ballydarown Glebe	KC	01
047 BOLSTER	Richard	6	son		Ballydarown Glebe	KC	01
048 BAKER	Michael	40	head lab		Ballydarown Glebe	KC	01
048 BAKER	Margaret	35	wife		Ballydarown Glebe	KC	01
048 BAKER	Ann	10	dau		Ballydarown Glebe	KC	01
048 BAKER	Michael	7	son		Ballydarown Glebe	KC	01
048 BAKER	John	3	son		Ballydarown Glebe	KC	01
048 CASEY	Kate	9	niec		Ballydarown Glebe	KC	01
048 CASEY	John	3	neph		Ballydarown Glebe	KC	01
049 WATSON	John	56	head pensioner		Ballydarown Glebe	KC	01
049 WATSON	Ann	44	wife		Ballydarown Glebe	KC	01
049 WATSON	Mary	16	dau		Ballydarown Glebe	KC	01
049 WATSON	William	11	son		Ballydarown Glebe	KC	01
049 WATSON	Ann	8	dau		Ballydarown Glebe	KC	01
049 WATSON	Jane	7	dau		Ballydarown Glebe	KC	01
049 WATSON	Rebecca	3	dau		Ballydarown Glebe	KC	01
050 CUNNINGHAM	Peter	70	head gatekeeper		Ballydarown Glebe	KC	01
050 CUNNINGHAM	Honora	62	wife		Ballydarown Glebe	KC	01
050 CUNNINGHAM	Charles	36	son lab		Ballydarown Glebe	KC	01
050 CUNNINGHAM	Peter	30	son pr.& glazier		Ballydarown Glebe	KC	01
050 CUNNINGHAM	Honora	24	dau		Ballydarown Glebe	KC	01
051 SHEEHAN	David	45	head clerk	empl. Mr. GERAN	Ballydarown Glebe	KC	01
051 SHEEHAN	Patrick	40	brot lab		Ballydarown Glebe	KC	01
052 MURRAY	Richard	40	head lab		Ballydarown Glebe	KC	01
052 MURRAY	Mary	40	wife		Ballydarown Glebe	KC	01
052 MURRAY	Mary	13	dau		Ballydarown Glebe	KC	01
052 MURRAY	Margaret	8	dau		Ballydarown Glebe	KC	01
052 McCARTHY	Honora	13	niec		Ballydarown Glebe	KC	01
053 QUIRK	Abigail	58	head farmer	widow	Ballydarown Glebe	KC	01
053 CAHILL	Ellen	34	dau		Ballydarown Glebe	KC	01
053 QUIRK	Mary	31	dau		Ballydarown Glebe	KC	01

053 QUIRK	Bridget	29	dau		Ballydarown Glebe	KC	01
053 QUIRK	Margaret	28	dau		Ballydarown Glebe	KC	01
053 QUIRK	Norry	27	dau		Ballydarown Glebe	KC	01
053 QUIRK	James	26	son farmer		Ballydarown Glebe	KC	01
053 QUIRK	Thomas	23	son farmer		Ballydarown Glebe	KC	01
053 CAHILL	Michael	8	gr/s		Ballydarown Glebe	KC	01
053 COLBERT	Denis	22	serv lab		Ballydarown Glebe	KC	01
053 COLBERT	Maurice	16	serv lab		Ballydarown Glebe	KC	01
054 DALY	Rev. James	53	head R.C. priest (note "e" in		Ballyderown	KC	02
054 HURLY	Ellen	40	serv hk	spelling of townland)	Ballyderown	KC	02
055 LEAMY	John	52	head lab	gatekeeper	Ballyderown	KC	02
055 LEAMY	Elizabeth	40	wife		Ballyderown	KC	02
056 BYRNES	William	40	head farmer		Ballyderown	KC	02
056 BYRNES	Catherine	34	wife		Ballyderown	KC	02
056 BYRNES	Mary	6	dau		Ballyderown	KC	02
056 BYRNES	Ellen	4	dau		Ballyderown	KC	02
056 BYRNES	Eliza	11m	dau		Ballyderown	KC	02
056 EGAN	Eliza	25	serv		Ballyderown	KC	02
056 DORAN	Jeremiah	22	serv lab		Ballyderown	KC	02
056 GRIFFIN	Patrick	18	serv lab		Ballyderown	KC	02
056 DORAN	William	16	serv lab		Ballyderown	KC	02
056 DORAN	Catherine	12	serv		Ballyderown	KC	02
057 HIGGINS	Elizabeth	na	head	senior, away	Ballyderown	KC	02
057 HIGGINS	Elizabeth	23	dau		Ballyderown	KC	02
057 HIGGINS	Martha	20	dau woolen mfg		Ballyderown	KC	02
057 HIGGINS	Anne	17	dau		Ballyderown	KC	02
057 HIGGINS	Susan	14	dau		Ballyderown	KC	02
057 HIGGINS	Jane	11	dau		Ballyderown	KC	02
057 HIGGINS	Chessy	9	dau		Ballyderown	KC	02
057 CONROY	Margaret	26	serv		Ballyderown	KC	02
057 DUNDAN	Edmond	26	visi		Ballyderown	KC	02
058 BRIEN	Honora	49	head mfg		Ballyderown	KC	02
058 BRIEN	Mary	25	dau		Ballyderown	KC	02
058 BRIEN	Bridget	19	dau factory		Ballyderown	KC	02
058 BRIEN	Allice	13	dau		Ballyderown	KC	02
058 BRIEN	Margaret	10	dau		Ballyderown	KC	02
058 BRIEN	Mary	24	na mfg	spinster	Ballyderown	KC	02
058 BRIEN	John	15	brot mfg		Ballyderown	KC	02
058 BRIEN	Catherine	20	sist mfg	(family No.	Ballyderown	KC	02
058 PRICE	Mary	27	visi	omitted)	Ballyderown	KC	02
058 BRIEN	Bridget	8	sist		Ballyderown	KC	02
059 ROCHE	Allice	46	head mfg	spinster	Ballyderown	KC	02
059 ROCHE	William	6	neph		Ballyderown	KC	02
060 RIORDAN	John	46	head woolen spin.		Ballyderown	KC	02
060 RIORDAN	Judith	38	wife		Ballyderown	KC	02
060 RIORDAN	Catherine	17	dau		Ballyderown	KC	02
060 RIORDAN	John	16	son		Ballyderown	KC	02

060	RIORDAN	Mary	11	dau		Ballyderown	KC	02
060	RIORDAN	Hanna	10	dau		Ballyderown	KC	02
060	RIORDAN	Michael	7	son		Ballyderown	KC	02
060	RIORDAN	Ellen	5	dau		Ballyderown	KC	02
060	RIORDAN	William	4	son		Ballyderown	KC	02
060	RIORDAN	Thomas	2	son		Ballyderown	KC	02
061	MAHONY	Jane	20	serv		Ballyderown	KC	02
062	CASEY	Patrick	33	head lab		Ballyderown	KC	02
062	CASEY	Mary	30	wife		Ballyderown	KC	02
062	CASEY	Norry	8	dau		Ballyderown	KC	02
062	CASEY	Patrick	6 m	son		Ballyderown	KC	02
063	CRONAN	Patrick	50	head lab		Ballyderown	KC	02
063	CRONAN	Judith	49	wife		Ballyderown	KC	02
063	CRONAN	Patrick	26	son		Ballyderown	KC	02
063	CRONAN	Johanna	20	dau		Ballyderown	KC	02
063	CRONAN	Eliza	9	dau		Ballyderown	KC	02
063	BARRY	James	26	visi		Ballyderown	KC	02
064	DORAN	Bridget	50	head	widow	Ballyderown	KC	03
064	DORAN	Jeremiah	19	son lab		Ballyderown	KC	03
064	DORAN	William	15	son		Ballyderown	KC	03
064	DORAN	Catherine	13	dau		Ballyderown	KC	03
065	CROWE	Ann	49	wife to crewman	husband in Co.Antrim	Ballyderown	KC	03
065	CROWE	Mary	11	niec		Ballyderown	KC	03
066	MOORE	Stephen	26	head lord	or LORD KILWORTH	Ballyderown	KC	03
066	NORRIS	William	45	serv lab		Ballyderown	KC	03
066	NORRIS	Johanna	40	wife to servant		Ballyderown	KC	03
066	LYONS	Michael	14	serv to Wm.NORRIS		Ballyderown	KC	03
067	TOBIN	Julia	40	wife	hus. Edw. in America	Ballyhenden	KC	12
067	TOBIN	Thomas	16	son lab		Ballyhenden	KC	12
067	TOBIN	Michael	16	son		Ballyhenden	KC	12
067	TOBIN	John	12	son		Ballyhenden	KC	12
067	TOBIN	Mary	9	dau		Ballyhenden	KC	12
067	TOBIN	Edmond	6	son		Ballyhenden	KC	12
068	ROCHE	James	37	head steward	to Mr.SULLIVAN	Ballyhenden	KC	12
068	STACK	Thomas	30	serv lab	(STUCK?)	Ballyhenden	KC	12
068	ROCHE	Thomas	30	serv lab		Ballyhenden	KC	12
068	COLEMAN	Catherine	28	serv milkmaid		Ballyhenden	KC	12
069	CRONAN	Patrick	24	head lab		Ballyhenden	KC	12
069	CRONAN	Ellen	28	wife		Ballyhenden	KC	12
070	DUNN	John	42	head lab		Ballyhenden	KC	12
070	DUNN	Mary	40	wife		Ballyhenden	KC	12
070	DUNN	John	20	son lab		Ballyhenden	KC	12
070	DUNN	Jeremiah	19	son lab		Ballyhenden	KC	12
070	DUNN	Hannah	15	dau		Ballyhenden	KC	12

070 DUNN	Michael	14	son		Ballyhenden	KC	12
070 DUNN	Jane	11	dau		Ballyhenden	KC	12
071 CALLAGHAN	John	65	head farmer		Ballyhenden	KC	12
071 CALLAGHAN	Bridget	44	wife		Ballyhenden	KC	12
071 CALLAGHAN	Edmond	16	son lab		Ballyhenden	KC	12
071 CALLAGHAN	Norry	14	dau		Ballyhenden	KC	12
071 CALLAGHAN	Michael	14	son		Ballyhenden	KC	12
071 CALLAGHAN	John	7	son		Ballyhenden	KC	12
071 CALLAGHAN	Michael	56	brot		Ballyhenden	KC	12
072 RYAN	William	56	head farmer		Ballyhenden	KC	12
072 RYAN	Honora	60	wife		Ballyhenden	KC	12
072 RYAN	Patrick	24	son lab		Ballyhenden	KC	12
072 TOUEL	Denis	30	serv		Ballyhenden	KC	12
072 WALSH	Mary	23	serv		Ballyhenden	KC	12
073 CRONAN	Daniel	25	head farmer		Ballyhenden	KC	12
073 CRONAN	John	20	brot lab		Ballyhenden	KC	12
073 CRONAN	Terence	18	brot lab		Ballyhenden	KC	12
073 CRONAN	Patrick	15	brot lab		Ballyhenden	KC	12
073 CRONAN	Edward	13	brot lab		Ballyhenden	KC	12
073 CRONAN	Michael	7	brot lab		Ballyhenden	KC	12
073 BARRY	Thomas	25	serv lab		Ballyhenden	KC	12
073 CONROY	Elizabeth	23	serv		Ballyhenden	KC	12
073 CONROY	Bridget	25	serv		Ballyhenden	KC	12
074 SULLIVAN	Andrew	72	head lab		Ballyhenden	KC	13
074 SULLIVAN	Johanna	56	wife		Ballyhenden	KC	13
074 KELEHER	Bridget	12	niec		Ballyhenden	KC	13
075 KEATING	Bridget	32	head farmer	widow	Ballyhenden	KC	13
075 KEATING	Bridget	8	dau		Ballyhenden	KC	13
075 KEATING	James	7	son		Ballyhenden	KC	13
075 KEATING	John	5	son		Ballyhenden	KC	13
075 KEATING	Eliza	3	dau		Ballyhenden	KC	13
075 BRIEN	John	30	serv lab		Ballyhenden	KC	13
075 BOWLER	John	28	serv lab		Ballyhenden	KC	13
075 FLEMMING	Michael	31	serv lab		Ballyhenden	KC	13
075 VERLING	Hannah	33	serv		Ballyhenden	KC	13
076 KENT	David	35	head farmer		Ballyhenden	KC	13
076 KENT	Ellen	30	wife		Ballyhenden	KC	13
076 KENT	David	5	son		Ballyhenden	KC	13
076 KENT	Ellen	3	dau		Ballyhanden	KC	13
076 KENT	John	2	son		Ballyhenden	KC	13
076 KENT	Elizabeth	3 m	dau		Ballyhenden	KC	13
076 KELEHER	Mary	50	aunt	aunt-in-law	Ballyhenden	KC	13
076 KEEFFE	Margaret	25	serv		Ballyhenden	KC	13
076 MORONEY	James	16	serv		Ballyhenden	KC	13
515 O'DONNELL	John	32	head farmer		Ballylackan	LE	17
515 O'DONNELL	Mary	32	wife		Ballylackan	LE	17
515 O'DONNELL	John	8	son		Ballylackan	LE	17

515	O'DONNELL	Edmond	7	son		Ballylackan	LE	17
515	O'DONNELL	Patrick	5	son		Ballylackan	LE	17
515	O'DONNELL	Owen	4	son		Ballylackan	LE	17
515	CLANCY	William	22	serv lab		Ballylackan	LE	17
515	CLANCY	Thomas	24	serv lab		Ballylackan	LE	17
515	BYRNES	Patrick	13	serv lab		Ballylackan	LE	17
515	FLYNN	Ellen	21	serv		Ballylackan	LE	17
515	CLANCY	Mary	20	serv		Ballylackan	LE	17
516	DALY	Denis	80	head lab		Ballylackan	LE	17
516	DALY	Mary	38	dau		Ballylackan	LE	17
516	DALY	Margaret	36	dau		Ballylackan	LE	17
517	JOYCE	Carey	59	head farmer		Ballylackan	LE	17
517	JOYCE	Bridget	50	wife		Ballylackan	LE	17
517	JOYCE	Sarah	28	dau		Ballylackan	LE	17
517	JOYCE	Bridget	22	dau		Ballylackan	LE	17
517	JOYCE	Kate	18	dau		Ballylackan	LE	17
517	JOYCE	Ellen	16	dau		Ballylackan	LE	17
517	JOYCE	Carey	9	son		Ballylackan	LE	17
517	QUIRK	Mary	19	serv		Ballylackan	LE	17
517	PARKER	Eliza	35	serv		Ballylackan	LE	17
517	CAINE	Michael	15	serv		Ballylackan	LE	17
517	SULLIVAN	Mary	40	serv		Ballylackan	LE	17
517	MILLER	James	20	serv lab		Ballylackan	LE	17
517	WALL	Patrick	23	serv lab		Ballylackan	LE	17
517	JOYCE	Michael	21	serv		Ballylackan	LE	17
517	LENEHAN	Patrick	50	serv lab		Ballylackan	LE	17
518	KELEHER	Michael	47	head farmer		Ballylackan	LE	17
518	KELEHER	Johanna	35	wife		Ballylackan	LE	17
518	KELEHER	Timothy	12	son		Ballylackan	LE	17
518	KELEHER	Eliza	10	dau		Ballylackan	LE	17
518	KELEHER	Michael	8	son		Ballylackan	LE	17
518	KELEHER	Mary	7	dau		Ballylackan	LE	17
518	KELEHER	John	5	son		Ballylackan	LE	17
518	SHEEHAN	Daniel	27	serv		Ballylackan	LE	17
518	BURKE	Margaret	28	serv		Ballylackan	LE	17
519	BROWNE	Catherine	60	head farmer	widow	Ballylackan	LE	17
519	BROWNE	Edmond	30	son farmer		Ballylackan	LE	17
519	BROWNE	Margaret	24	dau		Ballylackan	LE	17
519	BROWNE	Mary	22	dau		Ballylackan	LE	17
519	BROWNE	Ellen	20	dau		Ballylackan	LE	17
519	BROWNE	Patrick	17	son		Ballylackan	LE	17
519	BROWNE	Bridget	14	dau		Ballylackan	LE	17
519	BROWNE	James	11	son		Ballylackan	LE	17
519	COUGHLAN	Timothy	28	serv		Ballylackan	LE	17
519	O'BRIEN	Thomas	30	serv		Ballylackan	LE	17
519	CAHILL	John	60	brot		Ballylackan	LE	17
520	FLYNN	Thomas	40	head lab		Ballylackan	LE	17
520	FLYNN	Johanna	37	wife		Ballylackan	LE	17
520	FLYNN	Ellen	15	dau		Ballylackan	LE	17

520 FLYNN	Mary	13	dau		Ballylackan	LE	17
520 FLYNN	Catherine	11	dau		Ballylackan	LE	17
520 FLYNN	Ann	9	dau		Ballylackan	LE	17
520 FLYNN	James	7	son		Ballylackan	LE	17
520 FLYNN	Thomas	5	son		Ballylackan	LE	17
520 FLYNN	John	3	son		Ballylackan	LE	17
521 JOYCE	James	72	head farmer		Ballylackan	LE	18
521 JOYCE	Catherine	67	wife		Ballylackan	LE	18
521 JOYCE	Edmond	36	son		Ballylackan	LE	18
521 JOYCE	Mary	30	dau		Ballylackan	LE	18
521 JOYCE	James	13	son	(rel. checked)	Ballylackan	LE	18
521 JOYCE	John	11	son		Ballylackan	LE	18
521 JOYCE	Michael	9	son		Ballylackan	LE	18
521 JOYCE	Catherine	8	dau		Ballylackan	LE	18
521 JOYCE	Mary	6	dau		Ballylackan	LE	18
521 JOYCE	Edmond	2	son		Ballylackan	LE	18
521 JOYCE	Julia	2	gr/d		Ballylackan	LE	18
521 O'BRIEN	Michael	20	serv		Ballylackan	LE	18
521 HARRIS	Catherine	16	serv		Ballylackan	LE	18
521 BURKE	Johanna	67	visi		Ballylackan	LE	18
522 AHERN	David	60	head farmer		Ballylackan	LE	18
522 AHERN	Johanna	55	wife		Ballylackan	LE	18
522 AHERN	John	22	son		Ballylackan	LE	18
522 AHERN	Thomas	20	son		Ballylackan	LE	18
522 AHERN	Patrick	16	son		Ballylackan	LE	18
522 AHERN	Patrick	67	brot		Ballylackan	LE	18
522 WALSH	James	27	serv lab		Ballylackan	LE	18
522 ROCHE	Jane	21	serv		Ballylackan	LE	18
522 SULLIVAN	John	13	serv		Ballylackan	LE	18
523 HENNESY	Mary	40	wife dressmaker	husb. in America	Ballylackan	LE	18
523 HENNESY	William	13	son		Ballylackan	LE	18
523 HENNESY	Ellen	9	dau		Ballylackan	LE	18
523 HENNESY	Allice	7	dau		Ballylackan	LE	18
523 HENNESY	Robert	4	son		Ballylackan	LE	18
524 HEAFY	Thomas	30	head shoemaker		Ballylackan	LE	18
524 HEAFY	Julia	34	wife	(age 24?)	Ballylackan	LE	18
524 HEAFY	Hannah	25	sist		Ballylackan	LE	18
525 DRISCOLL	Patrick	32	head farmer	(age blurred)	Ballylackan	LE	18
525 DRISCOLL	Ellen	35	wife		Ballylackan	LE	18
525 DRISCOLL	David	7	son		Ballylackan	LE	18
525 DRISCOLL	Mary	4	dau		Ballylackan	LE	18
525 BYRNES	William	15	serv		Ballylackan	LE	18
526 SLATTERY	Johanna	65	head	widow	Ballylackan	LE	18
526 SLATTERY	Mary	32	sist	(age & rel. sic)	Ballylackan	LE	18
526 SLATTERY	Johanna	11	sist	(age & rel. sic)	Ballylackan	LE	18
527 GREEHY	Patrick	47	head farmer		Ballylackan	LE	18
527 GREEHY	Julia	30	wife		Ballylackan	LE	18

527 GREEHY	Patrick	10	son		Ballylackan	LE	18
527 GREEHY	Catherine	8	dau		Ballylackan	LE	18
527 GREEHY	John	18m	son		Ballylackan	LE	18
527 BLAKE	Maurice	15	rel.		Ballylackan	LE	18
528 BYRNES	Garrett	29	head lab		Ballylackan	LE	18
528 BYRNES	Margaret	25	wife		Ballylackan	LE	18
528 BYRNES	Ellen	2	dau		Ballylackan	LE	18
528 BYRNES	Bridget	60	moth		Ballylackan	LE	18
529 COFFEE	Thomas	52	head farmer		Ballylackan	LE	18
529 COFFEE	Ellen	70	wife	(age sic)	Ballylackan	LE	19
529 COFFEE	John	20	son		Ballylackan	LE	18
529 COFFEE	Elizabeth	19	dau		Ballylackan	LE	18
529 COFFEE	Catherine	16	dau		Ballylackan	LE	18
529 COFFEE	Mary	14	dau		Ballylackan	LE	18
529 COFFEE	Jeremiah	10	son		Ballylackan	LE	18
529 SLATTERY	John	33	rel.	relative	Ballylackan	LE	18
530 O'BRIEN	William	41	head lab		Ballylackan	LE	18
530 O'BRIEN	Elizabeth	38	wife		Ballylackan	LE	18
530 O'BRIEN	Margaret	9	dau		Ballylackan	LE	18
530 O'BRIEN	Hannah	8	dau		Ballylackan	LE	18
530 O'BRIEN	Elizabeth	6 m	dau	(2 yrs 6 mo? unclear)	Ballylackan	LE	18
531 MILLER	Thomas	50	head lab		Ballylackan	LE	19
531 MILLER	Margaret	45	wife		Ballylackan	LE	19
531 MILLER	Richard	25	son lab		Ballylackan	LE	19
531 MILLER	Denis	23	son carpenter		Ballylackan	LE	19
531 MILLER	Margaret	12	dau		Ballylackan	LE	19
531 MILLER	Elizabeth	5	dau		Ballylackan	LE	19
532 McCARTHY	Michael	45	head lab		Ballylackan	LE	19
532 McCARTHY	Ellen	45	wife		Ballylackan	LE	19
532 McCARTHY	John	16	son		Ballylackan	LE	19
532 McCARTHY	Michael	14	son		Ballylackan	LE	19
532 McCARTHY	Jeremiah	9	son		Ballylackan	LE	19
532 McCARTHY	Ellen	6	dau		Ballylackan	LE	19
532 McCARTHY	Bridget	5	dau		Ballylackan	LE	19
532 McCARTHY	James	9 m	son	(age illegible)	Ballylackan	LE	19
533 SULLIVAN	William	40	head lab		Ballylackan	LE	19
533 SULLIVAN	Alice	43	wife		Ballylackan	LE	19
533 SULLIVAN	Ellen	13	dau		Ballylackan	LE	19
533 SULLIVAN	William	9	son		Ballylackan	LE	19
534 FLYNN	Ellen	80	head	widow	Ballylackan	LE	19
534 FLYNN	Catherine	40	dau		Ballylackan	LE	19
534 FLYNN	Maurice	25	son		Ballylackan	LE	19
535 FLYNN	Timothy	31	head lab		Ballylackan	LE	19
535 FLYNN	Ellen	9	dau		Ballylackan	LE	19
535 FLYNN	Margaret	3	dau		Ballylackan	LE	19

-21-

536 BURKE	Ann	55	head	widow	Ballylackan	LE	19
536 BURKE	Mary	22	dau		Ballylackan	LE	19
536 BEGLY	Timothy	1 w	gr/s		Ballylackan	LE	19
537 HEALY	John	52	head farmer		Ballylackan	LE	19
537 HEALY	Ellen	52	wife		Ballylackan	LE	19
537 HEALY	Catherine	23	dau		Ballylackan	LE	19
537 HEALY	Johanna	19	dau		Ballylackan	LE	19
537 HEALY	John	16	son		Ballylackan	LE	19
537 HEALY	Ellen	15	dau		Ballylackan	LE	19
537 HEALY	Mary	8	dau		Ballylackan	LE	19
538 McCRAITH	Mary	40	head	widow	Ballylackan	LE	19
538 MYLES	Patrick	15	son	(surname ckd)	Ballylackan	LE	19
077 JOYCE	John	42	head blacksmith		Ballyvoskillikin	KC	03
077 JOYCE	Mary	30	wife		Ballyvoskillikin	KC	03
077 JOYCE	Catherine	7	dau		Ballyvoskillikin	KC	03
077 JOYCE	Margaret	5	dau		Ballyvoskillikin	KC	03
077 JOYCE	Michael	6 m	son		Ballyvoskillikin	KC	03
077 McAULIFFE	Timothy	18	none apprentice		Ballyvoskillikin	KC	03
078 LYONS	Mary	18	head	spinster	Ballyvoskillikin	KC	03
078 LYONS	Ellen	16	sist		Ballyvoskillikin	KC	03
078 LYONS	Honora	8	sist		Ballyvoskillikin	KC	03
079 CALLAGHAN	John	34	head lab		Ballyvoskillikin	KC	03
079 CALLAGHAN	Catherine	28	wife		Ballyvoskillikin	KC	03
079 CALLAGHAN	Johanna	8	dau		Ballyvoskillikin	KC	03
079 CALLAGHAN	Mary	9 m	dau		Ballyvoskillikin	KC	03
079 CALLAGHAN	Bridget	36	sist		Ballyvoskillikin	KC	03
079 McAULIFFE	Mary	60	visi		Ballyvoskillikin	KC	03
079 McAULIFFE	Catherine	21	visi		Ballyvoskillikin	KC	03
079 McAULIFFE	Jeremiah	13	visi		Ballyvoskillikin	KC	03
080 JOYCE	Terence	35	head farmer		Ballyvoskillikin	KC	03
080 JOYCE	Honora	65	moth		Ballyvoskillikin	KC	03
080 RIORDAN	Patrick	22	serv lab		Ballyvoskillikin	KC	03
080 LEARY	Patrick	50	serv lab		Ballyvoskillikin	KC	03
080 POWER	Ellen	25	serv		Ballyvoskillikin	KC	03
081 MULCAHY	Owen	39	head blacksmith		Ballyvoskillikin	KC	03
081 MULCAHY	Johanna	32	wife		Ballyvoskillikin	KC	03
081 MULCAHY	Daniel	14	son		Ballyvoskillikin	KC	03
081 MULCAHY	Garrett	12	son		Ballyvoskillikin	KC	03
081 MULCAHY	John	10	son		Ballyvoskillikin	KC	03
081 MULCAHY	Michael	8	son		Ballyvoskillikin	KC	03
081 MULCAHY	Mary	4	dau		Ballyvoskillikin	KC	03
081 MULCAHY	Ellen	2	dau		Ballyvoskillikin	KC	03
081 MULCAHY	Denis	2 m	son		Ballyvoskillikin	KC	03
081 McCARTHY	Timothy	20	none journeyman		Ballyvoskillikin	KC	03
081 FITZGERALD	Bridget	10	serv		Ballyvoskillikin	KC	03
082 O'NEILL (sic) James		60	head lab		Ballyvoskillikin	KC	04

082 O'NEIL	Mary	60	wife		Ballyvoskillikin	KC	04
082 O'NEIL	James	23	son lab		Ballyvoskillikin	KC	04
082 O'NEIL	Margaret	20	dau		Ballyvoskillikin	KC	04
082 O'NEIL	Bridget	17	dau		Ballyvoskillikin	KC	04
083 BURKE	Thomas	60	head pedlar		Ballyvoskillikin	KC	04
083 BURKE	Mary	50	wife		Ballyvoskillikin	KC	04
083 BURKE	Catherine	9	dau		Ballyvoskillikin	KC	04
084 CALLAGHAN	Mary	65	head	widow	Ballyvoskillikin	KC	04
084 CALLAGHAN	Daniel	40	son lab		Ballyvoskillikin	KC	04
084 CALLAGHAN	Mary	30	D/L		Ballyvoskillikin	KC	04
084 CALLAGHAN	George	5	gr/s		Ballyvoskillikin	KC	04
084 CALLAGHAN	Mary	3	gr/d		Ballyvoskillikin	KC	04
084 CALLAGHAN	George	30	son lab		Ballyvoskillikin	KC	04
084 CALLAGHAN	Mary	23	dau		Ballyvoskillikin	KC	04
084 CALLAGHAN	John	20	son lab		Ballyvoskillikin	KC	04
084 CALLAGHAN	Norry	18	dau		Ballyvoskillikin	KC	04
085 SAUL	Henry	26	head gentleman	Esq.,farmer	Boherdeveroge	KC	04
085 CROWLY	Mary	30	serv		Boherdeveroge	KC	04
085 MORRISON	James	25	serv		Boherdeveroge	KC	04
085 FENTON	Wiliam	20	serv		Boherdeveroge	KC	04
086 MURPHY	Michael	60	head farmer		Boherdeveroge	KC	04
086 MURPHY	Mary	50	wife		Boherdeveroge	KC	04
086 MURPHY	Johanna	27	dau		Boherdeveroge	KC	04
086 MURPHY	John	25	son lab		Boherdeveroge	KC	04
086 MURPHY	Margaret	17	dau		Boherdeveroge	KC	04
086 MURPHY	David	16	son lab		Boherdeveroge	KC	04
086 MURPHY	Patrick	14	son lab		Boherdeveroge	KC	04
086 MURPHY	Bridget	12	dau		Boherdeveroge	KC	04
086 MURPHY	John	40	serv lab		Boherdeveroge	KC	04
086 KELEHER	Patrick	18	serv lab		Boherdeveroge	KC	04
086 FRAZIER	Thomas	30	serv lab		Boherdeveroge	KC	04
086 RYAN	Cornelius	30	serv lab		Boherdeveroge	KC	04
086 FENNESY	John	25	serv lab		Boherdeveroge	KC	04
086 REA	Mary	70	visi		Boherdeveroge	KC	04
643 COLLIS	William Cooke	68	head magistrate	Esq.	Castlecooke	MA	19
643 COLLIS	Elizabeth	65	wife		Castlecooke	MA	19
643 COLLIS	John T.	32	son	Esq.	Castlecooke	MA	19
643 BARRY	Ann	25	niec		Castlecooke	MA	19
643 CAMPION	Benjamin	24	visi		Castlecooke	MA	19
643 FINN	John	36	serv		Castlecooke	MA	19
643 WHELAN	Bridget	32	serv house maid		Castlecooke	MA	19
643 WHELAN	Catherine	32	serv kitchen maid		Castlecooke	MA	19
644 CODY	David	41	head steward		Castlecooke	MA	19
644 CODY	Mary	35	wife		Castlecooke	MA	19
644 CODY	Mary	12	dau		Castlecooke	MA	19
644 CODY	Johanna	11	dau		Castlecooke	MA	19
644 CODY	Thomas	9	son		Castlecooke	MA	19
644 CODY	Edmond	7	son		Castlecooke	MA	19

644 CODY	Jane	2	dau		Castlecooke	MA	19
644 CODY	Margaret	10m	dau		Castlecooke	MA	19
644 TROY	Julia	60	M/L		Castlecooke	MA	19
645 DONOUGHUE	Johanna	35	head	widow	Castlecooke	MA	19
645 DONOUGHUE	Patrick	11	son	(spelled Donoghue)	Castlecooke	MA	19
645 DONOUGHUE	Thomas	9	son	(spelled Donoghue)	Castlecooke	MA	19
645 DONOUGHUE	Maurice	3	son	(spelled Donoghue)	Castlecooke	MA	19
645 COPPINGER	Rebecca	12	niec		Castlecooke	MA	19
646 LANE	Ellen	70	head	widow	Castlecooke	MA	19
646 LANE	John	33	son		Castlecooke	MA	19
646 LANE	Henry	31	son		Castlecooke	MA	19
646 LANE	Goen	29	son	(given name ckd.)	Castlecooke	MA	19
646 McCRAITH	Hannah	60	sist		Castlecooke	MA	19
647 STANTON	Bridget	55	head	widow	Castlecooke	MA	19
647 STANTON	Bridget	20	dau		Castlecooke	MA	19
647 STANTON	Catherine	20	niec		Castlecooke	MA	19
648 AMBROSE	Patrick	na	head lab		Castlecooke	MA	20
648 AMBROSE	Ellen	na	wife		Castlecooke	MA	20
648 AMBROSE	Patrick	21	son lab		Castlecooke	MA	20
648 AMBROSE	Robert	19	son lab		Castlecooke	MA	20
648 AMBROSE	David	17	son lab		Castlecooke	MA	20
648 AMBROSE	James	14	son		Castlecooke	MA	20
648 AMBROSE	Catherine	10	niec		Castlecooke	MA	20
649 ROCHE	Thomas	40	head lab		Castlecooke	MA	20
649 ROCHE	Margaret	38	wife		Castlecooke	MA	20
649 ROCHE	Johanna	17	dau		Castlecooke	MA	20
649 ROCHE	Maurice	14	son		Castlecooke	MA	20
649 ROCHE	James	12	son		Castlecooke	MA	20
649 ROCHE	Catherine	10	dau		Castlecooke	MA	20
649 ROCHE	Margaret	8	dau		Castlecooke	MA	20
649 ROCHE	Ellen	4	dau		Castlecooke	MA	20
650 BURKE	David	68	head schoolmaster		Castlecooke	MA	20
650 BURKE	Julia	54	wife		Castlecooke	MA	20
651 SHEEHAN	James	57	head lab		Castlecooke	MA	20
651 SHEEHAN	Bridget	53	wife		Castlecooke	MA	20
651 SHEEHAN	Jane	13	dau		Castlecooke	MA	20
652 GREEN	William	70	head lab	living alone	Castlecooke	MA	20
653 AHERN	Margaret	39	head	widow	Castlecooke	MA	20
653 AHERN	Mary	9	dau		Castlecooke	MA	20
653 AHERN	Margaret	5	dau		Castlecooke	MA	20
654 LANE	Richard	37	head lab		Castlecooke	MA	20
654 LANE	Mary	35	wife		Castlecooke	MA	20
654 LANE	Ellen	8	dau		Castlecooke	MA	20
654 LANE	Mary	6	dau		Castlecooke	MA	20

654	LANE	John	4	son		Castlecooke	MA	20
654	LANE	Catherine	2	dau		Castlecooke	MA	20
654	CUNNINGHAM	Patrick	56	visi		Castlecooke	MA	20
655	FINN	John	36	serv		Castlecooke	MA	20
655	FINN	Ellen	34	wife		Castlecooke	MA	20
655	FINN	Catherine	11	dau		Castlecooke	MA	20
655	FINN	Nancy	8	dau		Castlecooke	MA	20
655	FINN	Patrick	6	son		Castlecooke	MA	20
655	FINN	Thomas	5	son		Castlecooke	MA	20
655	FINN	Mary	2	dau		Castlecooke	MA	20
655	FINN	John	2	son		Castlecooke	MA	20
655	LYONS	Bridget	60	M/L		Castlecooke	MA	20
656	MOHER	Edmond	58	head farmer		Castlecooke	MA	20
656	MOHER	Mary	43	wife		Castlecooke	MA	20
656	MOHER	Ellen	20	dau		Castlecooke	MA	20
656	MOHER	Honora	18	dau		Castlecooke	MA	20
656	MOHER	Mary	16	dau		Castlecooke	MA	20
656	MOHER	James	15	son		Castlecooke	MA	20
656	MOHER	William	10	son		Castlecooke	MA	20
656	MOHER	Johanna	8	dau		Castlecooke	MA	20
656	MOHER	Catherine	6	dau		Castlecooke	MA	20
656	MOHER	Bridget	10m	dau		Castlecooke	MA	20
657	DONEGAN	John	64	head farmer		Castlecooke	MA	20
657	DONEGAN	Ellen	15	dau		Castlecooke	MA	20
657	DONEGAN	Johanna	11	dau		Castlecooke	MA	20
657	DONEGAN	Margaret	9	dau		Castlecooke	MA	20
657	DONEGAN	Thomas	8	son		Castlecooke	MA	20
658	LONDRIGAN	Thomas	70	head farmer		Castlecooke	MA	21
658	LONDRIGAN	Mary	70	wife		Castlecooke	MA	21
658	LONDRIGAN	Daniel	30	son farmer		Castlecooke	MA	21
658	LONDRIGAN	Ann	30	dau		Castlecooke	MA	21
658	LONDRIGAN	Margaret	4	gr/d		Castlecooke	MA	21
658	LONDRIGAN	Mary	2	gr/d		Castlecooke	MA	21
659	FITZGERALD	Garrett	59	head lab		Castlecooke	MA	21
658	FITZGERALD	Mary	59	wife		Castlecooke	MA	21
659	FITZGERALD	Bartholomew	31	son lab		Castlecooke	MA	21
659	FITZGERALD	Catherine	26	D/L		Castlecooke	MA	21
659	FITZGERALD	Honora	19	dau		Castlecooke	MA	21
659	FITZGERALD	John	1	gr/s		Castlecooke	MA	21
659	DALY	William	16	neph		Castlecooke	MA	21
551	TWOMY	Thomas	64	head lab		Coolalisheen	LE	21
551	TWOMY	Mary	58	wife	(listed as dau)	Coolalisheen	LE	21
551	TWOMY	Patrick	26	son lab		Coolalisheen	LE	21
551	TWOMY	Maurice	17	son lab		Coolalisheen	LE	21
551	TWOMY	Johanna	15	dau		Coolalisheen	LE	21
551	BYRNES	Elizabeth	12	serv		Coolalisheen	LE	21
552	TWOMY	Patrick	53	head lab		Coolalisheen	LE	21

552	TWOMY	Ann	40	wife		Coolalisheen	LE	21
552	TWOMY	Patrick	20	son		Coolalisheen	LE	21
552	TWOMY	Michael	17	son		Coolalisheen	LE	21
552	TWOMY	Thomas	15	son		Coolalisheen	LE	21
553	POWER	Charles	48	head lab		Coolalisheen	LE	21
553	POWER	Catherine	43	wife		Coolalisheen	LE	21
553	POWER	Michael	19	son lab		Coolalisheen	LE	21
553	POWER	Mary	14	dau		Coolalisheen	LE	21
553	POWER	Catherine	13	dau		Coolalisheen	LE	21
553	POWER	Richard	8	son		Coolalisheen	LE	21
553	POWER	Bridget	5	dau		Coolalisheen	LE	21
554	POWER	Richard	50	head lab		Coolalisheen	LE	21
554	POWER	Margaret	50	wife		Coolalisheen	LE	21
554	POWER	Thomas	18	son lab		Coolalisheen	LE	21
554	POWER	Ellen	16	dau		Coolalisheen	LE	21
554	POWER	Mary	14	dau		Coolalisheen	LE	21
554	POWER	Michael	12	son		Coolalisheen	LE	21
555	QUIRK	Thomas	40	head lab		Coolalisheen	LE	21
555	QUIRK	Mary	30	wife		Coolalisheen	LE	21
555	QUIRK	Denis	12	son		Coolalisheen	LE	21
555	QUIRK	Honora	10	dau		Coolalisheen	LE	21
555	QUIRK	James	7	son		Coolalisheen	LE	21
556	MAHONY	Daniel	50	head farmer		Coolalisheen	LE	21
556	MAHONY	Margaret	40	wife		Coolalisheen	LE	21
556	MAHONY	Bridget	10	dau		Coolalisheen	LE	21
556	MAHONY	David	45	brot		Coolalisheen	LE	21
556	LEAHY	Johanna	73	M/L		Coolalisheen	LE	21
556	MANGAN	Patrick	15	serv		Coolalisheen	LE	21
556	CALLAGHAN	Ellen	40	serv	(age blurred)	Coolalisheen	LE	21
557	HEALY	Thomas	40	head lab		Coolalisheen	LE	22
557	HEALY	Ellen	60	wife	(aged checked)	Coolalisheen	LE	22
557	HEALY	Mary	27	dau		Coolalisheen	LE	22
558	DONOVAN	Johanna	60	head	widow	Coolalisheen	LE	22
558	DONOVAN	John	30	son		Coolalisheen	LE	22
558	DONOVAN	Simon	28	son		Coolalisheen	LE	22
558	DONOVAN	Patrick	18	son		Coolalisheen	LE	22
559	MULCAHY	John	40	head caretaker	to Mr. Campion	Coolalisheen	LE	22
559	MULCAHY	Mary	30	wife		Coolalisheen	LE	22
559	MULCAHY	Ellen	4	dau		Coolalisheen	LE	22
559	MULCAHY	Mary	4 m	dau		Coolalisheen	LE	22
559	MULCAHY	Michael	8	neph		Coolalisheen	LE	22
559	BLAKE	William	32	Br/L		Coolalisheen	LE	22
559	BLAKE	Mary	60	M/L		Coolalisheen	LE	22
560	WALSH	Mary	57	head hk		Coolalisheen	LE	22
560	CROTTY	Mary	25	niec		Coolalisheen	LE	22
560	BARRY	John	34	visi		Coolalisheen	LE	22

561 DORAN	David	40	head lab		Coolalisheen	LE	22
561 DORAN	Judith	36	wife		Coolalisheen	LE	22
561 DORAN	David	13	son		Coolalisheen	LE	22
561 DORAN	Thomas	10	son		Coolalisheen	LE	22
561 DORAN	Elizabeth	7	dau		Coolalisheen	LE	22
561 DORAN	Mary	1	dau		Coolalisheen	LE	22
561 FLYNN	Johanna	30	S/L		Coolalisheen	LE	22
562 LOMASNEY	Judith	50	head hk	husb. in America	Coolalisheen	LE	22
563 CORBITT	Judith	60	head farmer	widow	Coolalisheen	LE	22
563 CORBITT	Timothy	30	son farmer		Coolalisheen	LE	22
563 CORBITT	Catherine	28	dau		Coolalisheen	LE	22
563 CORBITT	Cornelius	26	son farmer		Coolalisheen	LE	22
563 CORBITT	Hannora	24	dau		Coolalisheen	LE	22
563 MANGAN	James	20	serv lab		Coolalisheen	LE	22
564 BARRY	Mary	60	head	widow	Coolalisheen	LE	22
564 BARRY	James	35	son lab		Coolalisheen	LE	22
564 BARRY	John	27	son lab		Coolalisheen	LE	22
087 O'LEARY	William	38	head farmer	widower	Downing N	KC	22
087 O'LEARY	Jeremiah	6	son		Downing N	KC	22
087 O'LEARY	James	4	son		Downing N	KC	22
087 CARROL	Johanna	30	serv		Downing N	KC	22
088 CURTIN	William	34	head cattle dealr	cattle dealer	Downing N	KC	22
088 CURTIN	Hannora (sic)	32	wife		Downing N	KC	22
088 CURTIN	James	5	son		Downing N	KC	22
088 CURTIN	John	4	son		Downing N	KC	22
088 CURTIN	Hannora (sic)	2	dau		Downing N	KC	22
088 CURTIN	James	70	fath		Downing N	KC	22
088 AHERN	John	40	B/L		Downing N	KC	22
088 CAULEY	Bridget	40	visi		Downing N	KC	22
089 ROCHE	Martin	50	head lab		Downing N	KC	22
089 ROCHE	Patrick	20	son lab		Downing N	KC	22
089 ROCHE	John	16	son		Downing N	KC	22
089 ROCHE	James	14	son		Downing N	KC	22
090 DONOVAN	Jeremiah	40	head ploughman		Downing N	KC	22
090 DONOVAN	Ellen	45	wife		Downing N	KC	22
090 DONOVAN	Patrick	14	son		Downing N	KC	22
090 DONOVAN	Ellen	12	dau		Downing N	KC	22
090 DONOVAN	Bridget	10	dau		Downing N	KC	23
090 DONOVAN	Michael	8	son		Downing N	KC	23
090 DONOVAN	William	6	son		Downing N	KC	23
091 DENNEHY	Bridget	50	head	widow	Downing N	KC	23
091 DENNEHY	Catherine	16	dau		Downing N	KC	23
091 DENNEHY	Johanna	14	dau		Downing N	KC	23
091 DENNEHY	William	12	son		Downing N	KC	23
091 DENNEHY	Robert	9	son		Downing N	KC	23

092 RONAN	Catherine	60	head	widow, alone	Downing N	KC	23
093 CROTTY	Rodger	40	head carpenter		Downing N	KC	23
093 CROTTY	Margaret	40	wife		Downing N	KC	23
093 CROTTY	Catherine	12	dau		Downing N	KC	23
093 CROTTY	Mary	10	dau		Downing N	KC	23
093 CROTTY	John	8	son		Downing N	KC	23
093 CROTTY	James	4	son		Downing N	KC	23
094 O'DONNELL	John	51	head lab		Downing N	KC	23
094 O'DONNELL	Julia	40	wife		Downing N	KC	23
094 O'DONNELL	Ann	13	dau		Downing N	KC	23
094 O'DONNELL	James	12	son		Downing N	KC	23
094 O'DONNELL	John	11	son		Downing N	KC	23
094 O'DONNELL	Eliza	9	dau		Downing N	KC	23
094 O'DONNELL	Julia	7	dau		Downing N	KC	23
094 O'DONNELL	Cornelius	3	son		Downing N	KC	23
095 O'DONNELL	James	35	head farmer		Downing N	KC	23
095 O'DONNELL	Mary	25	wife		Downing N	KC	23
095 O'DONNELL	Mary	9	dau		Downing N	KC	23
095 O'DONNELL	Timothy	7	son		Downing N	KC	23
095 O'DONNELL	Honora	2	dau		Downing N	KC	23
096 O'DONNELL	Honora	35	head farmer	single woman	Downing N	KC	23
096 KELLY	Catherine	45	serv		Downing N	KC	23
097 CURTIN	Thomas	30	head cattle deal.	cattle dealer & lab	Downing N	KC	23
097 CURTIN	Johanna	28	wife		Downing N	KC	23
097 CURTIN	James	11	son		Downing N	KC	23
097 CURTIN	Timothy	8	son		Downing N	KC	23
098 O'NEIL	James	30	head lab		Downing N	KC	23
098 O'NEIL	Bridget	25	wife		Downing N	KC	23
098 O'NEIL	Richard	7 m	son		Downing N	KC	23
099 McNAMARA	Daniel	70	head farmer		Downing N	KC	23
099 McNAMARA	Mary	60	wife		Downing N	KC	23
099 McNAMARA	William	33	son lab		Downing N	KC	23
099 McNAMARA	J. W.	32	son lab		Downing N	KC	23
099 McNAMARA	Daniel	28	son lab		Downing N	KC	23
099 McNAMARA	Ellen	24	dau		Downing N	KC	23
099 McNAMARA	Bridget	17	dau		Downing N	KC	23
099 DALY	John	21	serv lab		Downing N	KC	23
099 DALY	Patrick	16	serv lab		Downing N	KC	23
099 DALY	Ann	45	niec		Downing N	KC	23
100 DRISCOLL	Cornelius	35	head lab		Downing N	KC	23
100 DRISCOLL	Ann	21	wife		Downing N	KC	23
100 DRISCOLL	Cornelius	3 m	son		Downing N	KC	23
101 KEEFFE	Cornelius	30	head lab		Downing N	KC	23
101 KEEFFE	Margaret	25	wife		Downing N	KC	23
101 KEEFFE	Mary	1 m	dau		Downing N	KC	23

102 HAYES	John	40	head farmer		Downing N	KC	23
102 HAYES	Eliza	32	wife		Downing N	KC	23
102 HAYES	David	5	son		Downing N	KC	23
102 HAYES	James	3	son		Downing N	KC	23
				(See Appendix for			
103 RYAN	William	6	son	thirty missing	Downing N	KC	24
103 RYAN	Mary	2	dau	records.)	Downing N	KC	24
104 HENNESY	Mary	35	head	widow	Downing N	KC	24
104 HENNESY	Thomas	14	son		Downing N	KC	24
104 HENNESY	James	10	son		Downing N	KC	24
104 HENNESY	Margaret	7	dau		Downing N	KC	24
105 LINEHAN	Michael	46	head schoolmaster		Downing N	KC	24
105 LINEHAN	Ellen	41	wife		Downing N	KC	24
105 LINEHAN	Timothy	15	son		Downing N	KC	24
105 LINEHAN	Ellen	13	dau		Downing N	KC	24
105 LINEHAN	Jeremiah	11	son		Downing N	KC	24
105 LINEHAN	Mary	9	dau		Downing N	KC	24
105 LINEHAN	Bridget	7	dau		Downing N	KC	24
105 LINEHAN	Michael	5	son		Downing N	KC	24
106 COUGHLAN	Judith	44	head	widow	Downing N	KC	24
106 COUGHLAN	Mary	22	dau		Downing N	KC	24
106 COUGHLAN	James	19	son		Downing N	KC	24
106 COUGHLAN	Jeremiah	17	son		Downing N	KC	24
106 COUGHLAN	William	10	son		Downing N	KC	24
106 COUGHLAN	Bartholomew	8	son		Downing N	KC	24
107 SULLIVAN	Bridget	70	head	widow	Downing N	KC	24
107 SULLIVAN	Martin	36	son		Downing N	KC	24
107 SULLIVAN	Edmond	34	son		Downing N	KC	24
107 COUGHLAN	Catherine	40	dau		Downing N	KC	24
107 COUGHLAN	William	11	gr/s		Downing N	KC	24
107 COUGHLAN	John	9	gr/s		Downing N	KC	24
107 COUGHLAN	Bridget	7	gr/d		Downing N	KC	24
108 DALY	David	50	head lab		Downing N	KC	24
108 DALY	Simon	24	brot		Downing N	KC	24
108 DALY	Eliza	18	sist		Downing N	KC	24
108 DALY	Catherine	16	sist		Downing N	KC	24
108 DALY	Mary	14	dau		Downing N	KC	24
109 TOBIN	John	50	head lab		Downing N	KC	24
109 TOBIN	Mary	46	wife		Downing N	KC	24
109 TOBIN	Mary	18	dau		Downing N	KC	24
109 TOBIN	Margaret	16	dau		Downing N	KC	24
109 TOBIN	Ellen	14	dau		Downing N	KC	24
109 TOBIN	Patrick	13	son		Downing N	KC	24
109 TOBIN	James	7	son		Downing N	KC	24
109 TOBIN	Margaret	80	moth		Downing N	KC	24
109 DALY	James	2	visi		Downing N	KC	24
110 O'LEARY	Ellen	60	head	widow	Downing N	KC	24

110 O'LEARY	Hannah	28	dau			Downing N	KC	24

111 O'BRIEN	Michael	68	head caretaker			Downing S	KC	24
111 O'BRIEN	Margaret	63	wife			Downing S	KC	24
111 O'BRIEN	Cornelius	16	son			Downing S	KC	24

112 HENDLEY	Arthur	40	head gentleman			Downing S	KC	24
112 HENDLEY	Francis	24	wife			Downing S	KC	24
112 HENDLEY	Mary	60	sist			Downing S	KC	24
112 HENDLEY	Phebe	50	sist			Downing S	KC	24
112 NORCOTT	Richard P.	59	F/L			Downing S	KC	24
112 NORCOTT	Edward	15	B/L			Downing S	KC	24
112 HENDLEY	Eliza	19	niec			Downing S	KC	24
112 LEAHY	Mary	15	serv			Downing S	KC	24
112 QUINLAN	Richard	20	serv			Downing S	KC	24
112 WILKINSON	William	12	serv			Downing S	KC	24
112 PRICE	Kate	20	serv			Downing S	KC	24
112 PRICE	Mary	30	serv			Downing S	KC	24
112 PRICE	Michael	5	son	son to Mary		Downing S	KC	24
112 STARKIE	Thomas	52	serv	serv. to Wm.Norcott		Downing S	KC	24

113 RICE	Thomas	27	head farmer			Downing S	KC	25
113 RICE	Edmond	39	brot			Downing S	KC	25
113 HEFFERNAN	Michael	60	serv			Downing S	KC	25
113 McCRAITH	James	50	serv herdsman			Downing S	KC	25
113 HENNESY	David	14	serv lab			Downing S	KC	25
113 CASEY	Ellen	52	serv milkmaid			Downing S	KC	25
113 TWOMY	Hannah	25	serv dairymaid			Downing S	KC	25

114 ASHBY	William	32	head ploughman			Downing S	KC	25
114 ASHBY	Ellen	40	wife			Downing S	KC	25
114 ASHBY	Michael	6	son			Downing S	KC	25
114 ASHBY	William	3	son			Downing S	KC	25
114 ASHBY	Mary	3	dau			Downing S	KC	25
114 MEADE	Honora	12	serv			Downing S	KC	25

115 CAHILL	Patrick	52	head quarryman			Downing S	KC	25
115 CAHILL	Julia	32	wife			Downing S	KC	25
115 CAHILL	Patrick	6 w	son			Downing S	KC	25
115 CAHILL	Catherine	70	visi			Downing S	KC	25

116 O'LEARY	Peter	48	head cattle dlr	jobber in cattle		Downing S	KC	25
116 O'LEARY	Margaret	56	sist			Downing S	KC	25
116 O'FLANAGAN	Ellen	78	cous			Downing S	KC	25

117 QUINLAN	Johanna	55	head	widow		Downing S	KC	25
117 QUINLAN	Ann	24	dau			Downing S	KC	25
117 QUINLAN	John	16	son			Downing S	KC	25
117 MOLONE	Ann	77	S/L			Downing S	KC	25
117 HENDLEY	Mary	9	gr/d			Downing S	KC	25

185 PIERCE	John P.	33	head gent.farmer	Esq.		Glanseskin	KW	28
185 PIERCE	Ann	28	wife			Glanseskin	KW	28
185 PIERCE	William	8	son			Glanseskin	KW	28

185	PIERCE	John	5	son	Glanseskin	KW	28
185	PIERCE	Ann	3	dau	Glanseskin	KW	28
185	PIERCE	Mary	1	dau	Glanseskin	KW	28
185	BRIEN	Mary	38	serv	Glanseskin	KW	28
185	BRIEN	Terence	45	serv	Glanseskin	KW	28
185	SENNOTT	Margaret	25	serv	Glanseskin	KW	28
185	DOODY	Bridget	26	serv	Glanseskin	KW	28
186	BANFIELD	Thomas	62	head pensioner	Glanseskin	KW	29
186	BANFIELD	Mary	50	wife	Glanseskin	KW	29
186	BANFIELD	Thomas	15	son	Glanseskin	KW	29
187	ATKINS	John	45	head pensioner	Glanseskin	KW	29
187	ATKINS	Mary	25	wife	Glanseskin	KW	29
187	ATKINS	Thomas	2	son	Glanseskin	KW	29
188	MORONEY	William	22	head miller	Glanseskin	KW	29
188	MORONEY	David	25	brot	Glanseskin	KW	29
188	MORONEY	Margaret	18	sist	Glanseskin	KW	29
188	O'CONNOR	Mary	5	niec	Glanseskin	KW	29
189	MAGNER	John	59	head farmer	Glanseskin	KW	29
189	MAGNER	Mary	58	wife	Glanseskin	KW	29
189	MAGNER	David	21	son	Glanseskin	KW	29
189	MAGNER	John	17	son	Glanseskin	KW	29
189	MAGNER	Bridget	14	dau	Glanseskin	KW	29
189	MAGNER	Mary	9	dau	Glanseskin	KW	29
189	CONDON	William	50	visi	Glanseskin	KW	29
189	CONDON	Patrick	7	visi	Glanseskin	KW	29
190	RYAN	John	29	head surveyor farm surveyor & farmer	Glanseskin	KW	29
190	RYAN	Mary	22	wife	Glanseskin	KW	29
190	CASEY	Judith	9	S/L	Glanseskin	KW	29
191	TOBIN	Richard	52	head lab	Glanseskin	KW	29
191	TOBIN	Mary	10	dau	Glanseskin	KW	29
191	TOBIN	Thomas	4	son	Glanseskin	KW	29
191	TOBIN	Maurice	54	brot	Glanseskin	KW	29
192	VEALE	Abigail	56	head	widow	Glanseskin	KW	29
192	VEALE	Thomas	26	son	Glanseskin	KW	29
192	CONNOLY	Dennis	16	neph	Glanseskin	KW	29
193	CURTIN	Catherine	67	head	widow	Glanseskin	KW	29
193	CURTIN	Michael	21	son	Glanseskin	KW	29
193	CURTIN	Jane	17	dau	Glanseskin	KW	29
193	CURTIN	Thomas	7	neph	Glanseskin	KW	29
193	CURTIN	Patrick	5	neph	Glanseskin	KW	29
194	HALLORAN	Patrick	53	head lab	Glanseskin	KW	29
194	HALLORAN	Mary	52	wife	Glanseskin	KW	29
194	HALLORAN	John	14	son	Glanseskin	KW	29
194	HALLORAN	William	11	son	Glanseskin	KW	29
194	McCRAITH	Julia	80	visi	Glanseskin	KW	29

195 MYLES	John	33	head lab		Glanseskin	KW	29
195 MYLES	Mary	31	wife		Glanseskin	KW	29
195 MYLES	William	16	son		Glanseskin	KW	29
195 MYLES	John	10	son		Glanseskin	KW	29
195 MYLES	Jeremiah	7	son		Glanseskin	KW	29
196 FANNING	Catherine	60	head	widow, living alone	Glanseskin	KW	29
197 WALSH	James	65	head haberdasher	living alone	Glanseskin	KW	29
198 QUINLAN	Denis	40	head lab		Glanseskin	KW	29
198 QUINLAN	Catherine	42	sist		Glanseskin	KW	29
198 QUINLAN	Margaret	26	sist		Glanseskin	KW	29
198 ELLAW	Nancy	50	sist		Glanseskin	KW	29
198 ELLAW	George	21	cous		Glanseskin	KW	29
198 ELLAW	Catherine	20	cous		Glanseskin	KW	29
199 TWOMY	Edmond	65	head lab		Glanseskin	KW	30
199 TWOMY	Mary	60	wife		Glanseskin	KW	30
200 WALSH	Mary	58	head	widow	Glanseskin	KW	30
200 WALSH	Michael	34	son		Glanseskin	KW	30
201 ROCHE	Richard	63	head weighmaster		Glanseskin	KW	30
201 ROCHE	Julia	56	wife		Glanseskin	KW	30
201 WALSH	Mary	10	niec		Glanseskin	KW	30
202 GALAVAN	David	64	head lab		Glanseskin	KW	30
202 GALAVAN	Mary	55	wife		Glanseskin	KW	30
202 GALAVAN	David	18	son		Glanseskin	KW	30
203 BRIEN	Terence	45	head lab		Glanseskin	KW	30
203 BRIEN	Mary	39	wife		Glanseskin	KW	30
203 BRIEN	Julia	6	dau		Glanseskin	KW	30
118 TEULON	Peter	62	head gentleman	Esq.	Glenwood	KC	25
118 CLANCY	Thomas	45	serv		Glenwood	KC	25
118 BROWN	Catherine	40	serv		Glenwood	KC	25
118 SULLIVAN	Eliza	20	serv		Glenwood	KC	25
119 CONDON	Johanna	24	head dressmaker	widow	Glenwood	KC	25
119 CONDON	Patrick	5	son		Glenwood	KC	25
119 FOLEY	Eliza	20	visi		Glenwood	KC	25
120 HARRINGTON	James	54	head steward		Glenwood	KC	25
120 HARRINGTON	Johanna	48	wife		Glenwood	KC	25
120 HARRINGTON	Mary	20	dau		Glenwood	KC	25
120 HARRINGTON	Johanna	18	dau		Glenwood	KC	25
120 HARRINGTON	John	15	son		Glenwood	KC	25
120 HARRINGTON	Ellen	13	dau		Glenwood	KC	25
120 HARRINGTON	Michael	11	son		Glenwood	KC	25
120 HARRINGTON	James	8	son		Glenwood	KC	25

204	BYRNES	Eugene	44	head farmer	Landlord Earl of	Graig	KW	26
204	BYRNES	Bridget	40	wife	Mt. Cashell	Graig	KW	26
204	BYRNES	John	13	son		Graig	KW	26
204	BYRNES	David	9	son		Graig	KW	26
204	BYRNES	Hannah	7	dau		Graig	KW	26
204	BYRNES	Catherine	5	dau		Graig	KW	26
204	BYRNES	Richard	3	son		Graig	KW	26
204	BYRNES	Margaret	2	dau		Graig	KW	26
204	BYRNES	Bridget	2	dau		Graig	KW	26
204	CALLAGHAN	Johanna	60	M/L		Graig	KW	26
204	KENNEDY	Eliza	12	niec		Graig	KW	26
204	CALLAGHAN	Ellen	23	serv		Graig	KW	26
204	DWYER	John	60	serv lab		Graig	KW	26
204	CROWE	William	40	serv lab		Graig	KW	26
204	McCARTHY	Michael	30	serv lab		Graig	KW	26
205	GERAN	John	39	head lab		Graig	KW	26
205	GERAN	Julia	6	dau		Graig	KW	26
205	McNAMARA	Margaret	48	na	widow	Graig	KW	26
205	McNAMARA	Eliza	17	dau	dau to wid McNAMARA	Graig	KW	26
205	McNAMARA	Edmond	15	son	son to wid McNAMARA	Graig	KW	26
205	McNAMARA	John	11	son	son to wid McNAMARA	Graig	KW	26
206	HANLON	James	39	head cattle job.	jobber in cattle	Graig	KW	26
206	HANLON	Mary	30	wife		Graig	KW	26
206	HANLON	Richard	27	brot		Graig	KW	26
206	HANLON	James	84	fath		Graig	KW	26
207	CALLAGHAN	William	34	head lab		Graig	KW	27
207	CALLAGHAN	Honnora	30	wife		Graig	KW	27
207	CALLAGHAN	Julia	6	dau		Graig	KW	27
207	CALLAGHAN	Hannora	4	dau		Graig	KW	27
207	CALLAGHAN	Michael	2	dau		Graig	KW	27
208	FENTON	Daniel	50	head jobber		Graig	KW	27
208	FENTON	Catherine	48	wife		Graig	KW	27
208	FENTON	John	18	son		Graig	KW	27
208	FENTON	Rodger	16	son		Graig	KW	27
208	FENTON	Catherine	14	dau		Graig	KW	27
208	FENTON	Mary	12	dau		Graig	KW	27
208	FENTON	Thomas	7	son		Graig	KW	27
208	FENTON	Simon	4	son		Graig	KW	27
209	KELEHER	Cornelius	50	head farmer		Graig	KW	27
209	KELEHER	Mary	41	wife		Graig	KW	27
209	KELEHER	Eliza	19	dau		Graig	KW	27
209	KELEHER	Mary	15	dau		Graig	KW	27
209	KELEHER	John	12	son		Graig	KW	27
209	KELEHER	Hannah	8	dau		Graig	KW	27
209	KELEHER	Margaret	5	dau		Graig	KW	27
210	SULLIVAN	Timothy	30	head farmer		Graig	KW	27
210	SULLIVAN	Ellen	25	wife		Graig	KW	27
210	SULLIVAN	Ellen	4	dau		Graig	KW	27

210 SULLIVAN	Margaret	2	dau		Graig	KW	27
211 RYAN	William	56	head farmer	also 1/2 pay Lieut.	Graig	KW	27
211 RYAN	Ann	35	wife		Graig	KW	27
211 RYAN	John	19	son		Graig	KW	27
211 RYAN	William	17	son		Graig	KW	27
211 RYAN	Jane	33	serv	(same surname)	Graig	KW	27
211 RYAN	Thomas	27	serv lab	(same surname)	Graig	KW	27
212 MONTGOMERY	Howard	52	head wood ranger		Graig	KW	27
212 MONTGOMERY	Johanna	41	wife		Graig	KW	27
212 MONTGOMERY	Frances	20	dau		Graig	KW	27
212 MONTGOMERY	Arabella	18	dau		Graig	KW	27
212 MONTGOMERY	Margaret	15	dau		Graig	KW	27
212 MONTGOMERY	John	13	son		Graig	KW	27
212 MONTGOMERY	Marta (sic)	9	dau		Graig	KW	27
212 MONTGOMERY	Johanna	6	dau		Graig	KW	27
212 MONTGOMERY	Susan	4	dau		Graig	KW	27
212 MONTGOMERY	Catherine	5 m	dau		Graig	KW	27
213 DONOVAN	Johanna	54	head	widow	Graig	KW	27
213 DONOVAN	John	31	son		Graig	KW	27
213 DONOVAN	Margaret	28	dau		Graig	KW	27
213 DONOVAN	Jeremiah	23	son		Graig	KW	27
213 DONOVAN	Cornelius	20	son		Graig	KW	27
213 DONOVAN	Norry	15	dau		Graig	KW	27
214 FITZGERALD	Johanna	50	head	widow	Graig	KW	27
214 FITZGERALD	Jane	20	dau		Graig	KW	27
214 FITZGERALD	Mary	14	dau		Graig	KW	27
214 FITZGERALD	William	8	son		Graig	KW	27
215 SHERLOCK	John	38	head lab		Graig	KW	27
215 SHERLOCK	Margaret	35	sist		Graig	KW	27
215 SHERLOCK	Patrick	15	neph		Graig	KW	27
216 HOWARD	John	53	head farmer		Graig	KW	28
216 HOWARD	Mary	52	wife		Graig	KW	28
216 HOWARD	Mary	27	dau		Graig	KW	28
216 HOWARD	Martin	24	son		Graig	KW	28
216 HOWARD	Bridget	21	dau		Graig	KW	28
216 HOWARD	William	18	son		Graig	KW	28
216 HOWARD	Michael	15	son		Graig	KW	28
216 HOWARD	James	12	son		Craig	KW	28
216 HOWARD	John	9	son		Graig	KW	28
216 SLATTERY	Thomas	27	visi		Graig	KW	28
217 SWEENY	Patrick	30	head farmer		Graig	KW	28
217 SWEENY	Mary	27	wife		Graig	KW	28
217 SWEENY	Julia	8	dau		Graig	KW	28
217 SWEENY	John	6	son		Graig	KW	28
217 SWEENY	Mary	4	dau		Graig	KW	28
217 SWEENY	Margaret	1	dau		Graig	KW	28

218 SHERLOCK	Edmond	40	head farmer		Graig	KW	28
218 SHERLOCK	Ellen	28	wife		Graig	KW	28
219 SWEENY	Mary	60	head	widow	Graig	KW	28
219 SWEENY	John	35	son		Graig	KW	28
219 SWEENY	Michael	32	son		Graig	KW	28
219 SWEENY	Margaret	27	dau		Graig	KW	28
219 ROCHE	John	12	visi		Graig	KW	28
220 HENNESY	Richard	65	head farmer		Graig	KW	28
220 HENNESY	Mary	50	wife		Graig	KW	28
220 HENNESY	Bridget	16	dau		Graig	KW	28
220 HENNESY	Patrick	10	son		Graig	KW	28
221 PIGOTT	William	48	head lab		Graig	KW	28
221 PIGOTT	Margaret	41	wife		Graig	KW	28
221 PIGOTT	Denis	20	son		Graig	KW	28
221 PIGOTT	John	18	son		Graig	KW	28
221 PIGOTT	Margaret	16	dau		Graig	KW	28
221 PIGOTT	Cornelius	14	son		Graig	KW	28
221 PIGOTT	Catherine	14	dau		Graig	KW	28
221 PIGOTT	Thomas	12	son		Graig	KW	28
221 PIGOTT	Johanna	3	dau		Graig	KW	28
222 COSGROVE	James	27	head lab		Graig	KW	28
222 COSGROVE	Mary	28	wife		Graig	KW	28
222 COSGROVE	Margaret	na	dau		Graig	KW	28
222 CORBAN	James	17	visi		Graig	KW	28
121 HICKEY	Simon	48	head steward	(emp.name illegible)	Gurtone	KC	26
121 HICKEY	Jane	46	wife		Gurtone	KC	26
121 HICKEY	Michael	15	son		Gurtone	KC	26
121 HICKEY	Bridget	12	dau		Gurtone	KC	26
121 HICKEY	Simon	10	son		Gurtone	KC	26
121 HICKEY	Mary	7	dau		Gurtone	KC	26
121 HICKEY	Peter	3	son		Gurtone	KC	25
122 NORRIS	Thomas	49	head ploughman	(age unclear)	Gurtone	KC	26
122 NORRIS	Margaret	46	wife	(age unclear)	Gurtone	KC	26
122 NORRIS	Ellen	17	dau		Gurtone	KC	26
122 NORRIS	Bridget	14	dau		Gurtone	KC	26
122 NORRIS	Julia	14	dau		Gurtone	KC	26
122 NORRIS	Maurice	12	son		Gurtone	KC	26
122 NORRIS	John	8	son		Gurtone	KC	26
122 NORRIS	Mary	6	dau		Gurtone	KC	26
122 NORRIS	Catherine	2	dau		Gurtone	KC	26
122 McCAULEY	James	31	S/L		Gurtone	KC	26
123 SULLIVAN	James	33	head ploughman	(emp.name illegible)	Gurtone	KC	26
123 MOLOWPY	Patrick	24	serv watchman		Gurtone	KC	26
123 RYAN	Patrick	58	serv shepherd		Gurtone	KC	26
123 CROTTY	Honora	30	serv housemaid		Gurtone	KC	26
123 DENNEHY	Ellen	52	serv dairymaid		Gurtone	KC	26

565	COLEMAN	John	34	head farmer		Kielbeg	LE	54
565	LANE	John	20	serv lab		Kielbeg	LE	54
565	FITZGERALD	Denis	21	serv ploughman		Kielbeg	LE	54
566	CANE	Mary	40	head	widow	Kielbeg	LE	54
566	CANE	Michael	13	son		Kielbeg	LE	54
566	CANE	Mary	11	dau		Kielbeg	LE	54
566	CANE	Ellen	10	dau		Kielbeg	LE	54
223	ROCHE	David	32	head caretaker		Kilally E	KW	52
223	ROCHE	Mary	30	wife		Kilally E	KW	52
223	ROCHE	John	4	son		Kilally E	KW	52
223	ROCHE	Margaret	1	dau		Kilally E	KW	52
223	ROCHE	Margaret	75	M/L	(mother?)	Kilally E	KW	52
224	CLIFFORD	Patrick	40	head lab		Kilally E	KW	52
224	CLIFFORD	Catherine	36	wife		Kilally E	KW	52
224	CLIFFORD	Margaret	16	dau		Kilally E	KW	52
224	CLIFFORD	Patrick	9	son		Kilally E	KW	52
225	FITZGERALD	James	42	head lab		Kilally E	KW	52
225	FITZGERALD	Hannah	40	wife		Kilally E	KW	52
225	FITZGERALD	William	18	son		Kilally E	KW	52
225	FITZGERALD	Julia	15	dau		Kilally E	KW	52
225	FITZGERALD	Robert	11	son		Kilally E	KW	52
225	FITZGERALD	Patrick	13	son		Kilally E	KW	52
225	FITZGERALD	James	7	son		Kilally E	KW	52
226	WALSH	Patrick	53	head farmer		Kilally W	KW	52
226	WALSH	Ellen	48	wife		Kilally W	KW	52
226	WALSH	Terence	24	son		Kilally W	KW	52
226	WALSH	Eliza	20	dau		Kilally W	KW	52
226	WALSH	Catherine	18	dau		Kilally W	KW	52
226	WALSH	Patrick	16	son		Kilally W	KW	52
226	WALSH	Ellen	14	dau		Kilally W	KW	52
226	WALSH	Margaret	12	dau		Kilally W	KW	52
226	WALSH	James	10	son		Kilally W	KW	52
226	McCRAITH	John	25	serv lab		Kilally W	KW	52
226	MAGNER	Edward	15	serv lab		Kilally W	KW	52
227	HESKIN	Alexander	60	head farmer		Kilally W	KW	52
227	HESKIN	Mary	55	wife		Kilally W	KW	52
227	HESKIN	Patrick	30	son		Kilally W	KW	52
227	HESKIN	Eliza	25	dau		Kilally W	KW	52
227	HESKIN	Edmond	20	son		Kilally W	KW	52
227	HESKIN	Margaret	16	dau		Kilally W	KW	52
227	HESKIN	Alexander	13	son		Kilally W	KW	52
227	HESKIN	Alexander	21	neph		Kilally W	KW	52
227	COURTNEY	Ellen	53	serv		Kilally W	KW	52
227	COURTNEY	Patrick	16	serv		Kilally W	KW	52
228	FANNING	Margaret	45	head	widow	Kilally W	KW	52
228	FANNING	David	19	son lab		Kilally W	KW	52
228	FANNING	Margaret	12	dau		Kilally W	KW	52

228 FANNING	Johanna	10	dau			Kilally W	KW	52
229 KENNEDY	Michael	30	head	lab		Kilally W	KW	52
229 RICE	Ellen	16	lodg			Kilally W	KW	52
229 RICE	Hannah	14	lodg			Kilally W	KW	52
230 HESKIN	Edmond	60	head	lab		Kilally W	KW	52
230 HESKIN	Catherine	30	dau			Kilally W	KW	52
230 HESKIN	William	25	son	lab		Kilally W	KW	52
230 HESKIN	Edmond	17	son			Kilally W	KW	52
231 PIGOTT	Margaret	56	head		widow	Kilally W	KW	53
231 PIGOTT	Edmond	25	son	lab		Kilally W	KW	53
231 PIGOTT	Maurice	20	son	lab		Kilally W	KW	53
231 PIGOTT	John	14	son	lab		Kilally W	KW	53
232 BRIEN	Mary	80	head	farmer	widow	Kilally W	KW	53
232 BRIEN	Patrick	36	son	farmer		Kilally W	KW	53
232 BRIEN	Mary	30	dau			Kilally W	KW	53
232 BRIEN	Margaret	5	gr/d			Kilally W	KW	53
232 BRIEN	Mary	9 m	gr/d			Kilally W	KW	53
232 BRIEN	Daniel	30	cous			Kilally W	KW	53
232 COLBERT	Ann	20	serv			Kilally W	KW	53
233 BRIEN	Terence	38	head	farmer		Kilally W	KW	53
233 BRIEN	Margaret	35	wife			Kilally W	KW	53
233 BRIEN	William	36	brot			Kilally W	KW	53
233 PIGOTT	Catherine	13	niec			Kilally W	KW	53
233 PIGOTT	Thomas	9	neph			Kilally W	KW	53
234 BRIEN	John	50	head	farmer		Kilally W	KW	53
234 BRIEN	Bridget	36	wife			Kilally W	KW	53
234 BRIEN	William	18	son			Kilally W	KW	53
234 BRIEN	Margaret	16	dau			Kilally W	KW	53
234 BRIEN	Denis	10	son			Kilally W	KW	53
234 BRIEN	Catherine	7	dau			Kilally W	KW	53
234 BRIEN	Nicholas	8 m	son			Kilally W	KW	53
235 CARROLL	Julia	18	na	hk		Kilally W	KW	53
235 CARROLL	Thomas	16	brot			Kilally W	KW	53
235 CARROLL	William	14	brot			Kilally W	KW	53
235 CARROLL	Anthony	12	son		(son?)	Kilally W	KW	53
235 CARROLL	Edmond	10	son		(son?)	Kilally W	KW	53
235 CARROLL	Eliza	8	son		(son! sic)	Kilally W	KW	53
236 FINN	Johanna	40	head		widow	Kilally W	KW	53
236 FINN	Margaret	7	dau			Kilally W	KW	53
236 CARROLL	Elizabeth	33	rel.		relative	Kilally W	KW	53
236 BRIEN	James	33	brot			Kilally W	KW	53
236 BRIEN	Catherine	14	niec			Kilally W	KW	53
236 BRIEN	Elizabeth	6	niec			Kilally W	KW	53
237 RIORDAN	Timothy	33	head	lab		Kilally W	KW	53
237 RIORDAN	Bridget	26	wife			Kilally W	KW	53

237 RIORDAN	Edward	11m	son		Kilally W	KW	53
237 AHERN	Catherine	40	lodg		Kilally W	KW	53
238 COURTNEY	George	64	head lab		Kilally W	KW	53
238 COURTNEY	Margaret	62	wife		Kilally W	KW	53
238 COURTNEY	Mary	29	dau		Kilally W	KW	53
238 COURTNEY	Michael	21	son		Kilally W	KW	53
238 COURTNEY	Ellen	19	dau		Kilally W	KW	53
239 BROUDER	Thomas	32	head farmer		Kilally W	KW	53
239 BROUDER	Mary	28	sist		Kilally W	KW	53
239 BROUDER	Johanna	25	sist		Kilally W	KW	53
239 BROUDER	William	20	brot		Kilally W	KW	53
239 MALONE	James	9	serv		Kilally W	KW	53
239 HANRAHAN	John	7	cous		Kilally W	KW	53
240 HANDLEY	Patrick	40	head farmer	(Kilally E or W?	Kilally W	KW	54
240 HANDLEY	Catherine	38	wife		Kilally W	KW	54
240 HANDLEY	Margaret	14	dau	(top of page	Kilally W	KW	54
240 HANDLEY	William	12	son	says west,	Kilally W	KW	54
240 HANDLEY	John	8	son	record says	Kilally W	KW	53
240 HANDLEY	Mary	6	dau	east)	Kilally W	KW	54
240 HANDLEY	Bridget	3	dau		Kilally W	KW	54
240 RIORDAN	Catherine	20	serv		Kilally W	KW	54
241 CARROLL	Mary	66	head	widow, (E or W?	Kilally W	KW	54
241 CARROLL	Patrick	28	son		Kilally W	KW	54
241 CARROLL	Julia	28	dau	(top of page	Kilally W	KW	54
241 CARROLL	Anthony	20	son	says west,	Kilally W	KW	54
241 CARROLL	Mary	18	dau	record says	Kilally W	KW	54
241 CARROLL	John	13	visi	east)	Kilally W	KW	54
241 CARROLL	Hannah	11	visi		Kilally W	KW	54
660 HUTCHINSON	William	65	head farmer		Kilclogh	MA	61
660 HUTCHINSON	Jane	64	wife		Kilclogh	MA	61
660 HUTCHINSON	John	33	son		Kilclogh	MA	61
660 HUTCHINSON	James	28	son		Kilclogh	MA	61
660 HUTCHINSON	Jane	26	dau		Kilclogh	MA	61
660 CRONIN	Elizabeth	20	serv		Kilclogh	MA	61
661 RICE	Richard	50	head farmer		Kilclogh	MA	61
661 RICE	Catherine	49	wife		Kilclogh	MA	61
661 RICE	Edward	18	son		Kilclogh	MA	61
661 RICE	John	16	son		Kilclogh	MA	61
661 RICE	Richard	13	son		Kilclogh	MA	61
661 RICE	Eliza	10	dau		Kilclogh	MA	61
661 RICE	Ellen	8	dau		Kilclogh	MA	61
661 RICE	Margaret	5	dau		Kilclogh	MA	61
661 BYRNES	Catherine	22	cous		Kilclogh	MA	61
662 GERAN	Catherine	38	head	widow	Kilclogh	MA	61
662 CASEY	Mary	22	lodg		Kilclogh	MA	61
662 BARRETT	Robert	1	none nursing		Kilclogh	MA	61

663 CLANCY	Patrick	40	head	lab		Kilclogh	MA	61
663 CLANCY	Catherine	38	wife			Kilclogh	MA	61
663 CLANCY	Ellen	20	dau			Kilclogh	MA	61
663 CLANCY	James	17	son			Kilclogh	MA	61
663 CLANCY	John	16	son			Kilclogh	MA	61
663 CLANCY	Bartholomew	7	son			Kilclogh	MA	61
663 CLANCY	William	5	son			Kilclogh	MA	61
664 HOGAN	John	32	head	lab		Kilclogh	MA	61
664 HOGAN	Ellen	30	wife			Kilclogh	MA	61
664 HOGAN	John	7	son			Kilclogh	MA	61
665 COUGHLAN	Thomas	40	head	lab		Kilclogh	MA	61
665 COUGHLAN	Catherine	30	wife			Kilclogh	MA	61
665 COUGHLAN	Mary	14	dau			Kilclogh	MA	61
665 COUGHLAN	John	9	son			Kilclogh	MA	61
666 MONTGOMERY	Thomas	30	head	lab		Kilclogh	MA	61
666 MONTGOMERY	Honnora	30	wife			Kilclogh	MA	61
666 MONTGOMERY	Mary	6	dau			Kilclogh	MA	61
666 ROCHE	Mary	60	M/L			Kilclogh	MA	61
667 LYNCH	John	35	head	farmer		Kilclogh	MA	61
667 LYNCH	Jane	36	wife			Kilclogh	MA	61
667 LYNCH	Mary	13	dau			Kilclogh	MA	61
667 LYNCH	Jane	11	dau			Kilclogh	MA	61
667 LYNCH	Thomas	9	son			Kilclogh	MA	61
667 LYNCH	Honora	7	dau			Kilclogh	MA	61
667 LYNCH	John	5	son			Kilclogh	MA	61
667 LYNCH	Elizabeth	3	dau			Kilclogh	MA	61
667 LYNCH	James	1	son			Kilclogh	MA	61
668 HOGAN	David	62	head	farmer		Kilclogh	MA	62
668 HOGAN	Johanna	59	wife			Kilclogh	MA	62
668 HOGAN	David	20	son			Kilclogh	MA	62
668 HOGAN	Michael	18	son			Kilclogh	MA	62
668 HOGAN	Ellen	16	dau			Kilclogh	MA	62
668 HOGAN	Honora	14	dau			Kilclogh	MA	62
669 FLANAGAN	Thomas	65	head	farmer	living alone	Kilclogh	MA	62
670 GRIFFIN	David	40	head	farmer		Kilclogh	MA	62
670 GRIFFIN	Ellen	35	wife			Kilclogh	MA	62
671 GRIFFIN	Edmond	30	head	farmer		Kilclogh	MA	62
671 GRIFFIN	Patrick	34	brot	farmer		Kilclogh	MA	62
671 GRIFFIN	Margaret	19	niec			Kilclogh	MA	62
671 GRIFFIN	David	15	neph			Kilclogh	MA	62
672 McCRAITH	John	60	head	lab	living alone	Kilclogh	MA	62
673 GRIFFIN	William	50	head	lab		Kilclogh	MA	62
673 GRIFFIN	Ellen	50	wife			Kilclogh	MA	62
673 GRIFFIN	George	22	son	lab		Kilclogh	MA	62

673 GRIFFIN	Michael	16	son			Kilclogh	MA	62
673 GRIFFIN	David	13	son			Kilclogh	MA	62
673 GRIFFIN	Mary	11	dau			Kilclogh	MA	62
674 BRIEN	Catherine	61	head farmer	widow		Kilclogh	MA	62
674 BRIEN	Thomas	27	son farmer			Kilclogh	MA	62
674 BRIEN	John	25	son farmer			Kilclogh	MA	62
674 BRIEN	Honora	18	dau			Kilclogh	MA	62
674 DUGGAN	James	15	serv			Kilclogh	MA	62
674 SULLIVAN	Arthur	5	visi			Kilclogh	MA	62
675 FOLEY	Patrick	30	head carpenter			Kilclogh	MA	62
675 FOLEY	Ann	26	wife			Kilclogh	MA	62
675 FOLEY	Catherine	6	dau			Kilclogh	MA	62
676 SWEENY	John	65	head farmer			Kilclogh	MA	62
676 SWEENY	Catherine	56	wife			Kilclogh	MA	62
676 SWEENY	Francis	32	son lab			Kilclogh	MA	62
676 SWEENY	Honora	28	dau			Kilclogh	MA	62
676 SWEENY	Mary	26	dau			Kilclogh	MA	62
676 SWEENY	Daniel	22	son			Kilclogh	MA	62
676 SWEENY	John	18	son			Kilclogh	MA	62
676 SWEENY	Thomas	16	son			Kilclogh	MA	62
676 SWEENY	Catherine	13	dau			Kilclogh	MA	62
676 SULLIVAN	Arthur	5	visi		(also with BRIEN)	Kilclogh	MA	62
677 DORNEY	Mary	52	head	widow		Kilclogh	MA	62
677 DORNEY	John	25	son lab			Kilclogh	MA	62
677 DORNEY	Catherine	21	dau			Kilclogh	MA	62
677 DORNEY	Edmond	18	son			Kilclogh	MA	62
677 DORNEY	Denis	13	son			Kilclogh	MA	62
677 DORNEY	Honora	10	dau			Kilclogh	MA	62
678 NUGENT	Catherine	40	head	widow		Kilclogh	MA	62
678 NUGENT	Patrick	10	son			Kilclogh	MA	62
678 NUGENT	Mary	8	dau			Kilclogh	MA	62
678 NUGENT	Michael	6	son			Kilclogh	MA	62
679 McCRAITH	John	55	head farmer			Kilclogh	MA	62
679 McCRAITH	Margaret	50	wife			Kilclogh	MA	62
679 McCRAITH	Thomas	22	son			Kilclogh	MA	62
679 McCRAITH	Michael	20	son			Kilclogh	MA	62
679 McCRAITH	Ellen	16	dau			Kilclogh	MA	62
679 McCRAITH	Ann	11	dau			Kilclogh	MA	62
680 AHERN	William	36	head lab			Kilclogh	MA	62
680 AHERN	Ellen	30	wife			Kilclogh	MA	62
681 AHERN	James	55	head farmer			Kilclogh	MA	63
681 AHERN	Johanna	45	wife			Kilclogh	MA	63
681 AHERN	Patrick	22	son farmer			Kilclogh	MA	63
681 AHERN	Johanna	20	dau			Kilclogh	MA	63
681 AHERN	Mary	18	dau	to America Apr 8 '53		Kilclogh	MA	63
681 AHERN	Catherine	14	dau			Kilclogh	MA	63
681 AHERN	Ellen	12	dau	to America Apr 8 '53		Kilclogh	MA	63

681	AHERN	Julia	10	dau		Kilclogh	MA	63
681	AHERN	Honora	8	dau		Kilclogh	MA	63
682	AHERN	Thomas	60	head farmer		Kilclogh	MA	63
682	AHERN	John	30	son		Kilclogh	MA	63
682	AHERN	Ellen	25	dau		Kilclogh	MA	63
682	AHERN	Thomas	22	son		Kilclogh	MA	63
683	WHITE	Thomas	70	head farmer		Kilclogh	MA	63
683	WHITE	Honora	26	dau		Kilclogh	MA	63
684	MORONY	Ellen	35	head farmer	widow	Kilclogh	MA	63
684	COLBERT	Ellen	16	dau		Kilclogh	MA	63
684	COLBERT	John	15	son		Kilclogh	MA	63
684	COLBERT	Bridget	7	dau		Kilclogh	MA	63
684	MORONY	Edward	6	son		Kilclogh	MA	63
685	MURRAY	John	40	head lab		Kilclogh	MA	63
685	MURRAY	Mary	40	wife		Kilclogh	MA	63
685	MURRAY	Patrick	6	son		Kilclogh	MA	63
685	MURRAY	Margaret	36	S/L		Kilclogh	MA	63
686	FLEMMING	Mary	80	head	widow	Kilclogh	MA	63
686	FLEMMING	Michael	30	son lab		Kilclogh	MA	63
686	KEEFFE	Catherine	27	dau		Kilclogh	MA	63
687	MOLOWPY	John	31	head farmer		Kilclogh	MA	63
687	MOLOWPY	Mary	33	sist		Kilclogh	MA	63
688	CASEY	James	32	head lab		Kilclogh	MA	63
688	CASEY	Johanna	24	wife		Kilclogh	MA	63
688	CASEY	John	5	son		Kilclogh	MA	63
688	CASEY	Michael	3	son		Kilclogh	MA	63
689	KEEFFE	Thomas	48	head lab		Kilclogh	MA	63
689	KEEFFE	Johanna	40	wife		Kilclogh	MA	63
689	KEEFFE	Daniel	13	son		Kilclogh	MA	63
689	KEEFFE	Thomas	10	son		Kilclogh	MA	63
690	FANNING	William	60	head farmer		Kilclogh	MA	63
690	FANNING	Mary	56	wife		Kilclogh	MA	63
690	FANNING	Cornelius	30	son lab		Kilclogh	MA	63
690	FANNING	John	28	son lab	to America Aug 3 '52	Kilclogh	MA	63
690	FANNING	James	13	son		Kilclogh	MA	63
691	WALSH	Catherine	39	head farmer	widow	Kilclogh	MA	63
691	WALSH	Honora	13	dau		Kilclogh	MA	63
691	WALSH	Mary	10	dau		Kilclogh	MA	63
691	WALSH	John	7	son		Kilclogh	MA	63
691	WALSH	Johanna	5	dau		Kilclogh	MA	63
567	SHEEHAN	Denis	38	head farmer		Kilmurry N	LE	56
567	SHEEHAN	Mary	37	wife		Kilmurry N	LE	56
567	SHEEHAN	Mary	9	dau		Kilmurry N	LE	56

567 SHEEHAN	Bridget	6	dau		Kilmurry N	LE	56
567 SHEEHAN	Mary	60	moth		Kilmurry N	LE	56
568 LANDE	James	35	head serv		Kilmurry N	LE	56
568 LANDE	Mary	35	wife		Kilmurry N	LE	56
568 LANDE	Edward	15	son		Kilmurry N	LE	56
568 LANDE	William	14	son		Kilmurry N	LE	56
568 LANDE	Patrick	10	son		Kilmurry N	LE	56
568 LANDE	Hannah	8	dau		Kilmurry N	LE	56
569 MACKESY	Thomas	40	head lab		Kilmurry N	LE	56
569 MACKESY	Mary	35	wife		Kilmurry N	LE	56
569 MACKESY	James	14	son		Kilmurry N	LE	56
569 MACKESY	Patrick	12	son		Kilmurry N	LE	56
569 MACKESY	Mary	10	dau		Kilmurry N	LE	56
569 MACKESY	Johanna	8	dau		Kilmurry N	LE	56
569 MACKESY	Thomas	4	son		Kilmurry N	LE	56
569 MACKESY	Elizabeth	1	dau		Kilmurry N	LE	56
570 CONNELLY	John	40	head farmer		Kilmurry N	LE	56
570 CONNELLY	Johanna	9	dau		Kilmurry N	LE	56
570 CONNELLY	Denis	7	son		Kilmurry N	LE	56
570 CONNELLY	Michael	3	son		Kilmurry N	LE	56
571 FITZGERALD	Michael	38	head stone mason		Kilmurry N	LE	56
571 FITZGERALD	Ellen	37	wife		Kilmurry N	LE	56
572 CONNOLLY	Michael	36	head lab		Kilmurry N	LE	56
572 CONNOLLY	Judith	32	wife		Kilmurry N	LE	56
572 CONNOLLY	William	9	son		Kilmurry N	LE	57
572 CONNOLLY	James	7	son		Kilmurry N	LE	57
572 CONNOLLY	Ellen	5	dau		Kilmurry N	LE	57
572 CONNOLLY	Michael	2	son		Kilmurry N	LE	57
573 CONNOLLY	Patrick	42	head farmer		Kilmurry N	LE	57
573 CONNOLLY	Johanna	36	wife		Kilmurry N	LE	57
573 CONNOLLY	Elizabeth	10	dau		Kilmurry N	LE	57
573 CONNOLLY	Johanna	8	dau		Kilmurry N	LE	57
573 CONNOLLY	Mary	6	dau		Kilmurry N	LE	57
573 CONNOLLY	William	1	son		Kilmurry N	LE	57
573 CONNOLLY	Ellen	12	rel.	relative	Kilmurry N	LE	57
574 KEEFFE	Michael	33	head farmer		Kilmurry N	LE	57
574 KEEFFE	Mary	32	wife		Kilmurry N	LE	57
574 WALSH	Ellen	60	lodg		Kilmurry N	LE	57
574 DUNN	Mary	43	lodg		Kilmurry N	LE	57
575 FLYNN	William	47	head lab		Kilmurry N	LE	57
575 FLYNN	Mary	40	wife		Kilmurry N	LE	57
575 FLYNN	Catherine	12	dau		Kilmurry N	LE	57
575 FLYNN	James	6	son		Kilmurry N	LE	57
576 AHERN	John	60	head farmer		Kilmurry N	LE	57
576 AHERN	James	30	son lab		Kilmurry N	LE	57

576 AHERN	Mary	27	dau		Kilmurry N	LE	57
576 AHERN	Timothy	25	son lab		Kilmurry N	LE	57
576 AHERN	Elizabeth	22	dau		Kilmurry N	LE	57
576 AHERN	John	18	son		Kilmurry N	LE	57
577 BARRY	Thomas	48	head farmer		Kilmurry N	LE	57
577 BARRY	Julia	42	wife		Kilmurry N	LE	57
577 BARRY	Mary	18	dau		Kilmurry N	LE	57
577 BARRY	Richard	16	son lab		Kilmurry N	LE	57
577 BARRY	Catherine	12	dau		Kilmurry N	LE	57
577 BARRY	Ellen	8	dau		Kilmurry N	LE	57
577 BARRY	Bridget	6	dau		Kilmurry N	LE	57
577 BARRY	Catherine	40	sist		Kilmurry N	LE	57
578 TREHY	James	37	head farmer		Kilmurry N	LE	58
578 TREHY	Mary	29	wife		Kilmurry N	LE	58
578 TREHY	Edward	35	son	(brother?)	Kilmurry N	LE	58
578 TREHY	Patrick	6	son		Kilmurry N	LE	58
578 TREHY	Bridget	3	dau		Kilmurry N	LE	58
578 HICKEY	Johanna	12	lodg		Kilmurry N	LE	58
579 KERESY	Michael	43	head blacksmith		Kilmurry N	LE	58
579 KERESY	Margaret	44	wife		Kilmurry N	LE	58
579 KERESY	Mary	6	niec		Kilmurry N	LE	58
579 FEORE	Michael	25	none journeyman	blacksmith	Kilmurry N	LE	58
579 LENARD	William	17	none apprentice	(surname unclear)	Kilmurry N	LE	58
579 AHERN	Michael	23	serv lab		Kilmurry N	LE	58
579 MYLES	Mary	17	serv		Kilmurry N	LE	58
580 KELLY	John	50	head lab		Kilmurry N	LE	58
580 KELLY	Michael	37	brot lab		Kilmurry N	LE	58
580 KELLY	Mary	30	wife	wife to Michael	Kilmurry N	LE	58
580 KELLY	Mary	9	dau		Kilmurry N	LE	58
581 CONDON	Thomas	38	head farmer		Kilmurry N	LE	58
581 CONDON	Ellen	60	moth		Kilmurry N	LE	58
581 CONDON	Michael	35	brot		Kilmurry N	LE	58
581 KELEHER	Mary	22	niec		Kilmurry N	LE	58
581 AHERN	Owen	12	neph		Kilmurry N	LE	58
581 DALY	Jeremiah	20	serv		Kilmurry N	LE	58
582 RYAN	Phillip	60	head lab		Kilmurry N	LE	58
582 RYAN	Elizabeth	50	wife		Kilmurry N	LE	58
582 RYAN	Mary	29	dau		Kilmurry N	LE	58
582 RYAN	Ellen	26	dau		Kilmurry N	LE	58
582 RYAN	William	23	son lab		Kilmurry N	LE	58
582 RYAN	John	18	son lab		Kilmurry N	LE	58
582 CONNOLLY	Ellen	50	lodg		Kilmurry N	LE	58
582 CONNOLLY	John	17	son	son to Ellen	Kilmurry N	LE	58
582 CONNOLLY	Patrick	12	son		Kilmurry N	LE	58
582 CONNOLLY	William	6	son		Kilmurry N	LE	58
583 BRODERICK	John	60	head farmer		Kilmurry N	LE	58
583 BRODERICK	Mary	50	wife		Kilmurry N	LE	58

583	BRODERICK	Ellen	26	dau		Kilmurry N	LE	58
583	BRODERICK	Bridget	17	dau		Kilmurry N	LE	58
583	BRODERICK	Abby	14	dau		Kilmurry N	LE	58
583	BRODERICK	Margaret	14	dau		Kilmurry N	LE	58
583	BRODERICK	Denis	35	serv lab	(same surname)	Kilmurry N	LE	58
583	RYAN	James	33	serv lab		Kilmurry N	LE	58
583	HICKEY	Maurice	11	serv lab		Kilmurry N	LE	58
584	GRANT	Thomas H. J.	28	head magistrate	Esq.	Kilmurry S	LE	58
584	GRANT	Mrs.	na	wife	(given name na)	Kilmurry S	LE	58
584	GALLIGAN	Honora	55	serv		Kilmurry S	LE	58
584	BRIEN	Bridget	24	serv		Kilmurry S	LE	58
584	HALLORAN	John	40	serv butler		Kilmurry S	LE	58
584	TROY	John	16	serv foot page		Kilmurry S	LE	58
585	HENNESY	Andrew	35	head cider man		Kilmurry S	LE	58
585	HENNESY	Catherine	30	wife		Kilmurry S	LE	58
585	HENNESY	Patrick	4	son		Kilmurry S	LE	58
585	HENNESY	Ellen	2 m	dau		Kilmurry S	LE	58
585	HENNESY	Timothy	40	brot		Kilmurry S	LE	58
585	MILLER	Margaret	20	serv hk	to Mr. Grant	Kilmurry S	LE	58
586	COLEMAN	Michael	32	head farm bailiff		Kilmurry S	LE	58
586	COLEMAN	Mary	31	wife		Kilmurry S	LE	58
586	COLEMAN	Mary	3	dau		Kilmurry S	LE	58
586	COLEMAN	Michael	2	son		Kilmurry S	LE	58
586	LEAHY	Julia	29	serv		Kilmurry S	LE	58
586	LEAHY	Catherine	25	serv		Kilmurry S	LE	58
587	SULLIVAN	Michael	29	head farmer		Kilmurry S	LE	58
587	SULLIVAN	Stephen	24	brot		Kilmurry S	LE	58
587	SULLIVAN	Elizabeth	71	moth		Kilmurry S	LE	58
587	DOYLE	Owen	25	serv lab		Kilmurry S	LE	58
587	ROCHE	John	15	serv cow boy		Kilmurry S	LE	58
587	TWOMY	Margaret	26	serv dairy maid		Kilmurry S	LE	58
588	WHELAN	James	43	head coachman		Kilmurry S	LE	59
588	WHELAN	Ann	40	wife		Kilmurry S	LE	59
588	WHELAN	Francis	9	son		Kilmurry S	LE	59
588	WHELAN	James	7	son		Kilmurry S	LE	59
588	WHELAN	John	5	son		Kilmurry S	LE	59
588	WHELAN	Thomas	2	son		Kilmurry S	LE	59
588	WHELAN	Ann	8 m	dau		Kilmurry S	LE	59
588	BRIEN	Mary	20	serv		Kilmurry S	LE	59
589	MYLES	Thomas	58	head lab		Kilmurry S	LE	59
589	MYLES	Honora	58	wife		Kilmurry S	LE	59
589	MYLES	Eliza	14	dau		Kilmurry S	LE	59
589	MYLES	Honor	10	dau		Kilmurry S	LE	59
590	CROTTY	John	66	head farmer		Kilmurry S	LE	59
590	CROTTY	Eliza	60	wife lab		Kilmurry S	LE	59
590	CROTTY	Mary	30	dau		Kilmurry S	LE	59
590	CROTTY	John	24	son lab		Kilmurry S	LE	59

590 CROTTY	Michael	22	son lab		Kilmurry S	LE	59
590 MAHONY	Eliza	19	cous		Kilmurry S	LE	59
591 AHERN	Timothy	73	head farmer		Kilmurry S	LE	59
591 AHERN	Bridget	70	wife		Kilmurry S	LE	59
591 AHERN	James	40	son lab		Kilmurry S	LE	59
591 AHERN	John	32	son lab		Kilmurry S	LE	59
591 FLYNN	James	10	gr/s		Kilmurry S	LE	59
592 WHELAN	Patrick	52	head lab		Kilmurry S	LE	59
592 WHELAN	Honora	52	wife		Kilmurry S	LE	59
592 WHELAN	Nancy	16	dau		Kilmurry S	LE	59
592 WHELAN	Honora	13	dau		Kilmurry S	LE	59
592 CAREY	Mary	22	D/L		Kilmurry S	LE	59
593 HENNESY	James	40	head lab		Kilmurry S	LE	59
593 HENNESY	Bridget	40	wife		Kilmurry S	LE	59
593 HENNESY	Michael	8	son		Kilmurry S	LE	59
593 HENNESY	Pat	6	son		Kilmurry S	LE	59
593 HENNESY	Timothy	4	son		Kilmurry S	LE	59
594 BERMINGHAM	Mary	48	head	widow	Kilmurry S	LE	59
594 BERMINGHAM	Walter	13	son		Kilmurry S	LE	59
595 MAHONY	William	36	head lab		Kilmurry S	LE	59
595 MAHONY	John	28	brot		Kilmurry S	LE	59
595 MAHONY	Eliza	19	sist		Kilmurry S	LE	59
596 CASEY	Margaret	80	head	widow	Kilmurry S	LE	59
596 CUMMINS	Margaret	20	gr/d		Kilmurry S	LE	59
597 CASEY	Patrick	35	head farmer		Kilmurry S	LE	59
597 CASEY	Mary	32	wife		Kilmurry S	LE	59
597 FLYNN	Julia	12	st/d		Kilmurry S	LE	59
597 FLYNN	Emilia	10	st/d		Kilmurry S	LE	59
597 FLYNN	Edward	9	st/s		Kilmurry S	LE	59
597 FLYNN	Eliza	3	st/d		Kilmurry S	LE	59
597 MYLES	Thomas	34	serv		Kilmurry S	LE	59
597 DALY	Patrick	18	serv		Kilmurry S	LE	59
597 ELSWORTH	Thomas	30	lodg		Kilmurry S	LE	59
598 FLYNN	John	40	head farmer		Kilmurry S	LE	59
598 FLYNN	Julia	28	dau		Kilmurry S	LE	59
598 FLYNN	Edward	24	son		Kilmurry S	LE	59
598 FLYNN	James	19	son		Kilmurry S	LE	59
598 FLYNN	Eliza	17	dau		Kilmurry S	LE	59
598 FLYNN	Catherine	15	dau		Kilmurry S	LE	59
598 QUIRK	Mary	78	M/L		Kilmurry S	LE	59
598 VERLIN	Richard	26	serv lab		Kilmurry S	LE	59
599 KEATING	Thomas	32	head lab		Kilmurry S	LE	59
599 KEATING	Ellen	32	wife		Kilmurry S	LE	59
599 KEATING	Ellen	1	dau		Kilmurry S	LE	59
599 KEANE	Ellen	9	rel.	relative	Kilmurry S	LE	59

600 MURPHY	John	33	head ploughman		Kilmurry S	LE	60
600 MURPHY	Mary	38	wife		Kilmurry S	LE	60
600 MURPHY	John	5	son		Kilmurry S	LE	60
600 MURPHY	Edward	4	son		Kilmurry S	LE	60
600 MURPHY	Catherine	1	dau		Kilmurry S	LE	60
601 DONOUGHUE	Edward	40	head lab		Kilmurry S	LE	60
601 DONOUGHUE	Mary	40	wife		Kilmurry S	LE	60
601 DONOUGHUE	Thomas	8	son		Kilmurry S	LE	60
601 DONOUGHUE	Mary	5	dau		Kilmurry S	LE	60
602 SHEEHAN	Patrick	48	head farmer		Kilmurry S	LE	60
602 SHEEHAN	Ellen	32	wife		Kilmurry S	LE	60
602 SHEEHAN	Ellen	2	dau		Kilmurry S	LE	60
602 SHEEHAN	Francis	8 m	son		Kilmurry S	LE	60
602 FLYNN	Ellen	76	M/L		Kilmurry S	LE	60
603 CODY	James	40	head farmer		Kilmurry S	LE	60
603 CODY	Hannah	40	wife		Kilmurry S	LE	60
603 CODY	Ellen	9	dau		Kilmurry S	LE	60
603 CODY	Edward	7	son		Kilmurry S	LE	60
603 CODY	James	5	son		Kilmurry S	LE	60
603 CODY	Margaret	3	dau		Kilmurry S	LE	60
604 WALSH	John	60	head farmer		Kilmurry S	LE	60
604 WALSH	Bridget	50	wife		Kilmurry S	LE	60
604 WALSH	James	27	son		Kilmurry S	LE	60
604 WALSH	Margaret	25	dau		Kilmurry S	LE	60
604 WALSH	Mary	23	dau		Kilmurry S	LE	60
604 WALSH	Catherine	20	dau		Kilmurry S	LE	60
604 WALSH	Thomas	18	son		Kilmurry S	LE	60
604 WALSH	Patrick	16	son		Kilmurry S	LE	60
604 WALSH	Michael	14	son		Kilmurry S	LE	60
604 WALSH	David	11	son		Kilmurry S	LE	60
604 WALSH	John	5	son		Kilmurry S	LE	60
605 WALSH	Jeremiah	50	head lab		Kilmurry S	LE	60
605 WALSH	Mary	42	wife	d. Feb. 12 1852?	Kilmurry S	LE	60
605 WALSH	Margaret	18	dau	d. Feb. 12 1852?	Kilmurry S	LE	60
605 WALSH	Mary	16	dau		Kilmurry S	LE	60
605 WALSH	Patrick	13	son	(family entry	Kilmurry S	LE	60
605 WALSH	John	11	son	confusing)	Kilmurry S	LE	60
605 WALSH	Ellen	9	dau		Kilmurry S	LE	60
605 WALSH	David	7	son		Kilmurry S	LE	60
605 WALSH	Honora	5	dau		Kilmurry S	LE	60
605 WALSH	Ellen	18	dau	(2 Ellens? sic)	Kilmurry S	LE	60
606 SHANAHAN	Patrick	34	head farmer	and wood ranger	Kilmurry S	LE	60
606 SHANAHAN	Johanna	30	wife		Kilmurry S	LE	60
606 SHANAHAN	Margaret	7	dau		Kilmurry S	LE	60
606 SHANAHAN	Catherine	5	dau		Kilmurry S	LE	60
606 SHANAHAN	John	4	son		Kilmurry S	LE	60
606 SHANAHAN	Thomas	10m	son		Kilmurry S	LE	60
606 SHANAHAN	Margaret	32	sist		Kilmurry S	LE	60

606 SAVAGE	Edward	20	serv lab		Kilmurry S	LE	60
606 KELLY	John	12	serv		Kilmurry S	LE	60
607 BRIEN	Michael	36	head farmer		Kilmurry S	LE	60
607 BRIEN	Johanna	40	wife		Kilmurry S	LE	60
607 BRIEN	William	12	son		Kilmurry S	LE	60
607 BRIEN	John	10	son		Kilmurry S	LE	60
607 BRIEN	Thomas	8	son		Kilmurry S	LE	60
607 BRIEN	Patrick	6	son		Kilmurry S	LE	60
607 BRIEN	Johanna	4	dau		Kilmurry S	LE	60
607 BRIEN	Eliza	3	dau		Kilmurry S	LE	60
607 BRIEN	Timothy	42	serv	(same surname)	Kilmurry S	LE	60
607 BRIEN	Mary	20	serv	(same surname)	Kilmurry S	LE	60
608 COLEMAN	Ellen	58	head farmer	widow	Kilmurry S	LE	60
608 COLEMAN	Michael	18	neph farmer		Kilmurry S	LE	60
608 COLEMAN	John	16	neph		Kilmurry S	LE	60
608 COLEMAN	Margaret	21	niec		Kilmurry S	LE	61
608 BRIEN	James	28	serv lab		Kilmurry S	LE	61
608 MURRAY	Mary	16	serv		Kilmurry S	LE	61
608 MURRAY	Mary	46	serv	(2 Mary Murrays)	Kilmurry S	LE	61
608 WALL	Mary	40	serv		Kilmurry S	LE	61
609 TOBIN	John	53	head ploughman		Kilmurry S	LE	61
609 TOBIN	Honora	40	wife		Kilmurry S	LE	61
609 TOBIN	Michael	24	son		Kilmurry S	LE	61
609 TOBIN	James	21	son		Kilmurry S	LE	61
609 TOBIN	John	18	son		Kilmurry S	LE	61
609 TOBIN	Thomas	13	son		Kilmurry S	LE	61
610 SWEENY	Catherine	67	head	widow, lives alone	Kilmurry S	LE	61
611 MALONE	Patrick	40	head lab		Kilmurry S	LE	61
611 MALONE	Mary	38	sist		Kilmurry S	LE	61
611 MALONE	Margaret	36	sist		Kilmurry S	LE	61
242 SIMMONS	Helena	70	head	widow	Kilworth	KW	30
242 SIMMONS	Mary	40	dau		Kilworth	KW	30
242 McAULIFFE	Mary	50	serv		Kilworth	KW	30
243 WILLIAMS	John	36	head sportsman		Kilworth	KW	30
243 WILLIAMS	Charlotte	32	wife		Kilworth	KW	30
243 STRAPP	Catherine	9	visi		Kilworth	KW	30
244 MAHONY	David	26	head clerk		Kilworth	KW	30
244 MAHONY	Elizabeth	56	moth		Kilworth	KW	30
244 MAHONY	Kate	14	sist		Kilworth	KW	30
244 MAHONY	Daniel	11	brot		Kilworth	KW	30
245 SEXTON	Margaret	40	head	widow	Kilworth	KW	30
245 SEXTON	William	16	son		Kilworth	KW	30
245 SEXTON	Patrick	14	son		Kilworth	KW	30
245 SEXTON	Eliza	10	dau		Kilworth	KW	30
245 SEXTON	Ann	8	dau		Kilworth	KW	30

246 O'BRIEN	Jeremiah	30	head	publican		Kilworth	KW	30
246 O'BRIEN	Eliza	24	wife			Kilworth	KW	30
246 O'BRIEN	Michael	1	son			Kilworth	KW	30
246 SWAINE	Bridget	16	serv			Kilworth	KW	30
247 ELLARD	John	52	head	lab		Kilworth	KW	30
247 ELLARD	Johanna	48	wife			Kilworth	KW	30
247 ELLARD	Mary	21	dau			Kilworth	KW	30
247 ELLARD	Margaret	19	dau			Kilworth	KW	30
247 ELLARD	George	14	son			Kilworth	KW	30
247 ELLARD	Ellen	8	dau			Kilworth	KW	30
248 HALES	James	31	head	yeoman		Kilworth	KW	31
248 HALES	Mary	40	sist			Kilworth	KW	31
248 HALES	Patty	37	sist			Kilworth	KW	31
248 HALES	Eliza	24	sist			Kilworth	KW	31
249 ROCHE	William	47	head	blacksmith		Kilworth	KW	31
249 ROCHE	Mary	45	wife			Kilworth	KW	31
249 ROCHE	Thomas	22	son			Kilworth	KW	31
249 ROCHE	Ellen	18	dau			Kilworth	KW	31
249 ROCHE	John	16	son			Kilworth	KW	31
249 ROCHE	Julia	12	dau			Kilworth	KW	31
249 ROCHE	Andrew	10	son			Kilworth	KW	31
250 FITZGERALD	James	60	head	tailor		Kilworth	KW	31
250 FITZGERALD	Mary	56	wife			Kilworth	KW	31
250 FITZGERALD	James	20	son			Kilworth	KW	31
250 FITZGERALD	Garret	15	son			Kilworth	KW	31
250 FITZGERALD	Patrick	12	son			Kilworth	KW	31
251 NOLAN	Jeremiah	55	head	lab		Kilworth	KW	31
251 NOLAN	Mary	18	dau			Kilworth	KW	31
252 BOLAND	Thomas	57	head	lab		Kilworth	KW	31
252 BOLAND	Patrick	17	son			Kilworth	KW	31
253 CARROLL	Catherine	60	head		widow	Kilworth	KW	31
253 CARROLL	Mary	22	dau			Kilworth	KW	31
253 CARROLL	Catherine	17	dau			Kilworth	KW	31
253 HARDING	Ellen	32	lodg			Kilworth	KW	31
253 ROCHE	Thomas	5	son		son to Ellen HARDING	Kilworth	KW	31
254 SULLIVAN	Patrick	20	serv			Kilworth	KW	31
254 SULLIVAN	Ellen	14	sist			Kilworth	KW	31
254 SULLIVAN	Michael	12	brot			Kilworth	KW	31
255 SCANLON	William	30	head	rope maker		Kilworth	KW	31
255 SCANLON	Honora	23	wife			Kilworth	KW	31
255 SCANLON	Ellen	1	dau			Kilworth	KW	31
256 CROWE	John	50	head	gardener		Kilworth	KW	31
256 CROWE	Mary	40	wife			Kilworth	KW	31
256 CROWE	William	15	son			Kilworth	KW	31

256	CROWE	John	11	son	Kilworth	KW	31
256	CROWE	Thomas	10	son	Kilworth	KW	31
257	BURKE	John	50	head cooper	Kilworth	KW	31
257	BURKE	Johanna	38	wife	Kilworth	KW	31
257	BURKE	Eliza	15	dau	Kilworth	KW	31
257	BURKE	Margaret	13	dau	Kilworth	KW	31
257	BURKE	Bridget	9	dau	Kilworth	KW	31
257	BURKE	Richard	7	son	Kilworth	KW	31
257	BURKE	Edmond	5	son	Kilworth	KW	31
257	BURKE	Mary	2	dau	Kilworth	KW	31
257	BURKE	Ellen	6 m	dau	Kilworth	KW	31
258	CASEY	Denis	45	head shopkeeper	Kilworth	KW	31
258	CASEY	Mary	40	wife	Kilworth	KW	31
258	CASEY	Mary	10	dau	Kilworth	KW	31
258	CASEY	Ellen	9	dau	Kilworth	KW	31
258	CASEY	Norry	7	dau	Kilworth	KW	31
258	CASEY	Eliza	5	dau	Kilworth	KW	32
258	CASEY	Thomas	2	son	Kilworth	KW	32
258	CASEY	Bridget	1	dau	Kilworth	KW	32
258	GEARY	Patrick	26	serv lab	Kilworth	KW	32
258	ROCHE	Patrick	30	serv lab	Kilworth	KW	32
258	CROWE	Bridget	20	serv	Kilworth	KW	32
259	CASEY	John	30	head farmer	Kilworth	KW	32
259	CASEY	Mary	26	wife	Kilworth	KW	32
259	CASEY	Patrick	1 m	son	Kilworth	KW	32
260	DALY	Mary	50	head hk	Kilworth	KW	32
260	DONOUGHUE	Bridget	60	cous	Kilworth	KW	32
261	BOYCE	Mary	34	head private lady	Kilworth	KW	32
261	MULCAHY	Polly	11	visi	Kilworth	KW	32
261	BULL	Catherine	13	visi	Kilworth	KW	32
262	NORRIS	Michael	38	head shopkeeper	Kilworth	KW	32
262	NORRIS	Mary	34	wife	Kilworth	KW	32
262	NORRIS	Julia	10	dau	Kilworth	KW	32
262	NORRIS	Thomas	8	son	Kilworth	KW	32
262	NORRIS	Ellen	5	dau	Kilworth	KW	32
262	NORRIS	David	3	son	Kilworth	KW	32
262	NORRIS	Mary	8 m	dau	Kilworth	KW	32
262	QUINN	Bridget	18	serv	Kilworth	KW	32
263	CONDON	Patrick	46	head publican	Kilworth	KW	32
263	CONDON	Eliza	44	wife	Kilworth	KW	32
263	CONDON	Fanny	16	dau	Kilworth	KW	32
263	CONDON	Eliza	14	dau	Kilworth	KW	32
263	CONDON	Patrick	12	son	Kilworth	KW	32
263	CONDON	Arthur	10	son	Kilworth	KW	32
263	CONDON	Ellen	8	dau	Kilworth	KW	32
263	CASEY	John	28	serv lab	Kilworth	KW	32
263	SWAYN	Catherine	19	serv maid	Kilworth	KW	32

264 FEY	James	41	head postmaster		Kilworth	KW	32
264 FEY	Margaret	22	wife		Kilworth	KW	32
264 FEY	Henry	2	son		Kilworth	KW	32
265 MULCAHY	Catherine	46	head	widow living alone	Kilworth	KW	32
266 BARRETT	Edmond	25	head baker		Kilworth	KW	32
266 BARRETT	Mary	30	wife		Kilworth	KW	32
266 BARRETT	Cornelius	20	brot		Kilworth	KW	32
266 PIGOTT	William	45	rel.	relative	Kilworth	KW	32
266 O'BRIEN	Denis	35	none journeyman	journeyman baker	Kilworth	KW	32
266 CASEY	Norry	30	serv maid		Kilworth	KW	32
267 O'BRIEN	Thomas	36	head shopkeeper		Kilworth	KW	32
267 O'BRIEN	Mary	33	wife		Kilworth	KW	32
267 O'BRIEN	Denis	1 m	son		Kilworth	KW	32
267 CONDON	Ellen	40	serv maid		Kilworth	KW	32
268 MORROGH	James	53	head gentleman	Esq.	Kilworth	KW	33
268 MORROGH	Catherine	47	wife		Kilworth	KW	33
268 MORROGH	Edmond	27	son		Kilworth	KW	33
268 MORROGH	James	14	son		Kilworth	KW	33
268 MORROGH	Henry	12	son		Kilworth	KW	33
268 MORROGH	Michael	7	son		Kilworth	KW	33
268 MORROGH	George	5	son		Kilworth	KW	33
268 SMYTH	Alicia	45	sist		Kilwórth	KW	33
268 SMYTH	Edmond	18	neph		Kilworth	KW	33
268 WALSH	Michael	30	serv		Kilworth	KW	33
268 CASEY	Jane	23	serv		Kilworth	KW	33
268 LANE	Maria	28	serv		Kilworth	KW	33
268 ILARD	Margaret	24	serv		Kilworth	KW	33
269 LOMASNEY	Michael	49	head harnessmaker		Kilworth	KW	33
269 LOMASNEY	Mary	49	wife		Kilworth	KW	33
269 LOMASNEY	Mary	23	dau		Kilworth	KW	33
269 LOMASNEY	James	18	son	to America Aug.3 '52	Kilworth	KW	33
269 LOMASNEY	John	15	son		Kilworth	KW	33
269 LOMASNEY	Michael	13	son		Kilworth	KW	33
269 LOMASNEY	Daniel	10	son		Kilworth	KW	33
270 MILLS	Peter	41	head nailer		Kilworth	KW	33
270 MILLS	Margaret	35	wife		Kilworth	KW	33
270 MILLS	Ellen	16	dau		Kilworth	KW	33
270 MILLS	Stephen	15	son		Kilworth	KW	33
270 MILLS	John	12	son		Kilworth	KW	33
270 MILLS	Margaret	9	dau		Kilworth	KW	33
270 MILLS	Mary	6	dau		Kilworth	KW	33
270 MILLS	Hannah	3	dau		Kilworth	KW	33
271 YOUNG	John	28	head victualler		Kilworth	KW	33
271 YOUNG	Hannah	20	wife		Kilworth	KW	33
271 YOUNG	Matthias	1	son	(abbrev. Matts.)	Kilworth	KW	33
271 NUNAN	Mary	16	serv maid		Kilworth	KW	33

272	DORNEY	Thomas	50	head	stone mason		Kilworth	KW	33
272	DORNEY	Mary	46	wife			Kilworth	KW	33
272	DORNEY	Jeremiah	14	son			Kilworth	KW	33
272	DORNEY	Ann	8	dau			Kilworth	KW	33
272	DORNEY	Jeremiah	32	brot			Kilworth	KW	33
273	DUGGAN	Edmond	60	head	thatcher		Kilworth	KW	33
273	NOONAN	Catherine	50	serv	hk		Kilworth	KW	33
273	MAGNER	Mary	15	dau			Kilworth	KW	33
274	QUIRK	Mary	50	head	pauper	living alone	Kilworth	KW	33
275	SHERLOCK	James	29	head	victualler		Kilworth	KW	33
275	SHERLOCK	Catherine	25	wife			Kilworth	KW	33
275	FANNING	Margaret	12	serv	maid		Kilworth	KW	33
276	HOWE	Joseph	69	head	schoolmaster		Kilworth	KW	33
276	HOWE	Catherine	26	dau		to America	Kilworth	KW	33
276	HOWE	Ellen	23	dau			Kilworth	KW	33
276	HOWE	Edmond	22	son	shoemaker	to America Jun 3 '52	Kilworth	KW	33
276	HOWE	Catherine	10	niec			Kilworth	KW	33
277	HENNESY	John	24	head	farmer		Kilworth	KW	33
277	CORBAN	John	27	serv	lab		Kilworth	KW	33
277	MACKESY	James	30	serv	lab		Kilworth	KW	33
278	HANLON	John	46	head	shopkeeper		Kilworth	KW	34
278	HANLON	Ellen	37	wife			Kilworth	KW	34
278	HANLON	Mary	10	dau			Kilworth	KW	34
278	HANLON	Catherine	8	dau			Kilworth	KW	34
278	HANLON	James	4	son			Kilworth	KW	34
278	HANLON	John	8 m	son			Kilworth	KW	34
278	MULLINS	Michael	18	serv	lab		Kilworth	KW	34
279	SENNOTT	Patrick	57	head	victualler		Kilworth	KW	34
279	SENNOTT	Bridget	48	wife			Kilworth	KW	34
279	SENNOTT	Edmond	27	st/b		step brother	Kilworth	KW	34
279	SENNOTT	Patrick	19	son			Kilworth	KW	34
279	SENNOTT	Bridget	15	dau			Kilworth	KW	34
279	SENNOTT	Edmond	10	son			Kilworth	KW	34
279	SENNOTT	Ansty	8	dau			Kilworth	KW	34
279	SENNOTT	Mary	6	dau			Kilworth	KW	34
279	CASEY	Patrick	10	neph			Kilworth	KW	34
280	ROCHE	Catherine	39	head	lodgings	widow	Kilworth	KW	34
280	CORENCY	James	79	uncl			Kilworth	KW	34
280	CONDON	Mary	28	lodg			Kilworth	KW	34
280	MOLAN	Bridget	42	lodg			Kilworth	KW	34
280	SWEENY	Edward	60	lodg			Kilworth	KW	34
280	CORMACK	James	24	lodg			Kilworth	KW	34
281	GREEHY	John	28	head	lab		Kilworth	KW	34
281	GREEHY	Ellen	25	wife			Kilworth	KW	34

282	CREEDON	Thomas	40	head	blacksmith		Kilworth	KW	34
282	CREEDON	Catherine	50	wife			Kilworth	KW	34
282	FANNING	Eliza	34	st/d			Kilworth	KW	34
282	FANNING	Margaret	14	dau		dau to Eliza	Kilworth	KW	34
282	FANNING	John	12	son		son to Eliza	Kilworth	KW	34
282	FANNING	Edmond	9	son		son to Eliza	Kilworth	KW	34
283	RYAN	William	55	head	shopkeeper		Kilworth	KW	34
283	RYAN	Amelia	50				Kilworth	KW	34
283	RYAN	William	26	son			Kilworth	KW	34
283	RYAN	Patrick	24	son			Kilworth	KW	34
283	RYAN	David	22	son			Kilworth	KW	34
283	RYAN	John	20	son			Kilworth	KW	34
283	RYAN	Amelia	15	dau			Kilworth	KW	34
284	BRIEN	Catherine	61	head		widow	Kilworth	KW	34
284	BRIEN	Mary	32	dau			Kilworth	KW	34
284	BRIEN	John	28	son	shoemaker		Kilworth	KW	34
285	MYLES	Mary	60	head		widow	Kilworth	KW	34
285	MYLES	Johanna	28	dau			Kilworth	KW	34
285	MYLES	John	18	son	lab		Kilworth	KW	34
285	HOWE	Catherine	10	gr/d			Kilworth	KW	34
285	HOWE	Martin	8	gr/s			Kilworth	KW	34
285	HOWE	Mary	6	gr/d			Kilworth	KW	34
285	HOWE	Julia	1	gr/d			Kilworth	KW	34
286	DORNEY	John	30	head	stone mason		Kilworth	KW	34
286	DORNEY	Jeremiah	10	son			Kilworth	KW	34
287	CRANWELL	James	46	head	shopkeeper		Kilworth	KW	34
287	CRANWELL	Ann	48	wife			Kilworth	KW	34
287	CRANWELL	Julia	19	dau			Kilworth	KW	34
287	CRANWELL	Thomas	15	son			Kilworth	KW	34
287	CRANWELL	Mary	13	dau			Kilworth	KW	34
287	CRANWELL	Margaret	11	dau			Kilworth	KW	34
287	WADE	Mary	60	serv	maid		Kilworth	KW	34
288	COTTER	Michael	38	head	shoemaker		Kilworth	KW	35
288	COTTER	Hanna	39	wife			Kilworth	KW	35
288	COTTER	Patrick	14	son			Kilworth	KW	35
288	COTTER	Margaret	12	dau			Kilworth	KW	35
288	COTTER	Hanna	10	dau			Kilworth	KW	35
288	COTTER	Catherine	8	dau			Kilworth	KW	35
288	COTTER	John	6	son			Kilworth	KW	35
288	COTTER	Ellen	4	dau			Kilworth	KW	35
289	SCULLY	Edward	33	head	process serv	process server	Kilworth	KW	35
289	SCULLY	Mary	32	wife			Kilworth	KW	35
289	SCULLY	Daniel	10	son			Kilworth	KW	35
289	SCULLY	Maurice	8	son			Kilworth	KW	35
289	SCULLY	Margaret	6	dau			Kilworth	KW	35
289	SCULLY	Honora	4	dau			Kilworth	KW	35

289 SCULLY	Mary	1	dau		Kilworth	KW	35
289 HANLON	Ann	15	S/L		Kilworth	KW	35
290 CUNNINGHAM	Thomas	52	head sawyer		Kilworth	KW	35
290 CUNNINGHAM	John	21	son		Kilworth	KW	35
290 CUNNINGHAM	Patty	16	dau		Kilworth	KW	35
290 CUNNINGHAM	Frances	14	dau	(Francis?)	Kilworth	KW	35
290 CUNNINGHAM	Julia	10	dau		Kilworth	KW	35
290 CUNNINGHAM	Emelia	8	dau		Kilworth	KW	35
291 FLYNN	James	28	head shoemaker		Kilworth	KW	35
291 FLYNN	Hanna	27	wife		Kilworth	KW	35
291 FLYNN	Mary	5	dau		Kilworth	KW	35
291 FLYNN	Thomas	3	son		Kilworth	KW	35
291 FLYNN	Martin	8 m	son		Kilworth	KW	35
292 McCRAITH	Michael	62	head lab		Kilworth	KW	35
292 McCRAITH	Thomas	35	son		Kilworth	KW	35
292 McCRAITH	Mary	26	dau		Kilworth	KW	35
292 McCRAITH	Jeremiah	17	son		Kilworth	KW	35
292 McCRAITH	Margaret	12	dau		Kilworth	KW	35
293 KENNEDY	Ann	30	head	widow	Kilworth	KW	35
293 McCRAITH	Mary	20	sist		Kilworth	KW	35
293 KENNEDY	Mary	11	dau	dau to Ann	Kilworth	KW	35
293 KENNEDY	Eliza	7	dau		Kilworth	KW	35
294 DALY	Jeremiah	28	head carpenter		Kilworth	KW	35
294 DALY	Catherine	20	sist		Kilworth	KW	35
295 FITZGIBBON	Gerrard	22	head schoolmaster	Nat'l schoolmaster	Kilworth	KW	35
295 FITZGIBBON	Elizabeth	23	sist sch.mistress	school mistress	Kilworth	KW	35
296 CONNELL	Martin	36	head shoemaker	to America Oct 22'52	Kilworth	KW	35
296 CONNELL	Honora	36	wife	gone to America	Kilworth	KW	35
297 CONDON	John	34	head lab		Kilworth	KW	35
297 CONDON	Ann	32	wife		Kilworth	KW	35
297 CONDON	Patrick	14	son		Kilworth	KW	35
297 CONDON	Maurice	12	son		Kilworth	KW	35
298 DORLING	Michael	54	head lab	living alone	Kilworth	KW	35
299 MURPHY	Jeremiah	40	head weaver		Kilworth	KW	35
299 MURPHY	Mary	32	wife		Kilworth	KW	35
299 MURPHY	John	7	son		Kilworth	KW	35
299 MURPHY	Catherine	2	dau		Kilworth	KW	35
299 MURPHY	James	2 m	son		Kilworth	KW	35
300 POWER	Nicholas	30	head lab		Kilworth	KW	36
300 POWER	Mary	32	wife		Kilworth	KW	36
301 CARTHY	Mary	45	head	widow	Kilworth	KW	36
301 CARTHY	Catherine	15	dau		Kilworth	KW	36

301 CARTHY	Richard	10	son			Kilworth	KW	36
301 CARTHY	Patrick	6	son			Kilworth	KW	36
302 PIGOTT	Margaret	29	head	milliner		Kilworth	KW	36
302 PIGOTT	Johanna	26	sist			Kilworth	KW	36
303 FENNESY	Mary	40	head		widow	Kilworth	KW	36
303 FENNESY	Catherine	17	dau			Kilworth	KW	36
303 FENNESY	Bridget	15	dau			Kilworth	KW	36
303 FENNESY	Mary	13	dau			Kilworth	KW	36
303 FENNESY	Ellen	11	dau			Kilworth	KW	36
303 FENNESY	Michael	9	son			Kilworth	KW	36
303 FENNESY	Hanna	7	dau			Kilworth	KW	36
304 LYONS	Patrick	58	head	skinner		Kilworth	KW	36
304 LYONS	Margaret	50	wife			Kilworth	KW	36
304 LYONS	James	22	son	lab		Kilworth	KW	36
304 LYONS	Catherine	18	dau			Kilworth	KW	36
304 LYONS	Johanna	16	dau			Kilworth	KW	36
304 LYONS	Eliza	15	dau			Kilworth	KW	36
305 SHANAHAN	Martin	72	head	weaver		Kilworth	KW	36
305 SHANAHAN	Eliza	34	dau			Kilworth	KW	36
305 SHANAHAN	Ellen	10	gr/d			Kilworth	KW	36
305 SHANAHAN	Martin	8	gr/s			Kilworth	KW	36
305 SHANAHAN	Eliza	4	gr/d			Kilworth	KW	36
305 WATERS	James	50	lodg			Kilworth	KW	36
305 DONOUGHUE	John	30	lodg			Kilworth	KW	36
306 NORRIS	Mary	73	head		widow	Kilworth	KW	36
306 CLEARY	Catherine	40	lodg			Kilworth	KW	36
306 CLEARY	Catherine	20	dau	serv	dau to Catherine	Kilworth	KW	36
306 CLEARY	Johanna	12	dau			Kilworth	KW	36
307 LEE	John	50	head	lab	living alone	Kilworth	KW	36
308 SHANAHAN	Edward	50	head	lab		Kilworth	KW	36
308 SHANAHAN	Nancy	45	wife			Kilworth	KW	36
308 SHANAHAN	Patrick	30	son			Kilworth	KW	36
308 SHANAHAN	James	26	son			Kilworth	KW	36
308 SHANAHAN	Eliza	21	dau			Kilworth	KW	36
308 SHANAHAN	Edmond	18	son			Kilworth	KW	36
308 SHANAHAN	Daniel	14	son			Kilworth	KW	36
308 SHANAHAN	Catherine	10	dau			Kilworth	KW	36
308 SHANAHAN	Nancy	7	dau			Kilworth	KW	36
309 FLYNN	Ellen	50	head		widow	Kilworth	KW	36
309 FLYNN	Margaret	24	dau			Kilworth	KW	36
309 FLYNN	William	22	son	lab		Kilworth	KW	36
309 REDDING	Norry	46	lodg			Kilworth	KW	36
309 REDDING	Mary	11	dau		dau to Norry	Kilworth	KW	36
309 REDDING	William	9	son		son to Norry	Kilworth	KW	36
310 FLYNN	Catherine	30	head		widow	Kilworth	KW	36

310 FLYNN	Margaret	5	dau		Kilworth	KW	36
310 FLYNN	Mary	18m	dau		Kilworth	KW	36
310 SULLIVAN	Ann	18	lodg		Kilworth	KW	36
310 MEANY	Mary	20	S/L		Kilworth	KW	36
311 CASEY	Eugene	40	head carrman		Kilworth	KW	36
311 CASEY	Hanna	36	wife		Kilworth	KW	36
311 CASEY	John	20	son lab		Kilworth	KW	37
311 CASEY	Eliza	18	dau		Kilworth	KW	37
311 CASEY	William	16	son		Kilworth	KW	37
311 CASEY	Eugene	14	son		Kilworth	KW	37
311 CASEY	Margaret	12	dau		Kilworth	KW	37
311 CASEY	Redmond	9	son		Kilworth	KW	37
311 CASEY	Mary	7	dau		Kilworth	KW	37
311 CASEY	Hanna	21m	dau		Kilworth	KW	37
312 LOONEY	James	56	head steward	to Dr. OSBORNE	Kilworth	KW	37
312 LOONEY	Hanna	23	dau		Kilworth	KW	37
312 LOONEY	David	21	son		Kilworth	KW	37
312 LOONEY	Mary	10	dau	10 yrs 6 mo	Kilworth	KW	37
313 RICE	Ellen	50	head publican	widow	Kilworth	KW	37
313 RICE	John	23	son grocer		Kilworth	KW	37
313 RICE	Thomas	21	son		Kilworth	KW	37
313 RICE	Richard	19	son		Kilworth	KW	37
313 RICE	Catherine	17	dau		Kilworth	KW	37
313 RICE	Julia	10	dau		Kilworth	KW	37
313 RICE	Edward	8	son		Kilworth	KW	37
313 SWAIN	Catherine	16	visi		Kilworth	KW	37
313 FITZGERALD	Mary	27	serv		Kilworth	KW	37
313 RICE	Peter	24	serv	(same surname)	Kilworth	KW	37
313 BIBLE	Ellen	72	visi	widow	Kilworth	KW	37
313 GEARY	Daniel	43	visi		Kilworth	KW	37
314 McCRAITH	Eugene	58	head lab		Kilworth	KW	37
314 McCRAITH	Margaret	45	wife		Kilworth	KW	37
314 McCRAITH	Mary	17	dau		Kilworth	KW	37
314 McCRAITH	John	15	son		Kilworth	KW	37
314 McCRAITH	Patrick	13	son		Kilworth	KW	37
314 McCRAITH	Daniell	11	son	(sic)	Kilworth	KW	37
314 McCRAITH	Eugene	9	son		Kilworth	KW	37
314 McCRAITH	Michael	6	son		Kilworth	KW	37
315 BARRETT	Mary	56	head	single, living alone	Kilworth	KW	37
316 BRYAN	Ann	55	head conf.dealer	dlr.in confectionary	Kilworth	KW	37
316 RYAN	Mary	30	lodg		Kilworth	KW	37
317 HUDSON	Hannah	66	head	widow	Kilworth	KW	37
317 HUDSON	John	27	son		Kilworth	KW	37
318 QUINN	Terence	36	head stone mason		Kilworth	KW	37
318 QUINN	Mary	34	wife		Kilworth	KW	37
318 QUINN	John	8	son		Kilworth	KW	37

318 QUINN	Robert	6	son		Kilworth	KW	37
318 QUINN	Ellen	4	dau		Kilworth	KW	37
318 QUINN	Mary	3	dau		Kilworth	KW	37
318 QUINN	Fanny	1	dau		Kilworth	KW	37
318 SULLIVAN	Mary	21	dau	(daughter, sic)	Kilworth	KW	37
319 QUINN	John	65	head stone mason		Kilworth	KW	37
319 QUINN	Hannah	65	wife	d. Dec. 1852	Kilworth	KW	37
319 QUINN	James	34	na	to America Apr '52	Kilworth	KW	37
319 QUINN	Nanne	11	gr/d	(sic)	Kilworth	KW	37
320 CONNORS	Patrick	79	head victualler		Kilworth	KW	37
320 CONNORS	Julia	74	wife		Kilworth	KW	37
320 LONERGAN	Bridget	65	lodg		Kilworth	KW	37
321 RYAN	Thomas	30	head carman		Kilworth	KW	37
321 RYAN	Mary	27	wife		Kilworth	KW	37
321 RYAN	William	5	son		Kilworth	KW	37
321 RYAN	Amelia	3	dau		Kilworth	KW	37
321 RYAN	Ignatius	2	son		Kilworth	KW	38
321 MORIARTY	Ellen	25	serv		Kilworth	KW	38
322 EGAN	Margaret	50	head shopkeeper		Kilworth	KW	38
322 KENNY	Bridget	50	serv		Kilworth	KW	38
323 WALL	Patrick	52	head victualler		Kilworth	KW	38
323 WALL	Mary	48	wife		Kilworth	KW	38
323 WALL	Margaret	22	dau		Kilworth	KW	38
323 WALL	Michael	20	son		Kilworth	KW	38
323 WALL	Honora	18	dau		Kilworth	KW	38
323 WALL	Alexander	16	son		Kilworth	KW	38
323 WALL	Patrick	10	son		Kilworth	KW	38
324 YOUNG	William	55	head victualler		Kilworth	KW	38
324 YOUNG	Sarah	19	dau		Kilworth	KW	38
324 YOUNG	Pierce	18	son		Kilworth	KW	38
324 YOUNG	Ann	15	dau	to America May 9 '51	Kilworth	KW	38
324 YOUNG	Mary	13	dau		Kilworth	KW	38
324 YOUNG	Eliza	11	dau		Kilworth	KW	38
324 HENNESY	Ann	3	gr/d		Kilworth	KW	38
324 COUGHLAN	Eliza	10	visi		Kilworth	KW	38
325 QUINN	Bartholomew	28	head shoemaker		Kilworth	KW	38
325 QUINN	Mary	22	wife		Kilworth	KW	38
325 QUINN	Norry	3	dau		Kilworth	KW	38
325 QUINN	Edmond	10m	son		Kilworth	KW	38
325 QUINN	Catherine	50	moth		Kilworth	KW	38
326 McCRAITH	Maurice	48	serv		Kilworth	KW	38
326 McCRAITH	Norry	45	wife		Kilworth	KW	38
326 McCRAITH	John	20	son		Kilworth	KW	38
326 McCRAITH	Denis	18	son		Kilworth	KW	38
326 McCRAITH	Michael	14	son		Kilworth	KW	38
326 McCRAITH	Sarah	11	dau		Kilworth	KW	38

326	McCRAITH	Maurice	9	son		Kilworth	KW	38
326	McCRAITH	Margaret	3	dau	3 yrs 6 months	Kilworth	KW	38
326	McCRAITH	Thomas	28	brot		Kilworth	KW	38
327	WORRELL	Joseph	27	head doctor	now res.ofDr.T.Payne	Kilworth	KW	38
327	WORRELL	Eliza	23	wife	former residents	Kilworth	KW	38
327	WORRELL	Gertrude	10m	dau	former resident	Kilworth	KW	38
327	WORRELL	Ellen	68	moth	former resident	Kilworth	KW	38
327	MAHONY	Ellen	28	serv	(left with WORRELLS?)	Kilworth	KW	38
327	PAYNE	Thomas	na	none doctor	in res.of J.WORRELL	Kilworth	KW	38
328	GOVLDE	John	64	head carpenter	(ck'd surname spell.)	Kilworth	KW	38
328	GOVLDE	Mary	57	wife	listed as deceased	Kilworth	KW	38
328	GOVLDE	Ellen	26	dau		Kilworth	KW	38
328	GOVLDE	Mary	22	dau		Kilworth	KW	38
328	GOVLDE	William	20	son		Kilworth	KW	38
329	McCARTHY	Jeremiah	24	head Irish inspt.		Kilworth	KW	38
329	RANKIN	Thomas	80	na pauper		Kilworth	KW	38
329	RANKIN	Mary	52	dau		Kilworth	KW	38
329	DILLON	Eliza	76	na pauper		Kilworth	KW	38
329	KENNY	Ellen	19	na pauper	gone to America	Kilworth	KW	38
329	KENNY	Catherine	9	sist		Kilworth	KW	38
330	QUINN	James	54	head clerk	to Insp. CORBAN	Kilworth	KW	38
330	QUINN	James	18	son		Kilworth	KW	38
330	QUINN	David	12	son		Kilworth	KW	38
330	QUINN	Arthur	6	son		Kilworth	KW	38
330	QUINN	Eliza	46	sist	d. Oct. 1851	Kilworth	KW	38
330	QUINN	Catherine	38	sist		Kilworth	KW	38
331	NOLAN	John	70	head summons serv	to Seniscal Court	Kilworth	KW	39
331	NOLAN	Andrew	26	son serv		Kilworth	KW	39
331	QUINN	Ellen	34	dau	to America Jul 19'51	Kilworth	KW	39
331	QUINN	Johanna	4	gr/d	to America	Kilworth	KW	39
331	QUINN	John	2	gr/s	to America	Kilworth	KW	39
331	QUINN	David	11m	gr/s	to America	Kilworth	KW	39
332	ARMOR	Elizabeth	65	head hotel keeper	widow	Kilworth	KW	39
332	ARMOR	Mary	40	sist		Kilworth	KW	39
332	ARMOR	Mary	11	niec		Kilworth	KW	39
332	ARMOR	Henry	8	neph		Kilworth	KW	39
332	BURKE	Mary	30	serv	to America Mar. '53	Kilworth	KW	39
332	McCRAITH	Michael	24	serv		Kilworth	KW	39
333	CONNORS	John	45	head victualler	to America Apr 23'52	Kilworth	KW	39
333	CONNORS	John	15	son		Kilworth	KW	39
333	CONNORS	Maria	12	dau		Kilworth	KW	39
333	CONNORS	Catherine	7	dau		Kilworth	KW	39
333	CONNORS	Felicia	9	visi		Kilworth	KW	39
334	FINN	William	51	head victualler		Kilworth	KW	39
334	FINN	Bridget	45	wife	d. Oct. 4, 1852	Kilworth	KW	39
334	FINN	Michael	18	son		Kilworth	KW	39

334 FINN	Richard	15	son		Kilworth	KW	39
334 FINN	Hannah	8	dau		Kilworth	KW	39
334 FINN	Bridget	6	dau		Kilworth	KW	39
334 FINN	Jane	2	dau		Kilworth	KW	39
335 ANDREWS	Jane	70	head	widow	Kilworth	KW	39
335 HACKETT	Grizalda	55	S/L		Kilworth	KW	39
335 LUKEY	Eliza	45	visi		Kilworth	KW	39
335 SULLIVAN	Edward	52	visi M. minister		Kilworth	KW	39
335 CUNNINGHAM	Ann	27	serv		Kilworth	KW	39
335 WALSH	Abigail	27	serv		Kilworth	KW	39
335 FENNESY	Jeremiah	53	serv steward		Kilworth	KW	39
335 CONNORS	James	25	serv lab		Kilworth	KW	39
336 DUANE	Elizabeth	48	head	widow	Kilworth	KW	39
336 DUANE	John	25	son lab		Kilworth	KW	39
336 DUANE	Ann	16	dau		Kilworth	KW	39
336 DUANE	William	14	son		Kilworth	KW	39
337 CASEY	Bridget	40	head	widow	Kilworth	KW	39
337 McMAHON	Mary	25	niec		Kilworth	KW	39
338 CASEY	Mary	53	head	wid, Anthony's Rd.	Kilworth	KW	39
338 CASEY	Michael	20	son nailer		Kilworth	KW	39
338 CASEY	Edward	12	son		Kilworth	KW	39
338 CASEY	Edmond	9	lodg	(same surname)	Kilworth	KW	39
339 GEARY	John	42	head lab	Anthony's Rd.	Kilworth	KW	39
339 GEARY	Catherine	34	wife		Kilworth	KW	39
339 GEARY	Ellen	4	dau		Kilworth	KW	39
339 GEARY	James	2	son		Kilworth	KW	39
339 LONERGAN	Mary	12	niec		Kilworth	KW	39
340 SINNOTT	Michael	23	head victualler	Anthony's Rd.	Kilworth	KW	39
340 SINNOTT	Norry	13	sist		Kilworth	KW	39
341 FING	Sib	44	head	widow, Anthony's Rd.	Kilworth	KW	39
342 MOHER	Patrick	34	head ploughman	Anthony's Rd.	Kilworth	KW	39
342 MOHER	Mary	34	wife		Kilworth	KW	39
342 MOHER	Ellen	11	dau		Kilworth	KW	39
342 MOHER	Eliza	18m	dau		Kilworth	KW	39
342 FINLEY	Ellen	60	M/L		Kilworth	KW	39
343 COURTNEY	Patrick	36	head lab	Anthony's Rd.	Kilworth	KW	40
343 COURTNEY	Mary	34	wife		Kilworth	KW	40
343 COURTNEY	John	13	son		Kilworth	KW	40
343 COURTNEY	Kate	7	dau		Kilworth	KW	40
343 COURTNEY	John	17	neph		Kilworth	KW	40
344 LANE	William	65	head pensioner	d. June 14, 1851	Kilworth	KW	40
344 LANE	Mary	70	wife	Anthony's Rd.	Kilworth	KW	40
344 LANE	Jane	20	dau		Kilworth	KW	40
344 LANE	Catherine	17	dau		Kilworth	KW	40

345	HARTNETTY	Thomas	55	head lab	Anthony's Rd.	Kilworth	KW	40
345	HARTNETTY	John	26	son		Kilworth	KW	40
345	HARTNETTY	Catherine	17	dau		Kilworth	KW	40
345	HARTNETTY	Thomas	16	son		Kilworth	KW	40
346	SULLIVAN	Honora	56	head	Anthony's Rd., widow	Kilworth	KW	40
346	McCARTHY	Catherine	43	na	widow	Kilworth	KW	40
346	McCARTHY	Johanna	13	dau	dau to Catherine	Kilworth	KW	40
346	McCARTHY	Margaret	4	dau	4 yr 8 mo	Kilworth	KW	40
347	CONDON	William	40	head wood ranger	Anthony's Rd.	Kilworth	KW	40
347	CONDON	Catherine	36	wife		Kilworth	KW	40
347	CONDON	Mary	2	dau		Kilworth	KW	40
347	CONDON	Ellen	36	sist		Kilworth	KW	40
347	CASEY	Margaret	11	rel.	relative	Kilworth	KW	40
347	CARROLL	Mary	14	rel.	relative	Kilworth	KW	40
348	McCRAITH	Denis	32	head lab	to America Aug 24'52	Kilworth	KW	40
348	McCRAITH	Johanna	34	wife	Anthony's Rd.	Kilworth	KW	40
348	McCRAITH	John	7	son		Kilworth	KW	40
348	McCRAITH	Mary	4	dau		Kilworth	KW	40
348	McCRAITH	Michael	2	son		Kilworth	KW	40
348	CALLAGHAN	Mary	64	M/L		Kilworth	KW	40
348	McCRAITH	Denis	10	rel.	relative	Kilworth	KW	40
348	McCRAITH	Mary	7	rel.	relative	Kilworth	KW	40
348	McCRAITH	Norry	5	rel.	relative	Kilworth	KW	40
349	GUINEVAN	Pat	56	head weaver	Anthony's Rd.	Kilworth	KW	40
349	GUINEVAN	John	28	son		Kilworth	KW	40
349	GARRETT	Mary	48	lodg		Kilworth	KW	40
350	SEXTON	William	44	head broguemaker	Anthony's Rd.	Kilworth	KW	40
350	SEXTON	Mary	43	wife	(surname SENTON?)	Kilworth	KW	40
350	SEXTON	William	13	son	to America May 9,'51	Kilworth	KW	40
350	SEXTON	John	10	son		Kilworth	KW	41
350	SEXTON	Eliza	7	dau		Kilworth	KW	41
350	ROCHE	Norry	60	visi		Kilworth	KW	41
351	SULLIVAN	Jeremiah	40	head tailor	Anthony's Rd.	Kilworth	KW	41
351	SULLIVAN	Margaret	42	wife		Kilworth	KW	41
351	DONOVAN	Michael	9	rel.	relative	Kilworth	KW	41
351	McCARTHY	John	19	none journeyman		Kilworth	KW	41
352	HANLON	Johanna	60	head	widow, Anthony's Rd.	Kilworth	KW	41
352	HANLON	John	16	son		Kilworth	KW	41
352	HANLON	Honora	14	dau		Kilworth	KW	41
352	HANLON	Edmond	13	son		Kilworth	KW	41
352	CONDON	Ellen	73	lodg		Kilworth	KW	41
353	CONNORS	Margaret	70	head	Anthony's Rd.,widow	Kilworth	KW	41
353	CONNORS	Edmond	24	son broguemaker		Kilworth	KW	41
354	HANLON	Patrick	50	head cattle job.	jobber in cattle	Kilworth	KW	41
354	HANLON	Mary	40	wife	Anthony's Rd.	Kilworth	KW	41

354	HANLON	James	18	son			Kilworth	KW	41
354	HANLON	Patrick	16	son			Kilworth	KW	41
354	HANLON	Michael	15	son			Kilworth	KW	41
354	HANLON	John	14	son			Kilworth	KW	41
354	HANLON	Maurice	11	son			Kilworth	KW	41
354	HANLON	Mary	4	dau			Kilworth	KW	41
354	HANLON	Thomas	4	son			Kilworth	KW	41
354	HANLON	Margaret	4	dau			Kilworth	KW	41
355	HOLEHAN	Denis	36	head	shoemaker	Anthony's Rd.	Kilworth	KW	41
355	HOLEHAN	Julia	30	wife			Kilworth	KW	41
355	HOLEHAN	Patrick	8	son			Kilworth	KW	41
355	HOLEHAN	Mary	7	dau			Kilworth	KW	41
355	HOLEHAN	Michael	6	son			Kilworth	KW	41
355	HOLEHAN	Norry	3	dau			Kilworth	KW	41
355	HOLEHAN	Catherine	6 m	dau			Kilworth	KW	41
355	HOLEHAN	Patrick	40	brot	shoemaker		Kilworth	KW	41
355	CRONEEN	Mary	14	rel.		relative	Kilworth	KW	41
356	FITZGERALD	James	50	head	broguemaker	Anthony's Rd.	Kilworth	KW	41
356	FITZGERALD	Bridget	40	wife			Kilworth	KW	41
356	FITZGERALD	Patrick	17	son	broguemaker		Kilworth	KW	41
356	FITZGERALD	Catherine	11	dau			Kilworth	KW	41
356	FITZGERALD	Ellen	4	dau			Kilworth	KW	41
356	FITZGERALD	Margaret	35	S/L			Kilworth	KW	41
356	FITZGERALD	John	5	neph			Kilworth	KW	41
356	FITZGERALD	Mary	2	niec			Kilworth	KW	41
357	JOYCE	Ellen	54	head		Anthony's Rd.,widow	Kilworth	KW	41
357	JOYCE	Thomas	27	son	lab		Kilworth	KW	41
357	JOYCE	Patrick	16	son	lab		Kilworth	KW	41
358	CRONAN	Johanna	45	head		Anthony's Rd.,widow	Kilworth	KW	41
358	DOHERTY	Denis	21	son	lab		Kilworth	KW	41
359	SULLIVAN	James	40	head	shoemaker	family in poor house	Kilworth	KW	41
360	FINN	David	50	head	lab	Anthony's Rd.	Kilworth	KW	41
360	FINN	Margaret	48	wife			Kilworth	KW	41
360	FINN	Ellen	13	dau			Kilworth	KW	41
360	FINN	Nancy	11	dau			Kilworth	KW	41
360	FINN	Mary	7	dau			Kilworth	KW	41
361	RYAN	Elizabeth	60	head	pauper	Anthony's Rd.,widow	Kilworth	KW	41
361	RYAN	David	28	son	broguemaker		Kilworth	KW	41
362	HOLEHAN	John	29	head	lawyer	Anthony's Rd.	Kilworth	KW	41
362	HOLEHAN	Owen	27	brot			Kilworth	KW	41
362	HOLEHAN	Michael	25	brot			Kilworth	KW	41
362	HOLEHAN	Peter	19	brot			Kilworth	KW	41
362	HOLEHAN	Julia	15	sist			Kilworth	KW	41
362	HOLEHAN	Owen	56	uncl			Kilworth	KW	41
363	NORCOTT	William	75	head	gentleman	Esq.,Clogheen Rd.	Kilworth	KW	42

363 NORCOTT	Mary	66	wife		Kilworth	KW	42
363 NORCOTT	Catherine	33	dau		Kilworth	KW	42
363 NORCOTT	Helen	31	dau		Kilworth	KW	42
363 DOHERTY	Ellen	22	serv		Kilworth	KW	42
363 PIGOTT	Catherine	26	serv		Kilworth	KW	42
364 CLARKE	Edward	42	head schoolmaster & clerk,Clogheen Rd.		Kilworth	KW	42
364 CLARKE	Eliza	40	wife		Kilworth	KW	42
364 CLARKE	Eliza	15	dau		Kilworth	KW	42
364 CLARKE	Mary	13	dau		Kilworth	KW	42
364 CLARKE	Edward	10	son		Kilworth	KW	42
364 CLARKE	Thomas	9	son		Kilworth	KW	42
364 CLARKE	Alexander	6	son		Kilworth	KW	42
364 CLARKE	Hester	4	dau		Kilworth	KW	42
364 CLARKE	Richard	1	son		Kilworth	KW	42
364 BURCHILL	Thomas	70	F/L		Kilworth	KW	42
364 KENNY	Cornelius	14	serv		Kilworth	KW	42
365 QUINN	Ann	35	head	hus. David in Dublin	Kilworth	KW	42
365 QUINN	Richard	18	son	Clogheen Rd.	Kilworth	KW	42
365 QUINN	John	16	son	family moved to Dub.	Kilworth	KW	42
365 QUINN	Maria	15	dau		Kilworth	KW	42
365 QUINN	Margaret	13	dau		Kilworth	KW	42
365 QUINN	David	11	son		Kilworth	KW	42
365 QUINN	Ann	9	dau		Kilworth	KW	42
365 QUINN	George	5	son		Kilworth	KW	42
365 QUINN	Jane	4	dau		Kilworth	KW	42
366 FAWSITT	Edward	na	head	in form. QUINN house	Kilworth	KW	42
366 FAWSITT	Ann	4	dau	Clogheen Rd.	Kilworth	KW	42
366 FAWSITT	John	3	son		Kilworth	KW	42
366 FAWSITT	Arabella	2	dau		Kilworth	KW	42
367 BENNETT	Sophia	31	head schoolmistrs Clogheen Rd.		Kilworth	KW	42
367 DANIELS	Ann	13	visi		Kilworth	KW	42
368 MORAN	Eliza	63	head nurse tender Clogheen Rd.,widow		Kilworth	KW	42
368 THOMPSON	William	na	none subconstable sick in dispensary		Kilworth	KW	42
369 O'HARA	Patrick	28	head schoolmaster Main St.		Kilworth	KW	42
369 O'HARA	Elizabeth	30	sist		Kilworth	KW	42
369 O'HARA	Michael	6	neph	d.suddenly Apr 2 '51	Kilworth	KW	42
369 COONEY	Mary	40	visi		Kilworth	KW	42
369 MOHER	Norry	40	lodg		Kilworth	KW	42
370 SHEEHAN	Michael	55	head blacksmith	Main St.	Kilworth	KW	42
370 SHEEHAN	Thomas	20	son blacksmith		Kilworth	KW	42
370 SHEEHAN	Michael	18	son blacksmith		Kilworth	KW	42
370 SHEEHAN	John	13	son		Kilworth	KW	42
370 COLEMAN	Eliza	28	serv		Kilworth	KW	42
371 CURTIN	Mary	23	head hk	Main St.	Kilworth	KW	42
371 WALSH	Margaret	9	niec		Kilworth	KW	42
371 WALSH	Michael	7	neph		Kilworth	KW	42

371 WALSH	Julia	4	niec		Kilworth	KW	42
371 WALSH	Ann	18m	niec		Kilworth	KW	42
372 QUINN	Richard	35	head shopkeeper	Main St.	Kilworth	KW	42
372 QUINN	Ellen	33	wife		Kilworth	KW	42
372 QUINN	Margaret	14	dau		Kilworth	KW	42
372 QUINN	David	12	son		Kilworth	KW	42
372 QUINN	Richard	8	son		Kilworth	KW	42
372 QUINN	James	5	son		Kilworth	KW	42
372 QUINN	Mary	3	dau		Kilworth	KW	42
372 QUINN	Ellen	1	dau		Kilworth	KW	42
372 SHEEDY	Judith	44	serv		Kilworth	KW	42
373 LANDE	Edmond	45	head shopkeeper	Main St.d.Apr 11 '53	Kilworth	KW	42
373 LANDE	Mary	40	wife	d. Sep 15, 1852	Kilworth	KW	42
373 LANDE	William	17	na	(son?)	Kilworth	KW	42
373 LANDE	Kate	14	na	(dau?)	Kilworth	KW	42
373 GALLIGAN	Ellen	45	na	(surname illegible)	Kilworth	KW	42
374 GEARY	Daniel	57	head process serv	Main St.	Kilworth	KW	43
374 GEARY	Margaret	53	wife		Kilworth	KW	43
374 GEARY	Honora	27	dau		Kilworth	KW	43
374 GEARY	Johanna	24	dau		Kilworth	KW	43
374 GEARY	Margaret	15	dau		Kilworth	KW	43
375 CONNELL	William	74	head dealer&lodgr	Main St.d. Mar 1 '53	Kilworth	KW	43
375 CONNELL	John	35	son shoemaker		Kilworth	KW	43
375 CONNELL	Honora	24	dau		Kilworth	KW	43
375 CONNELL	Kate	14	gr/d		Kilworth	KW	43
376 CONNELL	Jeremiah	42	head shoemaker	Main St.	Kilworth	KW	43
376 CONNELL	Mary	36	wife		Kilworth	KW	43
376 CONNELL	Mary	10	dau		Kilworth	KW	43
376 COLLINS	James	30	na gardener		Kilworth	KW	43
377 WRIGHT	William	37	head millrite	Main St.	Kilworth	KW	43
377 WRIGHT	Jane	33	wife	fam. moved to Ahada	Kilworth	KW	43
377 WRIGHT	William	8	son		Kilworth	KW	43
377 WRIGHT	Alexander	6	son		Kilworth	KW	43
377 WRIGHT	Richard	4	son		Kilworth	KW	43
377 WRIGHT	Mary	2	dau		Kilworth	KW	43
377 WRIGHT	Nathaniel	1	son		Kilworth	KW	43
377 RIORDAN	Bridget	27	serv		Kilworth	KW	43
378 DANIELS	Michael	52	head constable	Main St.	Kilworth	KW	43
378 DANIELS	Susan	8	dau		Kilworth	KW	43
378 RYAN	Edmond	29	none A. constable		Kilworth	KW	43
378 HOLMES	William	25	none subconstable		Kilworth	KW	43
378 TORBETT	John	27	none subconstable		Kilworth	KW	43
378 HUGHES	Edward	25	none subconstable		Kilworth	KW	43
378 BONYNGE	James	21	none subconstable		Kilworth	KW	43
378 CALLAGHAN	John	30	none subconstable		Kilworth	KW	43
379 CONNORS	Mary	62	head	Pound Lane, widow	Kilworth	KW	43

379 CONNORS	Michael	26	son		Kilworth	KW	43
379 CONNORS	Catherine	20	dau		Kilworth	KW	43
380 CURTIN	Thomas	26	head lab	Pound Lane	Kilworth	KW	43
380 CURTIN	John	5	son		Kilworth	KW	43
380 CURTIN	Jane	18	sist		Kilworth	KW	43
381 HANLON	Edward	47	head lab	Pound Lane	Kilworth	KW	43
381 HANLON	Catherine	41	wife		Kilworth	KW	43
381 HANLON	John	20	son		Kilworth	KW	43
381 HANLON	Edward	16	son		Kilworth	KW	43
381 HANLON	Mary	13	dau		Kilworth	KW	43
381 HANLON	Catherine	11	dau		Kilworth	KW	43
381 HANLON	Ellen	35	rel.	relative	Kilworth	KW	43
382 KENNEDY	Cornelius	44	head pensioner	liv. alone, Pound Ln	Kilworth	KW	43
383 WALSH	Edmond	66	head tailor	liv. alone, Pound Ln	Kilworth	KW	43
384 MAHONY	Daniel	33	head carpenter	Pound Lane	Kilworth	KW	43
384 MAHONY	Jane	30	wife		Kilworth	KW	43
384 MAHONY	Daniel	6	son		Kilworth	KW	43
384 MAHONY	Michael	5	son		Kilworth	KW	43
384 MAHONY	Mary	2	dau		Kilworth	KW	43
385 McCARTHY	James	30	head tailor	Pound Lane	Kilworth	KW	43
385 McCARTHY	Bridget	35	wife		Kilworth	KW	43
385 McCARTHY	Charles	6	son		Kilworth	KW	43
385 McCARTHY	Kate	3	dau		Kilworth	KW	43
386 CORBITT	Timothy	50	head fidler	Pound Lane	Kilworth	KW	44
386 CORBITT	Catherine	52	wife		Kilworth	KW	44
386 CORBITT	Patrick	25	son		Kilworth	KW	44
386 CORBITT	Catherine	17	dau		Kilworth	KW	44
387 LINEHAN	Mary	42	wife	wife to Wm. LINEHAN	Kilworth	KW	44
387 LINEHAN	Ellen	17	dau	Pound Lane	Kilworth	KW	44
387 LINEHAN	Edmond	14	son		Kilworth	KW	44
388 CONNORS	William	40	head victualler	Pound Lane	Kilworth	KW	44
388 CONNORS	Ellen	41	wife		Kilworth	KW	44
388 CONNORS	Ann	17	dau		Kilworth	KW	44
388 CONNORS	Patrick	15	son		Kilworth	KW	44
388 CONNORS	Mary	10	dau		Kilworth	KW	44
388 CONNORS	Johanna	8	dau		Kilworth	KW	44
388 CONNORS	John	6	son		Kilworth	KW	44
388 CONNORS	William	5	son		Kilworth	KW	44
388 CONNORS	Thomas	3	son		Kilworth	KW	44
388 CONNORS	Mary	9	niec		Kilworth	KW	44
388 BRONIG	Johanna	34	S/L		Kilworth	KW	44
388 MAHONY	John	13	neph		Kilworth	KW	44

389 WHIBBS	Catherine	53	head		Pound Lane, widow	Kilworth	KW	44
389 WHIBBS	John	28	son			Kilworth	KW	44
389 WHIBBS	Michael	4	gr/s			Kilworth	KW	44
390 WHELAN	Isabella	46	head		Pound Lane, widow	Kilworth	KW	44
390 WHELAN	Mary	15	dau			Kilworth	KW	44
390 WHELAN	Margaret	12	dau			Kilworth	KW	44
390 WHELAN	Jane	7	dau			Kilworth	KW	44
391 MORONY	Honora	46	head		Pound Lane, widow	Kilworth	KW	44
391 MORONY	Jeremiah	23	son	lab		Kilworth	KW	44
391 MORONY	Richard	18	son	lab		Kilworth	KW	44
392 SHANAHAN	Patrick	55	head	lab	Pound Lane	Kilworth	KW	44
392 SHANAHAN	Mary	52	wife			Kilworth	KW	44
392 SHANAHAN	Edmond	21	son	lab		Kilworth	KW	44
392 SHANAHAN	Patrick	19	son	lab		Kilworth	KW	44
392 SHANAHAN	Margaret	17	dau			Kilworth	KW	44
392 SHANAHAN	Hannah	13	dau			Kilworth	KW	44
393 MALONE	Michael	60	head	cooper	removed to Fermoy	Kilworth	KW	44
393 MALONE	Mary	38	sis		Pound Ln.to Fermoy	Kilworth	KW	44
394 BRUNIG	Honora	70	head		Pound Lane, widow	Kilworth	KW	44
394 BRUNIG	Mary	38	dau			Kilworth	KW	44
395 BROUDER	Daniel	50	head	lab	Pound Lane	Kilworth	KW	44
395 BROUDER	Mary	47	wife			Kilworth	KW	44
395 BROUDER	Michael	17	son	lab		Kilworth	KW	44
395 BROUDER	Eliza	14	dau			Kilworth	KW	44
396 HOGAN	Mary	60	head		Pound Lane, widow	Kilworth	KW	44
396 HOGAN	Catherine	14	dau			Kilworth	KW	44
397 MYLES	Patrick	40	head	lab		Kilworth	KW	44
397 MYLES	Ellen	30	wife			Kilworth	KW	44
397 MYLES	Margaret	11	dau			Kilworth	KW	44
397 MYLES	Thomas	6	son			Kilworth	KW	44
398 HENDLEY	James	65	head	yeoman	Pound Lane	Kilworth	KW	44
398 HENDLEY	Arthur	70	na	pound keeper		Kilworth	KW	44
398 MAHONY	Catherine	48	niec			Kilworth	KW	44
398 SHEEDY	Mary	40	serv			Kilworth	KW	44
399 GOVLD	Henry	53	head	carpenter	Pound Lane	Kilworth	KW	45
399 GOVLD	Honora	23	dau			Kilworth	KW	45
399 GOVLD	Catherine	19	dau			Kilworth	KW	45
399 GOVLD	John	17	son			Kilworth	KW	45
399 GOVLD	Bridget	15	dau			Kilworth	KW	45
399 GOVLD	Henry	12	son			Kilworth	KW	45
400 MORONY	William	40	head	pauper	Pound Lane	Kilworth	KW	45
400 MORONY	Margaret	50	wife			Kilworth	KW	45
400 MORONY	Norry	15	dau			Kilworth	KW	45

400 MORONY	Richard	13	son		Kilworth	KW	45
400 MORONY	Daniel	10	son		Kilworth	KW	45
400 MORONY	William	8	son		Kilworth	KW	45
400 MORONY	John	5	son		Kilworth	KW	45
401 BRIEN	Elizabeth	55	head	Pound Lane, widow	Kilworth	KW	45
401 BRIEN	William	28	son lab		Kilworth	KW	45
401 BRIEN	Patrick	23	son		Kilworth	KW	45
401 BRIEN	Margaret	21	dau		Kilworth	KW	45
401 BRIEN	Julia	20	dau		Kilworth	KW	45
401 BRIEN	Elizabeth	19	dau		Kilworth	KW	45
401 BRIEN	John	17	son		Kilworth	KW	45
401 BRIEN	Johanna	15	dau		Kilworth	KW	45
402 MAHONY	David	40	head lab	Pound Lane	Kilworth	KW	45
402 MAHONY	Mary	40	wife		Kilworth	KW	45
402 MAHONY	Denis	21	son lab		Kilworth	KW	45
402 MAHONY	Catherine	17	dau		Kilworth	KW	45
402 MAHONY	John	10	son		Kilworth	KW	45
402 MAHONY	Mary	6	dau		Kilworth	KW	45
403 TROY	Patrick	48	head lab	removed to Macroney	Kilworth	KW	45
403 TROY	Mary	42	wife	Pound Lane, moved	Kilworth	KW	45
403 TROY	Patrick	14	son	moved	Kilworth	KW	45
403 TROY	Thomas	12	son	moved	Kilworth	KW	45
403 TROY	Hannah	10	dau	moved	Kilworth	KW	45
403 TROY	Mary	6	dau	moved	Kilworth	KW	45
403 QUINN	Michael	22	lodg	gone to England	Kilworth	KW	45
404 STANTON	Johanna	51	head	Pound Lane, widow	Kilworth	KW	45
404 STANTON	Mary	30	dau		Kilworth	KW	45
404 STANTON	Mary	24	gr/d	(granddaughter? sic)	Kilworth	KW	45
405 CASEY	William	21	head lab	Pound Lane	Kilworth	KW	45
405 CASEY	John	19	brot lab		Kilworth	KW	45
405 CASEY	Jeremiah	16	brot		Kilworth	KW	45
406 MURPHY	Johanna	40	head	Pound Lane, widow	Kilworth	KW	45
406 MURPHY	Mary	16	dau		Kilworth	KW	45
406 MURPHY	John	14	son		Kilworth	KW	45
406 MURPHY	Richard	12	son		Kilworth	KW	45
407 CASEY	Patrick	30	head lab	Pound Lane	Kilworth	KW	45
407 CASEY	Bridget	27	sist		Kilworth	KW	45
407 CASEY	Jeremiah	13	naph		Kilworth	KW	45
407 MADDEN	Michael	22	lodg lab		Kilworth	KW	45
408 COSGROVE	Mary	56	head	Pound Lane, widow	Kilworth	KW	45
408 COSGROVE	Richard	27	son lab		Kilworth	KW	45
408 COSGROVE	John	25	son lab		Kilworth	KW	45
408 COSGROVE	Terence	19	son lab		Kilworth	KW	45
409 SCANLON	Margaret	69	head	Pound Lane, widow	Kilworth	KW	45

409 SCANLON	James	40	son		Kilworth	KW	45
409 McAULIFFE	Mary	14	gr/d		Kilworth	KW	45
410 SHEEDY	Mary	52	head	Pound Lane, widow	Kilworth	KW	46
410 SHEEDY	John	23	son broguemaker		Kilworth	KW	46
411 CONDON	Mary	22	serv	Pound Ln, liv. alone	Kilworth	KW	46
412 MYLES	John	18	head lab	Pound Lane	Kilworth	KW	46
412 CASEY	Ellen	35	sist		Kilworth	KW	46
412 CASEY	Ellen	15	st/s	step sister	Kilworth	KW	46
412 McCRAITH	Catherine	55	lodg		Kilworth	KW	46
412 McNAMARA	Mary	52	lodg	widow	Kilworth	KW	46
412 McNAMARA	Margaret	26	dau	dau to Mary	Kilworth	KW	46
413 ILARD	Nicholas	50	head lab	Pound Lane	Kilworth	KW	46
413 ILARD	Ellen	45	wife		Kilworth	KW	46
413 ILARD	John	17	son		Kilworth	KW	46
413 ILARD	George	13	son		Kilworth	KW	46
413 ILARD	William	10	son		Kilworth	KW	46
413 ILARD	Michael	2	son		Kilworth	KW	46
414 CLEARY	Catherine	66	head	Pound Lane, widow	Kilworth	KW	46
414 MOLONY	Ellen	39	dau		Kilworth	KW	46
414 PRIOR	Julia	20	gr/d		Kilworth	KW	46
414 MOLONY	Mary	15	gr/d		Kilworth	KW	46
415 HAGARTY	Mary	60	head	Pound Lane, widow	Kilworth	KW	46
415 HAGARTY	Michael	35	son weaver		Kilworth	KW	46
415 HAGARTY	Edmond	26	son weaver		Kilworth	KW	46
415 HAGARTY	Richard	23	son weaver		Kilworth	KW	46
415 HAGARTY	Catherine	18	dau		Kilworth	KW	46
415 BRIEN	Julia	6	lodg		Kilworth	KW	46
124 MOAKLEY	John	50	head farmer	also Knockanabohelee	Knockanabohelly	KC	63
124 MOAKLEY	Margaret	40	wife		Knockanabohelly	KC	63
124 MOAKLEY	John	14	son		Knockanabohelly	KC	63
124 MOAKLEY	Andrew	11	son		Knockanabohelly	KC	63
124 MOAKLEY	Eliza	9	dau		Knockanabohelly	KC	63
124 MOAKLEY	Cathrine	8	dau		Knockanabohelly	KC	63
124 MOAKLEY	Margaret	3	dau		Knockanabohelly	KC	63
124 SULLIVAN	Denis	50	serv lab		Knockanabohelly	KC	63
124 ROCHE	John	51	serv lab		Knockanabohelly	KC	63
124 O'NEIL	Ellen	30	serv		Knockanabohelly	KC	63
125 WOODS	Ellen	40	head	widow	Knockanabohelly	KC	64
125 WOODS	Timothy	15	son		Knockanabohelly	KC	64
125 WOODS	Mary	14	dau		Knockanabohelly	KC	64
125 WOODS	Maurice	12	son		Knockanabohelly	KC	64
125 WOODS	Bartholomew	9	son		Knockanabohelly	KC	64
125 WOODS	Catherine	7	dau		Knockanabohelly	KC	64
126 CONNORS	Thomas	50	head farmer		Knockanabohelly	KC	64
126 CONNORS	Catherine	45	wife		Knockanabohelly	KC	64

126	CONNORS	Bartholomew	22	son		Knockanabohelly	KC	64
126	CONNORS	Michael	21	son		Knockanabohelly	KC	64
126	CONNORS	Catherine	19	dau		Knockanabohelly	KC	64
126	CONNORS	John	17	son		Knockanabohelly	KC	64
127	McCRAITH	Rodger	43	head farmer		Knockanabohelly	KC	64
127	McCRAITH	Ellen	40	wife		Knockanabohelly	KC	64
127	McCRAITH	Bridget	11	dau		Knockanabohelly	KC	64
127	McCRAITH	Edmond	9	son		Knockanabohelly	KC	64
127	McCRAITH	Catherine	8	dau		Knockanabohelly	KC	64
127	McCRAITH	Rodger	2	son		Knockanabohelly	KC	64
128	TOBIN	Catherine	60	head farmer	widow	Knockanabohelly	KC	64
128	TOBIN	Edmond	35	son farmer		Knockanabohelly	KC	64
128	TOBIN	Mary	25	dau		Knockanabohelly	KC	64
416	NORRIS	Patrick	46	head lab		Knockanohill	KW	30
416	NORRIS	Mary	40	wife		Knockanohill	KW	30
416	NORRIS	Michael	16	son		Knockanohill	KW	30
416	NORRIS	Patrick	13	son		Knockanohill	KW	30
416	NORRIS	John	10	son		Knockanohill	KW	30
416	NORRIS	Mary	4	dau		Knockanohill	KW	30
417	WALSH	John	48	head gardener	widower	Knockanohill	KW	30
417	WALSH	Mary	11	dau		Knockanohill	KW	30
417	WALSH	Ellen	9	dau		Knockanohill	KW	30
417	WALSH	Catherine	7	dau		Knockanohill	KW	30
417	WALSH	Bridget	4	dau		Knockanohill	KW	30
417	WALSH	Ellen	5	aunt	aunt in law,age chkd	Knockanohill	KW	30
417	RIAL	Edward	23	B/L		Knockanohill	KW	30
612	CLANCY	Jane	50	head	widow	Knockaskehane	LE	54
612	CLANCY	Patrick	21	son lab		Knockaskehane	LE	54
612	CLANCY	Denis	18	son lab		Knockaskehane	LE	54
612	CLANCY	John	16	son lab		Knockaskehane	LE	54
613	SHEEHAN	Thomas	35	head lab		Knockaskehane	LE	54
613	SHEEHAN	Ellen	37	wife		Knockaskehane	LE	54
613	SHEEHAN	William	8	son		Knockaskehane	LE	54
613	CASHEEN	Ellen	30	lodg		Knockaskehane	LE	54
613	FITZGERALD	Patrick	19	lodg		Knockaskehane	LE	54
614	MAHONY	Patrick	40	head lab		Knockaskehane	LE	54
614	MAHONY	Catherine	30	wife		Knockaskehane	LE	54
614	MAHONY	John	9	son		Knockaskehane	LE	54
615	CLANCY	Daniel	40	head lab		Knockaskehane	LE	54
615	CLANCY	Margaret	74	wife	(age checked, 47?)	Knockaskehane	LE	54
615	CLANCY	Thomas	34	son lab		Knockaskehane	LE	54
615	CLANCY	Patrick	27	son lab		Knockaskehane	LE	54
615	CLANCY	Mary	24	dau		Knockaskehane	LE	54
616	ROCHE	James	20	head schoolmaster		Knockaskehane	LE	54
616	ROCHE	Ellen	60	moth		Knockaskehane	LE	54

616 ROCHE	Maurice	14	brot		Knockaskehane	LE	54
617 CLANCY	Catherine	65	head	widow, lives alone	Knockaskehane	LE	54
618 CLANCY	John	59	head farmer		Knockaskehane	LE	54
618 CLANCY	Johanna	53	wife		Knockaskehane	LE	54
618 CLANCY	Mary	20	dau		Knockaskehane	LE	54
618 CLANCY	Denis	17	son lab		Knockaskehane	LE	54
618 CLANCY	Thomas	13	son		Knockaskehane	LE	54
618 CLANCY	John	12	son		Knockaskehane	LE	55
618 CLANCY	Ellen	9	dau		Knockaskehane	LE	55
619 NUNAN	John	50	head lab		Knockaskehane	LE	55
619 NUNAN	Ellen	35	wife		Knockaskehane	LE	55
619 COLLIS	Thomas	16	st/s		Knockaskehane	LE	55
619 NUNAN	Mary	13	dau		Knockaskehane	LE	55
619 NUNAN	Catherine	11	dau		Knockaskehane	LE	55
619 NUNAN	Patrick	10	son		Knockaskehane	LE	55
619 NUNAN	John	8	son		Knockaskehane	LE	55
619 NUNAN	William	4	son		Knockaskehane	LE	55
619 NUNAN	Richard	2	son		Knockaskehane	LE	55
619 NUNAN	Mary	4 m	dau		Knockaskehane	LE	55
620 COLEMAN	Johanna	60	head farmer	widow	Knockaskehane	LE	55
620 COLEMAN	Michael	30	son farmer		Knockaskehane	LE	55
620 COLEMAN	Margaret	28	dau		Knockaskehane	LE	55
620 COLEMAN	Ellen	24	dau		Knockaskehane	LE	55
620 COLEMAN	William	23	son farmer		Knockaskehane	LE	55
620 COLEMAN	Alice	21	dau		Knockaskehane	LE	55
620 COLEMAN	Mary	19	dau		Knockaskehane	LE	55
620 COLEMAN	Johanna	17	dau		Knockaskehane	LE	55
621 COLEMAN	Ellen	40	head	widow	Knockaskehane	LE	55
621 COLEMAN	William	15	son lab		Knockaskehane	LE	55
622 REALLY	James	34	head lab		Knockaskehane	LE	55
622 REALLY	Catherine	30	wife		Knockaskehane	LE	55
622 REALLY	Catherine	10	dau		Knockaskehane	LE	55
622 REALLY	Mary	6	dau		Knockaskehane	LE	55
622 REALLY	Eliza	4	dau		Knockaskehane	LE	55
623 VERLIN	Ellen	30	head	widow	Knockaskehane	LE	55
623 VERLIN	Patrick	32	son	(son? sic)	Knockaskehane	LE	55
624 SWEENY	Mary	60	head	widow	Knockaskehane	LE	55
624 SWEENY	Mary	32	dau		Knockaskehane	LE	55
625 SWEENY	John	40	lab		Knockaskehane	LE	55
625 SWEENY	Mary	29	wife		Knockaskehane	LE	55
625 SWEENY	Patrick	9	son		Knockaskehane	LE	55
625 SWEENY	Michael	4	son		Knockaskehane	LE	55
625 SWEENY	Michael	40	lodg lab	(same surname)	Knockaskehane	LE	55
626 ROCHE	James	60	head lab		Knockaskehane	LE	55

626 ROCHE	Johanna	58	wife		Knockaskehane	LE	55
626 ROCHE	Mary	20	dau		Knockaskehane	LE	55
626 ROCHE	Johanna	17	dau		Knockaskehane	LE	55
627 BRIEN	Bridget	40	head		Knockaskehane	LE	55
627 BRIEN	Margaret	18	dau		Knockaskehane	LE	55
627 BRIEN	John	15	son		Knockaskehane	LE	55
627 BRIEN	Michael	8	son		Knockaskehane	LE	55
628 BRIEN	Denis	50	head tailor		Knockaskehane	LE	55
628 BRIEN	Bridget	12	dau		Knockaskehane	LE	55
628 BRIEN	Catherine	12	dau		Knockaskehane	LE	55
628 BRIEN	Ellen	9	dau		Knockaskehane	LE	55
629 MYLES	Michael	57	head farmer		Knockaskehane	LE	55
629 MYLES	Sarah	37	wife		Knockaskehane	LE	55
629 MYLES	William	19	son		Knockaskehane	LE	55
629 MYLES	John	17	son		Knockaskehane	LE	55
629 MYLES	Ellen	15	dau		Knockaskehane	LE	56
629 MYLES	Bartholomew	10	son		Knockaskehane	LE	56
629 MYLES	Jane	8	dau		Knockaskehane	LE	56
629 MYLES	Jeremiah	6	son		Knockaskehane	LE	56
629 MYLES	Johanna	3	dau		Knockaskehane	LE	56
630 ROCHE	Thomas	40	head farmer		Knockaskehane	LE	56
630 ROCHE	Ellen	35	wife		Knockaskehane	LE	56
630 ROCHE	John	28	brot		Knockaskehane	LE	56
630 O'BRIEN	Catherine	50	serv		Knockaskehane	LE	56
631 MURPHY	Elizabeth	47	head	widow	Knockaskehane	LE	56
631 MURPHY	Mary	13	dau		Knockaskehane	LE	56
631 MURPHY	David	11	son		Knockaskehane	LE	56
631 SHANAHAN	Mary	65	moth		Knockaskehane	LE	56
632 BRIEN	Mary	50	head	widow	Knockaskehane	LE	56
632 BRIEN	Bridget	21	dau		Knockaskehane	LE	56
632 BRIEN	Anthony	17	son		Knockaskehane	LE	56
632 BRIEN	Patrick	12	son		Knockaskehane	LE	56
632 BRIEN	John	10	son		Knockaskehane	LE	56
632 DIGEEN	William	40	lodg		Knockaskehane	LE	56
632 DIGEEN	Bridget	33	wife	wife to William	Knockaskehane	LE	56
632 DIGEEN	Daniel	4	son		Knockaskehane	LE	56
632 MURRY	Daniel	60	lodg		Knockaskehane	LE	56
632 MURRY	James	31	son	son to Daniel	Knockaskehane	LE	56
633 CAMPION	Thomas	40	head gentleman	Esq.	Leitrim	LE	64
633 CAMPION	Ann	29	wife		Leitrim	LE	64
633 CAMPION	William	27	brot		Leitrim	LE	64
633 BROUDER	Honora	58	serv		Leitrim	LE	64
633 BROUDER	Catherine	23	serv		Leitrim	LE	64
633 BROUDER	William	18	serv		Leitrim	LE	64
633 BROUDER	Honora	13	serv		Leitrim	LE	64
633 CLEARY	William	19	serv	to T. Campion, Esq.	Leitrim	LE	64

633 CLEARY	John	15	serv			Leitrim	LE	64
633 FITZGERALD	Maryanne	10	dau		illeg.	Leitrim	LE	64
634 HALY	Maurice	57	head farmer			Leitrim	LE	64
634 HALY	Elizabeth	58	wife			Leitrim	LE	64
634 HALY	John	25	son			Leitrim	LE	64
634 HALY	Jane	19	dau			Leitrim	LE	64
634 HALY	Elizabeth	17	dau			Leitrim	LE	64
634 HALY	Maurice	15	son			Leitrim	LE	64
634 HALY	Thomas	12	son			Leitrim	LE	64
635 RICE	Thomas	61	head stone mason			Leitrim	LE	64
635 RICE	Margaret	52	wife			Leitrim	LE	64
636 KEEFFE	Daniel	53	head steward	to Mr. Campion		Leitrim	LE	64
636 KEEFFE	Catherine	27	wife			Leitrim	LE	64
636 KEEFFE	Bridget	15	dau			Leitrim	LE	64
637 CLANCY	John	42	head farmer			Leitrim	LE	64
637 CLANCY	Mary	36	wife			Leitrim	LE	64
637 CLANCY	Margaret	7	dau			Leitrim	LE	64
637 CLANCY	Kate	6	dau			Leitrim	LE	64
637 CLANCY	Bridget	5	dau			Leitrim	LE	64
637 CLANCY	Patrick	3	son			Leitrim	LE	64
637 CLANCY	John	6 m	son			Leitrim	LE	64
637 MAHONY	William	24	serv ploughman			Leitrim	LE	64
637 ROCHE	John	17	serv herdsman			Leitrim	LE	64
637 WOODS	Judith	19	serv			Leitrim	LE	64
637 WOODS	Margaret	14	serv	(surname illegible)		Leitrim	LE	64
637 O'BRIEN	James	14	serv			Leitrim	LE	64
638 ROCHE	William	50	head lab			Leitrim	LE	64
638 ROCHE	Mary	10	dau			Leitrim	LE	64
638 ROCHE	John	6	son			Leitrim	LE	64
639 CLANCY	Thomas	55	head lab			Leitrim	LE	64
639 CLANCY	Bridget	43	wife			Leitrim	LE	64
640 CLANCY	Patrick	40	head farmer			Leitrim	LE	65
640 CLANCY	Margaret	27	wife			Leitrim	LE	65
640 CLANCY	Patrick	4	son			Leitrim	LE	65
640 CLANCY	Honora	3	dau			Leitrim	LE	65
640 CLANCY	Johanna	80	moth			Leitrim	LE	65
640 CLANCY	Catherine	38	sist			Leitrim	LE	65
640 FLYNN	John	30	serv			Leitrim	LE	65
641 CLANCY	William	35	head farmer			Leitrim	LE	65
641 CLANCY	Morgan	30	brot			Leitrim	LE	65
641 CLANCY	Margaret	26	sist			Leitrim	LE	65
641 CLANCY	John	50	cous			Leitrim	LE	65
641 MILLER	James	29	serv			Leitrim	LE	65
641 STANTON	Michael	20	serv			Leitrim	LE	65
641 BRIEN	Patrick	15	serv			Leitrim	LE	65
641 BRIEN	Ellen	24	serv			Leitrim	LE	65

642 BRIEN	Ellen	45	head	widow	Leitrim	LE	65
642 BRIEN	Mary	18	dau		Leitrim	LE	65
642 BRIEN	Michael	13	son		Leitrim	LE	65
129 BARRY	James	40	head farmer		Loughnahilly	KC	65
129 BARRY	Mary	50	wife		Loughnahilly	KC	65
129 BUCKLY	James	24	st/s		Loughnahilly	KC	65
129 HARRINGTON	John	15	st/s	(nephew?)	Loughnahilly	KC	65
129 BUCKLY	Phillip	22	neph	(step son?)	Loughnahilly	KC	65
129 CALLAGHAN	John	20	serv		Loughnahilly	KC	65
129 MOLOWPY	Mary	25	serv		Loughnahilly	KC	65
130 COURTNEY	Patrick	46	head lab		Loughnahilly	KC	65
130 COURTNEY	Catherine	45	wife		Loughnahilly	KC	65
130 COURTNEY	Bridget	18	dau		Loughnahilly	KC	65
130 COURTNEY	Patrick	10	son		Loughnahilly	KC	65
130 COURTNEY	Edmond	7	son		Loughnahilly	KC	65
692 RILEY	Joseph	45	head farmer	and huntsman	Macroney Lr	MA	66
692 RILEY	Mary	47	wife		Macroney Lr	MA	66
692 RILEY	Michael	14	son		Macroney Lr	MA	66
692 RILEY	Joseph	12	son		Macroney Lr	MA	66
692 RILEY	Elizabeth	10	dau		Macroney Lr	MA	66
692 NAGLE	John	20	serv		Macroney Lr	MA	66
692 WALSH	Julia	29	serv		Macroney Lr	MA	66
693 ROCHE	John	50	head miller	living alone	Macroney Lr	MA	66
694 WHELAN	Thomas	52	head river bail.	river baileff	Macroney Lr	MA	66
694 WHELAN	Johanna	40	wife		Macroney Lr	MA	66
694 WHELAN	Johanna	18	dau		Macroney Lr	MA	66
694 WHELAN	Michael	14	son		Macroney Lr	MA	66
694 WHELAN	Bridget	12	dau		Macroney Lr	MA	66
694 WHELAN	William	9	son		Macroney Lr	MA	66
694 WHELAN	Thomas	4	son		Macroney Lr	MA	66
696 CASEY	John	50	head farmer	family moved	Macroney Lr	MA	66
696 CASEY	Bridget	40	wife		Macroney Lr	MA	66
696 CASEY	William	18	son		Macroney Lr	MA	66
696 CASEY	John	17	son		Macroney Lr	MA	67
696 CASEY	Ellen	16	dau		Macroney Lr	MA	67
696 CASEY	Elizabeth	11	dau		Macroney Lr	MA	67
696 CASEY	Mary	6	dau		Macroney Lr	MA	67
696 CASEY	Daniel	4	son		Macroney Lr	MA	67
696 CASEY	Maurice	2	son		Macroney Lr	MA	67
696 SHEEHAN	Cornelius	17	serv		Macroney Lr	MA	67
696 MANSERGT	Michael	na	head	Esq.&fam.Casey Place	Macroney Lr	MA	67
697 DORAN	Edmond	40	head farmer		Macroney Lr	MA	67
697 DORAN	Mary	13	dau		Macroney Lr	MA	67
697 DORAN	Thomas	6	son		Macroney Lr	MA	67
697 DORAN	Patrick	2	son		Macroney Lr	MA	67
697 DORAN	Catherine	20	niec		Macroney Lr	MA	67

698 PENDERGAST	Edward	35	head farmer		Macroney Lr	MA	67
698 PENDERGAST	Mary	30	wife		Macroney Lr	MA	67
698 PENDERGAST	Catherine	7	dau		Macroney Lr	MA	67
698 PENDERGAST	Thomas	5	son		Macroney Lr	MA	67
698 PENDERGAST	Mary	3	dau		Macroney Lr	MA	67
699 BEGLY	Thomas	60	head lab		Macroney Lr	MA	67
699 BEGLY	Bridget	54	wife		Macroney Lr	MA	67
700 NORRIS	Michael	44	head wood ranger		Macroney Lr	MA	67
700 NORRIS	Ellen	30	wife		Macroney Lr	MA	67
700 NORRIS	Ellen	10	dau		Macroney Lr	MA	67
700 NORRIS	Bridget	8	dau		Macroney Lr	MA	67
700 NORRIS	Thomas	6	son		Macroney Lr	MA	67
700 NORRIS	Michael	1	son		Macroney Lr	MA	67
701 SWEENY	Daniel	71	head farmer		Macroney Lr	MA	67
701 SWEENY	Honora	68	wife		Macroney Lr	MA	67
701 SWEENY	Thomas	35	son		Macroney Lr	MA	67
701 SWEENY	John	30	son		Macroney Lr	MA	67
701 SWEENY	Honora	26	dau		Macroney Lr	MA	67
701 PENDERGAST	Thomas	15	serv		Macroney Lr	MA	67
702 CONNORS	William	40	head farmer	George HURST now at	Macroney Lr	MA	67
702 CONNORS	Mary	28	wife		Macroney Lr	MA	67
702 CONNORS	Daniel	11	son		Macroney Lr	MA	67
702 CONNORS	Mary	9	dau		Macroney Lr	MA	67
702 CONNORS	Patrick	7	son		Macroney Lr	MA	67
702 CONNORS	William	5	son		Macroney Lr	MA	67
702 CONNORS	Michael	3	son		Macroney Lr	MA	67
702 CONNORS	John	1	son		Macroney Lr	MA	67
702 McCRAITH	John	22	serv lab		Macroney Lr	MA	67
702 CONNORS	Bridget	20	serv	(same surname)	Macroney Lr	MA	67
702 FITZGERALD	Edward	40	serv lab		Macroney Lr	MA	67
702 LONDREGAN	Michael	39	serv lab		Macroney Lr	MA	67
703 McENERNAY	Patrick	53	head blacksmith		Macroney Lr	MA	67
703 McENERNAY	Catherine	50	wife		Macroney Lr	MA	67
703 McENERNAY	Mary	20	dau		Macroney Lr	MA	67
703 McENERNAY	Margaret	18	dau		Macroney Lr	MA	67
703 McENERNAY	Patrick	16	son		Macroney Lr	MA	67
703 McENERNAY	Catherine	14	dau		Macroney Lr	MA	67
703 McENERNAY	Bridget	11	dau		Macroney Lr	MA	67
703 McENERNAY	Jeremiah	5	son		Macroney Lr	MA	67
704 HEAFY	Mary	45	head	widow	Macroney Lr	MA	67
704 HEAFY	Ellen	16	dau		Macroney Lr	MA	67
704 HEAFY	Julia	11	dau		Macroney Lr	MA	67
704 HEAFY	Patrick	5	son		Macroney Lr	MA	67
705 LYONS	John	60	head farmer		Macroney Lr	MA	67
705 LYONS	Jane	50	wife		Macroney Lr	MA	67
705 LYONS	Catherine	19	dau		Macroney Lr	MA	67
705 LYONS	Denis	17	son		Macroney Lr	MA	67

705 LYONS	Michael	14	son		Macroney Lr	MA	67
705 LYONS	John	12	son		Macroney Lr	MA	67
705 LYONS	Mary	10	dau		Macroney Lr	MA	67
705 LYONS	Patrick	8	son		Macroney Lr	MA	67
705 LYONS	Ellen	6	dau		Macroney Lr	MA	67
706 FENNELL	Catherine	18	head hk	(FERRELL?)	Macroney Lr	MA	67
706 FENNELL	Thomas	15	brot		Macroney Lr	MA	67
706 FENNELL	Mary	12	sist		Macroney Lr	MA	67
706 FENNELL	Mary	20	serv	(same surname)	Macroney Lr	MA	67
706 MAHONY	Patrick	25	serv lab		Macroney Lr	MA	68
706 CASEY	Timothy	9	serv		Macroney Lr	MA	68
707 HEAFY	Johanna	40	head farmer	widow	Macroney Lr	MA	68
707 HEAFY	Margaret	13	dau		Macroney Lr	MA	68
707 HEAFY	Ellen	11	dau		Macroney Lr	MA	68
707 HEAFY	Patrick	8	son		Macroney Lr	MA	68
707 HEAFY	Amelia	6	dau		Macroney Lr	MA	68
707 HEAFY	Michael	2	son		Macroney Lr	MA	68
708 HEAFY	Maurice	54	head farmer		Macroney Lr	MA	68
708 HEAFY	Catherine	43	wife		Macroney Lr	MA	68
708 HEAFY	Patrick	17	son		Macroney Lr	MA	68
708 HEAFY	Daniel	15	son		Macroney Lr	MA	68
708 HEAFY	Ellen	13	dau		Macroney Lr	MA	68
708 HEAFY	Julia	11	dau		Macroney Lr	MA	68
708 HEAFY	Mary	9	dau		Macroney Lr	MA	68
708 HEAFY	Timothy	7	son		Macroney Lr	MA	68
709 WHELAN	John	70	head lab		Macroney Lr	MA	68
709 WHELAN	Eliza	25	dau		Macroney Lr	MA	68
709 WHELAN	Maurice	20	son		Macroney Lr	MA	68
709 WHELAN	Ellen	12	dau		Macroney Lr	MA	68
710 SAVAGE	Patrick	33	head lab		Macroney Lr	MA	68
710 SAVAGE	Jane	33	wife		Macroney Lr	MA	68
711 LYONS	James	40	head lab		Macroney Lr	MA	68
711 LYONS	Catherine	38	wife		Macroney Lr	MA	68
711 LYONS	Ellen	11	dau		Macroney Lr	MA	68
711 LYONS	Margaret	9	dau		Macroney Lr	MA	68
711 LYONS	John	7	son		Macroney Lr	MA	68
711 LYONS	William	4	son		Macroney Lr	MA	68
711 LYONS	Alice	2	dau		Macroney Lr	MA	68
712 KEEFFE	John	20	head lab		Macroney Lr	MA	68
712 KEEFFE	Margaret	28	wife		Macroney Lr	MA	68
712 KEEFFE	Margaret	1	dau		Macroney Lr	MA	68
713 SAVAGE	Johanna	60	head	widow, living alone	Macroney Lr	MA	68
714 STANTON	Jane	50	head	widow	Macroney Lr	MA	68
714 STANTON	John	25	son lab		Macroney Lr	MA	68
714 STANTON	Thomas	22	son lab		Macroney Lr	MA	68

714 STANTON	Mary	15	dau		Macroney Lr	MA	68
714 STANTON	Richard	13	son		Macroney Lr	MA	68
714 STANTON	Edmond	12	son		Macroney Lr	MA	68
715 LANE	James	36	head lab		Macroney Up	MA	68
715 LANE	Alice	32	wife		Macroney Up	MA	68
715 LANE	George	11	son		Macroney Up	MA	68
715 LANE	James	9	son		Macroney Up	MA	68
715 LANE	Mary	7	dau		Macroney Up	MA	68
715 LANE	John	5	son		Macroney Up	MA	68
715 LANE	Elizabeth	1	dau		Macroney Up	MA	68
716 TROY	John	34	head carpenter		Macroney Up	MA	68
716 TROY	Mary	32	wife		Macroney Up	MA	68
716 TROY	James	7	son		Macroney Up	MA	68
716 TROY	Maurice	5	son		Macroney Up	MA	68
716 TROY	Margaret	1	dau		Macroney Up	MA	68
717 FITZGERALD	James	50	head lab		Macroney Up	MA	68
717 FITZGERALD	Ann	40	wife		Macroney Up	MA	68
717 FITZGERALD	Mary	17	dau		Macroney Up	MA	68
718 KEEFFE	Thomas	40	head linen weaver		Macroney Up	MA	68
718 KEEFFE	Mary	40	wife		Macroney Up	MA	68
718 KEEFFE	Jeremiah	11	son		Macroney Up	MA	68
718 KEEFFE	Margaret	9	dau		Macroney Up	MA	68
718 KEEFFE	Ellen	7	dau		Macroney Up	MA	68
719 KEEFFE	Patrick	30	head lab		Macroney Up	MA	68
719 KEEFFE	Margaret	25	sist		Macroney Up	MA	68
719 CONDON	Thomas	16	neph		Macroney Up	MA	68
720 POWER	George	37	head lab		Macroney Up	MA	68
720 POWER	Ellen	30	wife		Macroney Up	MA	68
720 POWER	Mary	10	dau		Macroney Up	MA	68
720 POWER	Thomas	8	son		Macroney Up	MA	68
720 POWER	Ann	3	dau		Macroney Up	MA	68
721 GREEHY	Abina	40	head	wid.(given name chkd)	Macroney Up	MA	69
721 GREEHY	Thomas	14	son		Macroney Up	MA	69
722 McNAMARRA	Stephen	60	head shoemaker	(surname spell.chkd)	Macroney Up	MA	69
722 McNAMARRA	Catherine	56	wife		Macroney Up	MA	69
722 McNAMARRA	Margaret	20	dau		Macroney Up	MA	69
722 McNAMARRA	Andrew	14	son		Macroney Up	MA	69
723 HURLEY	Patrick	50	head lab		Macroney Up	MA	69
723 HURLEY	Bridget	42	wife		Macroney Up	MA	69
723 HURLEY	John	4	son		Macroney Up	MA	69
723 HURLEY	Bridget	1	dau		Macroney Up	MA	69
724 QUIRKE	Michael	40	head blacksmith		Macroney Up	MA	69
724 QUIRKE	Mary	30	wife		Macroney Up	MA	69

725	TORHILL	David	45	head carpenter		Macroney Up	MA	69
725	TORHILL	Bridget	40	wife		Macroney Up	MA	69
725	TORHILL	Mary	17	dau		Macroney Up	MA	69
725	TORHILL	Catherine	15	dau		Macroney Up	MA	69
725	TORHILL	Timothy	11	son		Macroney Up	MA	69
725	TORHILL	Bridget	9	dau		Macroney Up	MA	69
725	TORHILL	Alice	7	dau		Macroney Up	MA	69
725	TORHILL	Johanna	5	dau		Macroney Up	MA	69
726	GEELEHER	Elizabeth	43	wife	(to pensioner/na)	Macroney Up	MA	69
726	GEELEHER	Honora	13	dau		Macroney Up	MA	69
726	GEELEHER	James	11	son		Macroney Up	MA	69
726	GEELEHER	Maurice	9	son		Macroney Up	MA	69
726	GEELEHER	John	7	son		Macroney Up	MA	69
726	GEELEHER	Mary	5	dau		Macroney Up	MA	69
727	DONEGAN	Ellen	42	head farmer	widow	Macroney Up	MA	69
727	DONEGAN	Mary	20	dau		Macroney Up	MA	69
727	DONEGAN	Jeremiah	18	son		Macroney Up	MA	69
727	DONEGAN	Thomas	15	son		Macroney Up	MA	69
727	DONEGAN	Catherine	13	dau		Macroney Up	MA	69
727	DONEGAN	Ellen	11	dau		Macroney Up	MA	69
727	DONEGAN	Maurice	8	son		Macroney Up	MA	69
727	MAHONEY	Ellen	34	serv		Macroney Up	MA	69
727	RIORDAN	William	24	serv		Macroney Up	MA	69
727	CAREY	John	19	serv		Macroney Up	MA	69
728	SAVAGE	Michael	50	head ploughman		Macroney Up	MA	69
728	SAVAGE	Johanna	46	wife		Macroney Up	MA	69
728	SAVAGE	Maurice	16	son		Macroney Up	MA	69
728	SAVAGE	Ellen	8	dau		Macroney Up	MA	69
728	SAVAGE	John	4	son		Macroney Up	MA	69
729	LYONS	John	50	head farmer		Macroney Up	MA	69
729	LYONS	Ellen	48	wife		Macroney Up	MA	69
729	LYONS	John	14	son		Macroney Up	MA	69
729	LYONS	Alice	10	dau		Macroney Up	MA	69
729	LYONS	Ellen	8	dau		Macroney Up	MA	69
729	LYONS	Martin	5	son		Macroney Up	MA	69
730	GRIFFIN	Patrick	78	head farmer		Macroney Up	MA	69
730	GRIFFIN	Mary	60	wife		Macroney Up	MA	69
730	GRIFFIN	James	33	son		Macroney Up	MA	69
730	GRIFFIN	Thomas	31	son		Macroney Up	MA	69
730	GRIFFIN	Mary	31	dau		Macroney Up	MA	69
730	GRIFFIN	Patrick	29	son		Macroney Up	MA	69
730	GRIFFIN	Margaret	26	dau		Macroney Up	MA	69
730	GRIFFIN	Daniel	86	brot		Macroney Up	MA	69
730	GRIFFIN	Judith	95	sist		Macroney Up	MA	69
730	KEATING	Catherine	12	rel.	relative	Macroney Up	MA	69

731	MURPHY	John	50	head farmer		Macroney Up	MA	69
731	MURPHY	Catherine	56	wife		Macroney Up	MA	69
731	MURPHY	Honora	21	dau		Macroney Up	MA	69
731	MURPHY	Ellen	19	dau		Macroney Up	MA	69
731	MURPHY	Daniel	17	son		Macroney Up	MA	69
731	MURPHY	Bridget	15	dau		Macroney Up	MA	69
731	MURPHY	Catherine	13	dau		Macroney Up	MA	69
732	GEARY	Michael	40	head farmer		Macroney Up	MA	69
732	GEARY	Margaret	37	wife		Macroney Up	MA	69
732	GEARY	John	8	son		Macroney Up	MA	69
732	GEARY	Mary	37	sist		Macroney Up	MA	69
733	DALTON	Margaret	60	head	widow, living alone	Macroney Up	MA	69
734	DALTON	Margaret	50	head farmer	widow	Macroney Up	MA	69
734	DALTON	Mary	30	dau		Macroney Up	MA	69
734	DALTON	Margaret	24	dau		Macroney Up	MA	69
734	DALTON	William	22	son		Macroney Up	MA	69
734	DALTON	Denis	12	son		Macroney Up	MA	69
735	BOWLER	Judith	50	head	widow	Macroney Up	MA	70
735	BOWLER	Thomas	21	son lab		Macroney Up	MA	70
736	BYRNES	Maurice	52	head farmer		Macroney Up	MA	70
736	BYRNES	Ellen	48	wife		Macroney Up	MA	70
736	BYRNES	Michael	25	son		Macroney Up	MA	70
736	BYRNES	Catherine	23	dau		Macroney Up	MA	70
736	BYRNES	Ellen	21	dau		Macroney Up	MA	70
736	BYRNES	David	19	son		Macroney Up	MA	70
736	BYRNES	Eliza	17	dau		Macroney Up	MA	70
736	BYRNES	William	15	son		Macroney Up	MA	70
737	FOLEY	Johanna	50	head farmer	widow (age sic)	Macroney Up	MA	70
737	FOLEY	Margaret	37	dau		Macroney Up	MA	70
737	FOLEY	Mary	25	dau		Macroney Up	MA	70
737	FOLEY	Eliza	20	dau		Macroney Up	MA	70
737	DUGGAN	Martin	15	gr/s		Macroney Up	MA	70
737	DUGGAN	John	12	gr/s		Macroney Up	MA	70
737	DUGGAN	James	10	gr/s		Macroney Up	MA	70
737	FOLEY	Daniel	50	serv lab		Macroney Up	MA	70
737	MURPHY	Norry	11	lodg		Macroney Up	MA	70
737	KELLY	Margaret	2	lodg		Macroney Up	MA	70
738	BARRY	David	50	head lab		Macroney Up	MA	70
738	BARRY	Margaret	50	wife		Macroney Up	MA	70
739	MURPHY	Honora	59	head	widow	Macroney Up	MA	70
739	MURPHY	Ellen	20	dau		Macroney Up	MA	70
739	MURPHY	Honora	16	dau		Macroney Up	MA	70
740	HANLON	John	47	head farmer		Macroney Up	MA	70
740	HANLON	Catherine	48	wife		Macroney Up	MA	70
740	HANLON	Ellen	20	dau		Macroney Up	MA	70

740 HANLON	Mary	18	dau		Macroney Up	MA	70
741 MAHONY	Denis	60	head lab		Macroney Up	MA	70
741 MAHONY	Jane	50	wife		Macroney Up	MA	70
741 MAHONY	John	24	son		Macroney Up	MA	70
741 MAHONY	David	22	son		Macroney Up	MA	70
741 MAHONY	James	20	son		Macroney Up	MA	70
741 MAHONY	Ellen	18	dau		Macroney Up	MA	70
741 CASHERAN	Norry	55	visi		Macroney Up	MA	70
741 CASHERAN	Patrick	17	visi		Macroney Up	MA	70
742 DONEGAN	Maurice	60	head lab		Macroney Up	MA	70
742 DONEGAN	Margaret	48	wife		Macroney Up	MA	70
742 DONEGAN	Catherine	14	dau		Macroney Up	MA	70
742 DONEGAN	Margaret	13	dau		Macroney Up	MA	70
743 MOHER	Jeremiah	66	head farmer		Macroney Up	MA	70
743 MOHER	Ellen	50	wife		Macroney Up	MA	70
743 MOHER	Andrew	23	son		Macroney Up	MA	70
743 MOHER	Jeremiah	18	son		Macroney Up	MA	70
743 MOHER	Michael	16	son		Macroney Up	MA	70
743 MOHER	David	13	son		Macroney Up	MA	70
743 POWER	Johanna	20	serv		Macroney Up	MA	70
744 KANE	Michael	50	head lab		Macroney Up	MA	70
744 KANE	Ellen	50	wife		Macroney Up	MA	70
744 KANE	Johanna	12	dau		Macroney Up	MA	70
744 KANE	Dennis	10	son		Macroney Up	MA	70
744 KANE	Thomas	9	son		Macroney Up	MA	70
745 FENNESY	Michael	45	head farmer		Macroney Up	MA	70
745 FENNESY	Ellen	40	wife		Macroney Up	MA	70
745 FENNESY	Johanna	7	niec		Macroney Up	MA	70
746 MOHER	David	56	head lab		Macroney Up	MA	70
746 MOHER	Mary	50	wife		Macroney Up	MA	70
746 MOHER	Jane	21	dau		Macroney Up	MA	70
746 MOHER	Bridget	12	dau		Macroney Up	MA	70
746 MOHER	Richard	10	son		Macroney Up	MA	70
746 MOHER	Mary	8	dau		Macroney Up	MA	70
746 MOHER	David	7	son		Macroney Up	MA	70
747 McAULIFFE	Catherine	60	head	widow	Macroney Up	MA	70
747 McAULIFFE	Margaret	30	dau		Macroney Up	MA	70
747 McAULIFFE	Catherine	28	dau		Macroney Up	MA	70
748 WALSH	Mary	40	head farmer	widow	Macroney Up	MA	70
748 WALSH	Jeffery	17	son		Macroney Up	MA	70
748 WALSH	Mary	13	head		Macroney Up	MA	70
748 WALSH	Johanna	11	dau		Macroney Up	MA	70
748 WALSH	Bridget	9	dau		Macroney Up	MA	70
748 WALSH	Catherine	7	dau		Macroney Up	MA	71
748 WALSH	Margaret	3	dau		Macroney Up	MA	71

749	WHELAN	Judith	66	head	widow	Macroney Up	MA	71
749	WHELAN	Judith	24	dau		Macroney Up	MA	71
749	WHELAN	Pierce	21	son		Macroney Up	MA	71
749	WHELAN	Thomas	16	son		Macroney Up	MA	71
749	AHERN	Thomas	10	visi		Macroney Up	MA	71
749	McCOY	John	5	visi		Macroney Up	MA	71
750	BURKE	Mary	25	head hk	living alone	Macroney Up	MA	71
751	JOYCE	Elizabeth	66	head	widow	Macroney Up	MA	71
751	JOYCE	Elizabeth	24	dau		Macroney Up	MA	71
751	JOYCE	Michael	24	son		Macroney Up	MA	71
751	JOYCE	Ann	22	dau		Macroney Up	MA	71
751	JOYCE	Mary	20	dau		Macroney Up	MA	71
751	JOYCE	Ellen	18	dau		Macroney Up	MA	71
751	JOYCE	James	16	son		Macroney Up	MA	71
752	McCRAITH	Ann	32	head	wid. (age illegible)	Macroney Up	MA	71
752	POWER	John	28	visi		Macroney Up	MA	71
753	BRIEN	Margaret	30	head	widow	Macroney Up	MA	71
753	BRIEN	Mary	5	dau		Macroney Up	MA	71
753	BRIEN	Elizabeth	3	dau		Macroney Up	MA	71
753	BRIEN	Catherine	40	aunt		Macroney Up	MA	71
754	SLATTERY	Michael	50	head farmer		Macroney Up	MA	71
754	SLATTERY	Honora	41	wife		Macroney Up	MA	71
754	SLATTERY	Patrick	12	son		Macroney Up	MA	71
754	SLATTERY	John	11	son		Macroney Up	MA	71
754	SLATTERY	Mary	9	dau		Macroney Up	MA	71
754	SLATTERY	Timothy	7	son		Macroney Up	MA	71
754	SLATTERY	Julia	5	dau		Macroney Up	MA	71
754	BARRY	Richard	35	serv		Macroney Up	MA	71
418	CORBAN	Laurence	66	head magistrate	Esq.	Maryville	KW	65
418	CORBAN	Mary	24	dau		Maryville	KW	65
418	BURKE	Margaret	55	na	died	Maryville	KW	65
418	CORBAN	Eliza	53	sist		Maryville	KW	65
418	BURKE	George R.	30	neph		Maryville	KW	65
418	KEARNEY	John	50	serv		Maryville	KW	65
418	GERAN	Ellen	28	serv		Maryville	KW	65
418	CALLAGHAN	Margaret	20	serv		Maryville	KW	65
419	WRIGHT	George	28	head miller		Maryville	KW	65
419	WRIGHT	Eliza	27	wife		Maryville	KW	65
419	WRIGHT	William	3	son		Maryville	KW	65
419	HENRY	Mary	20	serv		Maryville	KW	65
420	CALLAGHAN	Timothy	65	head steward		Maryville	KW	65
420	CALLAGHAN	Honora	27	dau		Maryville	KW	65
420	CALLAGHAN	Catherine	17	dau		Maryville	KW	65
421	CONDON	David	50	head mill lab		Maryville	KW	65

421 CONDON	Margaret	18	dau		Maryville	KW	65
421 MAGNER	Eliza	65	aunt		Maryville	KW	65
422 NUNAN	Patrick	50	head lab		Maryville	KW	65
422 NUNAN	Margaret	40	wife		Maryville	KW	65
422 NUNAN	Thomas	22	son		Maryville	KW	65
423 KNOWLES	Henry	41	head lab		Monedrisane	KW	65
423 KNOWLES	Catherine	17	dau		Monedrisane	KW	65
423 KNOWLES	Thomas	15	son		Monedrisane	KW	65
423 KNOWLES	Amelia	7	dau		Monedrisane	KW	65
423 KEEFFE	Eliza	25	rel.	relative	Monedrisane	KW	65
424 NUNAN	John	60	head blacksmith		Monedrisane	KW	65
424 NUNAN	Deborah	50	wife		Monedrisane	KW	65
425 RYAN	Michael	55	head shepherd	fam.moved, Kilmurry	Monedrisane	KW	66
425 RYAN	Julia	39	wife		Monedrisane	KW	66
425 RYAN	Catherine	9	dau		Monedrisane	KW	66
425 RYAN	Mary	7	dau		Monedrisane	KW	66
425 RYAN	Michael	3 m	son		Monedrisane	KW	66
425 NUGENT	Mary	28	serv		Monedrisane	KW	66
425 O'DONNELL	John	16	serv		Monedrisane	KW	66
426 ROCHE	John	60	head lab		Monedrisane	KW	66
426 ROCHE	Ellen	50	wife		Monedrisane	KW	66
426 ROCHE	Johanna	12	dau		Monedrisane	KW	66
426 MULCAHY	Elizabeth	80	M/L		Monedrisane	KW	66
427 DALY	Thomas	60	head lab		Monedrisane	KW	66
427 DALY	Ellen	64	wife		Monedrisane	KW	66
427 DALY	John	26	son		Monedrisane	KW	66
427 COLBERT	Maurice	14	serv		Monedrisane	KW	66
428 FOUHY	John	58	head		Monedrisane	KW	66
428 FOUHY	Catherine	50	wife		Monedrisane	KW	66
428 FOUHY	Richard	20	son		Monedrisane	KW	66
428 FOUHY	David	17	son		Monedrisane	KW	66
428 FOUHY	John	14	son		Monedrisane	KW	66
428 FOUHY	Johanna	12	dau		Monedrisane	KW	66
428 FOUHY	Thomas	11	son		Monedrisane	KW	66
429 COURTNEY	Margaret	56	head	Town Kilworth, widow	Monedrisane	KW	46
429 COURTNEY	Thomas	26	son lab	New Road	Monedrisane	KW	46
429 COURTNEY	Alexander	16	son lab		Monedrisane	KW	46
430 SHANAHAN	Bridget	52	head	Town Kilworth, widow	Monedrisane	KW	46
430 SULLIVAN	Ellen	29	lodg		Monedrisane	KW	46
431 RYAN	Jeremiah	44	head pensioner	Town Kilworth	Monedrisane	KW	46
431 RYAN	Bridget	40	wife		Monedrisane	KW	46
431 RYAN	Catherine	12	dau		Monedrisane	KW	46
431 RYAN	Emmy	9	dau		Monedrisane	KW	46
431 RYAN	John	5	son		Monedrisane	KW	46

431 RYAN	Edmond	2	son		Monedrisane	KW	46
432 HORGAN	John	50	head weaver	Town Kilworth	Monedrisane	KW	46
432 HORGAN	Eliza	36	dau		Monedrisane	KW	46
432 HORGAN	John	23	son weaver		Monedrisane	KW	46
432 HORGAN	Michael	18	son weaver		Monedrisane	KW	46
432 HORGAN	Ellen	15	dau		Monedrisane	KW	46
433 RIORDAN	Bridget	56	head	Town Kilworth, wid	Monedrisane	KW	46
433 RIORDAN	William	36	son lab		Monedrisane	KW	46
433 RIORDAN	John	25	son lab		Monedrisane	KW	46
433 RIORDAN	Eliza	20	dau		Monedrisane	KW	46
434 COTTER	Margaret	60	head	Town Kilworth, wid	Monedrisane	KW	46
434 COTTER	Margaret	20	dau		Monedrisane	KW	46
434 COTTER	Honora	16	dau		Monedrisane	KW	46
435 McGRATH	Margaret	60	head pauper	Town Kilworth, wid	Monedrisane	KW	46
435 LEONARD	Mary	50	na	widow	Monedrisane	KW	46
435 LEONARD	Johanna	18	dau		Monedrisane	KW	46
435 LEONARD	Mary	16	dau		Monedrisane	KW	46
436 KEEFFE	Pat	na	head	(list. only as husb.)	Monedrisane	KW	47
436 KEEFFE	Johanna	30	wife	Town Kilworth	Monedrisane	KW	47
436 FARRELL	William	40	serv		Monedrisane	KW	47
436 FARRELL	Ellen	40	wife	wife of serv	Monedrisane	KW	47
436 FARRELL	Mary	13	dau		Monedrisane	KW	47
436 FARRELL	Michael	6	son		Monedrisane	KW	47
437 PIGOTT	Mary	70	head	Town Kilworth, wid	Monedrisane	KW	47
437 PIGOTT	Mary	24	dau		Monedrisane	KW	47
438 NORRIS	John	56	head lab	Town Kilworth	Monedrisane	KW	47
438 NORRIS	Margaret	58	wife		Monedrisane	KW	47
438 NORRIS	William	15	son		Monedrisane	KW	47
439 CRONAN	Michael	na	husb	in America	Monedrisane	KW	47
439 CRONAN	Catherine	48	wife	Town Kilworth	Monedrisane	KW	47
439 CRONAN	Patrick	14	son		Monedrisane	KW	47
439 CRONAN	Thomas	12	son		Monedrisane	KW	47
439 CRONAN	Bridget	10	dau		Monedrisane	KW	47
439 CRONAN	Catherine	5	dau		Monedrisane	KW	47
440 ELLARD	John	40	head h.carpenter	Town Kilworth	Monedrisane	KW	47
440 ELLARD	Mary	38	wife		Monedrisane	KW	47
440 ELLARD	John	17	son carpenter		Monedrisane	KW	47
440 ELLARD	Patrick	15	son		Monedrisane	KW	47
440 ELLARD	Margaret	13	dau		Monedrisane	KW	47
440 ELLARD	Joseph	11	son		Monedrisane	KW	47
440 ELLARD	Mary	7	dau		Monedrisane	KW	47
440 ELLARD	George	3	son		Monedrisane	KW	47
440 ELLARD	Ellen	9 m	dau		Monedrisane	KW	47

441 KINNEALY	William	38	head lab	Town Kilworth	Monedrisane	KW	47
441 KINNEALY	Johanna	34	wife		Monedrisane	KW	47
441 KINNEALY	Ellen	11	dau		Monedrisane	KW	47
441 KINNEALY	Mary	9	dau		Monedrisane	KW	47
441 KINNEALY	Patrick	7	son		Monedrisane	KW	47
442 CONDON	Johanna	60	head	Town Kilworth, wid	Monedrisane	KW	47
442 CONDON	William	38	son lab		Monedrisane	KW	47
442 CONDON	Richard	30	son lab		Monedrisane	KW	47
442 CONDON	Mary	8	gr/d		Monedrisane	KW	47
442 BRIEN	Mary	20	dau		Monedrisane	KW	47
443 CONDON	Catherine	54	head dlr.in fowl	Town Kilworth	Monedrisane	KW	47
443 CONDON	Eliza	44	sist		Monedrisane	KW	47
444 CREEDON	Patrick	73	head weaver	Town Kilworth	Monedrisane	KW	47
444 CREEDON	Catherine	68	wife		Monedrisane	KW	47
444 CREEDON	Ellen	13	rel.	relative	Monedrisane	KW	47
445 DALY	William, Rev.	37	head R.C.curate	Town Kilworth	Monedrisane	KW	47
445 BEGLY	Honora	33	serv		Monedrisane	KW	47
445 PINE	John	17	serv		Monedrisane	KW	47
445 FITZPATRICK	James C.	56	visi surgeon		Monedrisane	KW	47
446 BURKE	Edmond	39	head cooper	d. Nov 19, 1852	Monedrisane	KW	47
446 BURKE	Ellen	35	wife	Town of Kilworth	Monedrisane	KW	47
446 BURKE	David	12	son		Monedrisane	KW	47
446 BURKE	Margaret	5	dau		Monedrisane	KW	47
446 FOLEY	Nanne	7	rel.	relative	Monedrisane	KW	47
447 ARMOR	Arthur	70	head sher.bailiff	sheriff's bailiff	Monedrisane	KW	47
447 ARMOR	Mary	45	wife	Town Kilworth	Monedrisane	KW	47
447 ARMOR	Mary	24	dau		Monedrisane	KW	47
447 ERLES	Maria	3 m	gr/d		Monedrisane	KW	47
448 JOHNSON	Thomas	58	head gardener	Town Kilworth	Monedrisane	KW	48
448 JOHNSON	Mary	30	sist		Monedrisane	KW	48
449 CONDON	Richard	50	head lab	Town Kilworth	Monedrisane	KW	48
449 CONDON	Catherine	40	wife		Monedrisane	KW	48
449 CONDON	Mary	14	dau		Monedrisane	KW	48
449 CONDON	John	12	son		Monedrisane	KW	48
449 CONDON	Joseph	10	son		Monedrisane	KW	48
449 CONDON	Thomas	8	son		Monedrisane	KW	48
449 CONDON	Catherine	6	dau		Monedrisane	KW	48
450 SWAINE	Charles	50	head carrman	Town Kilworth	Monedrisane	KW	48
450 SWAINE	Honora	50	wife		Monedrisane	KW	48
450 SWAINE	Francis	24	son		Monedrisane	KW	48
450 SWAINE	Charles	13	son		Monedrisane	KW	48
451 TOBIN	John	68	head architect	Town Kilworth	Monedrisane	KW	48
451 POWER	Margaret	27	niec		Monedrisane	KW	48

452	LOMASNEY	John	45	head coachman	Town Kilworth	Monedrisane	KW	48
452	LOMASNEY	Mary	40	wife		Monedrisane	KW	48
452	LOMASNEY	Mary	16	dau		Monedrisane	KW	48
452	LOMASNEY	Matthew	14	son		Monedrisane	KW	48
452	LOMASNEY	Ellen	11	dau		Monedrisane	KW	48
452	LOMASNEY	John	8	son		Monedrisane	KW	48
452	LOMASNEY	Edmond	5	son		Monedrisane	KW	48
453	DALY	Michael	42	head carpenter	Town Kilworth	Monedrisane	KW	48
453	DALY	Catherine	40	wife		Monedrisane	KW	48
453	DALY	Michael	14	son		Monedrisane	KW	48
453	DALY	William	12	son		Monedrisane	KW	48
453	DALY	Ellen	10	dau		Monedrisane	KW	48
453	DALY	Mary	8	dau		Monedrisane	KW	48
453	DALY	John	5	son		Monedrisane	KW	48
453	DALY	Thomas	2	son		Monedrisane	KW	48
454	LODGE	Ann	77	head	Town Kilworth, wid	Monedrisane	KW	48
454	LODGE	George	38	son		Monedrisane	KW	48
455	NOLAN	Thomas	78	head pensioner	d. Jan 11, 1852	Monedrisane	KW	48
455	NOLAN	Mary	60	wife	Town Kilworth	Monedrisane	KW	48
455	NOLAN	Margaret	32	dau		Monedrisane	KW	48
455	NOLAN	Patrick	22	son		Monedrisane	KW	48
456	CURTIN	Ann	15	head	Town Kilworth	Monedrisane	KW	48
456	CURTIN	Margaret	10	na		Monedrisane	KW	48
457	DALY	John	66	head publican	d. May 11, 1851	Monedrisane	KW	48
457	DALY	Johanna	58	wife	Town Kilworth	Monedrisane	KW	48
457	DALY	Bridget	26	na		Monedrisane	KW	48
457	DALY	James	22	na		Monedrisane	KW	48
457	DALY	William	18	na		Monedrisane	KW	48
458	ROCHE	Garrett	45	head lab	Town Kilworth	Monedrisane	KW	48
458	ROCHE	Mary	40	wife		Monedrisane	KW	48
458	ROCHE	Catherine	19	dau		Monedrisane	KW	48
458	ROCHE	Bridget	17	dau		Monedrisane	KW	48
458	ROCHE	Margaret	13	dau		Monedrisane	KW	48
458	ROCHE	James	8	son		Monedrisane	KW	48
459	CROWLY	Mary	40	head	Town Kilworth, wid	Monedrisane	KW	48
459	CROWLY	Richard	17	son		Monedrisane	KW	48
459	CROWLY	Charles	15	son		Monedrisane	KW	49
459	CROWLY	Johanna	12	dau		Monedrisane	KW	49
459	CROWLY	Mary	10	dau		Monedrisane	KW	49
459	CROWLY	Anthony	3	son		Monedrisane	KW	49
459	HENNESY	James	19	rel.	relative	Monedrisane	KW	49
459	EGAN	Michael	22	lodg		Monedrisane	KW	49
460	KEATING	Catherine	60	head	Town Kilworth, wid	Monedrisane	KW	49
460	KEATING	John	36	na carrman		Monedrisane	KW	49
460	KEATING	Richard	28	son		Monedrisane	KW	49

460 KEATING	Catherine	22	dau		Monedrisane	KW	49
460 KEATING	Patrick	18	son		Monedrisane	KW	49
460 HENNESY	Catherine	10	gr/d		Monedrisane	KW	49
460 HENNESY	William	8	gr/s		Monedrisane	KW	49
460 HENNESY	Patrick	6	gr/s		Monedrisane	KW	49
460 HENNESY	Eliza	2	gr/d		Monedrisane	KW	49
461 TOBIN	Thomas	40	head lab	Town Kilworth	Monedrisane	KW	49
461 TOBIN	Catherine	37	wife		Monedrisane	KW	49
461 TOBIN	Mary	12	dau		Monedrisane	KW	49
461 TOBIN	Patrick	10	son		Monedrisane	KW	49
461 TOBIN	John	8	son		Monedrisane	KW	49
461 TOBIN	Thomas	6	son		Monedrisane	KW	49
461 TOBIN	James	4	son		Monedrisane	KW	49
462 BARRY	Edmond	58	head carpenter	Town Kilworth	Monedrisane	KW	49
462 BARRY	Hannah	23	dau		Monedrisane	KW	49
462 BARRY	Ellen	21	dau		Monedrisane	KW	49
462 BARRY	Ann	55	sist		Monedrisane	KW	49
463 McAULIFFE	Patrick	27	head shoemaker	Town Kilworth	Monedrisane	KW	49
463 McAULIFFE	Catherine	24	wife		Monedrisane	KW	49
463 McAULIFFE	Mary	6 m	dau		Monedrisane	KW	49
463 McAULIFFE	Ann	60	moth		Monedrisane	KW	49
463 McAULIFFE	Ellen	22	sist		Monedrisane	KW	49
463 McAULIFFE	Daniel	20	brot		Monedrisane	KW	49
463 DALY	James	57	uncl		Monedrisane	KW	49
464 CONDON	Edward	40	head broguemaker	Town Kilworth	Monedrisane	KW	49
464 CONDON	Margaret	44	wife		Monedrisane	KW	49
464 CONDON	John	13	son		Monedrisane	KW	49
464 CONDON	David	30	brot		Monedrisane	KW	49
465 POWER	Mary	35	serv	Town Kilworth	Monedrisane	KW	49
465 SEXTON	Eliza	12	dau		Monedrisane	KW	49
466 COTTER	Charles	60	head tailor	Town Kilworth	Monedrisane	KW	49
466 COTTER	Bridget	55	wife		Monedrisane	KW	49
466 COTTER	Mary	24	dau		Monedrisane	KW	49
466 COTTER	John	4	gr/s		Monedrisane	KW	49
467 KENNY	Thomas	38	head lab		Monedrisane	KW	49
467 KENNY	Mary	34	wife		Monedrisane	KW	49
467 KENNY	John	15	son		Monedrisane	KW	49
467 KENNY	Honora	11	dau		Monedrisane	KW	49
467 KENNY	Thomas	7	son		Monedrisane	KW	49
467 KENNY	James	2	son		Monedrisane	KW	49
468 AHERN	Johanna	60	head	Town Kilworth, wid	Monedrisane	KW	49
468 AHERN	John	23	son		Monedrisane	KW	49
468 AHERN	Catherine	22	dau		Monedrisane	KW	49
468 AHERN	James	20	son		Monedrisane	KW	49
468 AHERN	Margaret	60	rel.	relative	Monedrisane	KW	49

469 FITZGERALD	Marks	45	head	shoemaker	Town Kilworth	Monedrisane	KW	50
469 FITZGERALD	Bridget	45	wife			Monedrisane	KW	50
469 FITZGERALD	James	23	son			Monedrisane	KW	50
469 FITZGERALD	William	17	son			Monedrisane	KW	50
469 FITZGERALD	Ellen	16	dau			Monedrisane	KW	50
469 FITZGERALD	Marks	7	son			Monedrisane	KW	50
470 MORIARTY	John	19	head	shoemaker	Town Kilworth	Monedrisane	KW	50
470 MORIARTY	Catherine	20	sist			Monedrisane	KW	50
470 MORIARTY	Patrick	17	brot			Monedrisane	KW	50
470 MORIARTY	Marks	14	brot			Monedrisane	KW	50
471 SULLIVAN	Catherine	40	head	hk	Town Kilworth	Monedrisane	KW	50
471 CONROY	Catherine	16	lodg			Monedrisane	KW	50
471 ANDREWS	Ellen	40	lodg			Monedrisane	KW	50
471 ANDREWS	John	9	son		son to Ellen	Monedrisane	KW	50
472 READEY	James	40	head	carrman	Town Kilworth	Monedrisane	KW	50
472 READEY	Margaret	38	wife			Monedrisane	KW	50
472 READEY	James	15	son			Monedrisane	KW	50
472 READEY	Peter	12	son			Monedrisane	KW	50
472 READEY	Nancy	7	dau			Monedrisane	KW	50
472 READEY	Michael	4	son			Monedrisane	KW	50
472 READEY	Margaret	3	dau			Monedrisane	KW	50
473 GRIFFIN	Honora	60	head		Town Kilworth, wid	Monedrisane	KW	50
473 GRIFFIN	Matthew	33	son			Monedrisane	KW	50
474 WATTS	William	25	head	stonedresser	Town Kilworth	Monedrisane	KW	50
474 WATTS	Margaret	23	wife			Monedrisane	KW	50
474 WATTS	Richard	5	son			Monedrisane	KW	50
474 WATTS	Margaret	5	dau			Monedrisane	KW	50
475 SCULLY	Daniel	47	head	ploughman	Town Kilworth	Monedrisane	KW	50
475 SCULLY	Ellon (sic)	44	wife			Monedrisane	KW	50
475 SCULLY	Margaret	18	dau			Monedrisane	KW	50
475 SCULLY	Eliza	16	dau			Monedrisane	KW	50
475 SCULLY	Daniel	14	son			Monedrisane	KW	50
475 SCULLY	Mary	12	dau			Monedrisane	KW	50
475 SCULLY	Timothy	10	son			Monedrisane	KW	50
475 SCULLY	Martin	8	son			Monedrisane	KW	50
475 SCULLY	Hannah	6	dau			Monedrisane	KW	50
475 SCULLY	Ellen	2	dau			Monedrisane	KW	50
476 SCULLY	John	55	head	lab	Town Kilworth	Monedrisane	KW	50
476 SCULLY	Alice	57	sist			Monedrisane	KW	50
476 ANDREWS	Margaret	15	niec			Monedrisane	KW	50
476 SULLIVAN	Daniel	3	neph		3 yrs 9 mo	Monedrisane	KW	50
477 KENNY	Edward	57	head	lab	Town Kilworth	Monedrisane	KW	50
477 KENNY	Ansty	56	wife			Monedrisane	KW	50
477 KENNY	Margaret	26	dau			Monedrisane	KW	50
477 KENNY	Edmond	21	son	shoemaker		Monedrisane	KW	50
477 KENNY	Patrick	14	son			Monedrisane	KW	50

477	KENNY	Thomas	22	S/L	(checked S/L surname)	Monedrisane	KW	50
477	KENNY	Margaret	26	sist		Monedrisane	KW	50
478	CONDON	Elizabeth	57	head	Town Kilworth, wid	Monedrisane	KW	50
478	CONDON	Ellen	33	dau		Monedrisane	KW	50
478	CONDON	Jeremiah	30	son		Monedrisane	KW	50
479	DOWNEY	Catherine	76	head	Town Kilworth, wid	Monedrisane	KW	50
479	DOWNEY	Catherine	25	dau		Monedrisane	KW	50
479	DOWNEY	Michael	18	gr/s		Monedrisane	KW	50
480	TWOMY	Honora	30	head	Town Kilworth, wid	Monedrisane	KW	51
480	TWOMY	Mary	9	dau		Monedrisane	KW	51
480	TWOMY	Ellen	7	dau		Monedrisane	KW	51
480	TWOMY	Margaret	5	dau		Monedrisane	KW	51
481	MADDEN	Maurice	30	head lab	Town Kilworth	Monedrisane	KW	51
481	MADDEN	Bridget	25	wife		Monedrisane	KW	51
481	MADDEN	Thomas	3	son	3 yrs 9 mo	Monedrisane	KW	51
481	MADDEN	Julia	5 m	dau		Monedrisane	KW	51
481	CONROY	Bridget	50	M/L		Monedrisane	KW	51
481	CONROY	Ellen	20	S/L		Monedrisane	KW	51
482	NEIL	Mary	56	head	Town Kilworth, wid	Monedrisane	KW	51
482	HYDE	Nancy	55	lodg	widow	Monedrisane	KW	51
482	WHELAN	Ellen	23	dau		Monedrisane	KW	51
482	HYDE	Mary	15	dau		Monedrisane	KW	51
482	HYDE	Anne	14	dau		Monedrisane	KW	51
482	WHELAN	Mary	2 w	gr/d		Monedrisane	KW	51
483	McCRAITH	Maurice	40	head lab	Town Kilworth	Monedrisane	KW	51
483	McCRAITH	Eliza	36	wife		Monedrisane	KW	51
483	McCRAITH	Mary	9	dau		Monedrisane	KW	51
483	McCRAITH	Redmond	7	son		Monedrisane	KW	51
483	McCRAITH	Maurice	1	son		Monedrisane	KW	51
484	CONDON	Patrick	35	head shoemaker	Town Kilworth	Monedrisane	KW	51
484	CONDON	Julia	30	wife		Monedrisane	KW	51
484	CONDON	John	6	son		Monedrisane	KW	51
485	HENNESY	Patrick	40	head broguemaker	Town Kilworth	Monedrisane	KW	51
485	HENNESY	Mary	40	wife		Monedrisane	KW	51
485	HENNESY	Henry	11	son		Monedrisane	KW	51
485	HENNESY	Maurice	9	son		Monedrisane	KW	51
485	HENNESY	Anne	1	dau		Monedrisane	KW	51
486	McCRAITH	Redmond	60	head lab	Town Kilworth, alone	Monedrisane	KW	51
487	WALSH	Nancy	60	head	Town Kilworth, wid	Monedrisane	KW	51
487	WALSH	Michael	20	son		Monedrisane	KW	51
487	WALSH	Margaret	15	dau	15 yrs 6 mo	Monedrisane	KW	51
487	WALSH	Denis	13	son	13 yrs 6 mo	Monedrisane	KW	51
487	DUANE	John	22	lodg		Monedrisane	KW	51

488 CONNORS	Patrick	36	head broguemaker	Town Kilworth	Monedrisane	KW	51
488 CONNORS	Bridget	13	dau		Monedrisane	KW	51
488 HORGAN	John	25	lodg		Monedrisane	KW	51
489 HENNESY	Maurice	74	head broguemaker	Town Kilworth	Monedrisane	KW	51
489 HENNESY	James	40	son		Monedrisane	KW	51
489 HENNESY	John	38	son		Monedrisane	KW	51
489 HENNESY	Bridget	25	dau		Monedrisane	KW	51
490 SCULLY	Patrick	32	head lab	Town Kilworth	Monedrisane	KW	51
490 SCULLY	Catherine	30	wife		Monedrisane	KW	51
490 SCULLY	Daniel	17	son		Monedrisane	KW	51
490 SCULLY	James	16	son		Monedrisane	KW	51
490 SCULLY	Ann	14	dau		Monedrisane	KW	51
490 SCULLY	Alice	12	dau		Monedrisane	KW	51
490 SCULLY	Patrick	9	son		Monedrisane	KW	51
490 SCULLY	Michael	2	son	2 yrs 6 mo	Monedrisane	KW	51
491 SPALANE	Johanna	48	head	Town Kilworth, wid	Monedrisane	KW	51
491 SPALANE	Patrick	21	son		Monedrisane	KW	51
491 SPALANE	John	17	son		Monedrisane	KW	51
492 JONES	Ellen	60	head	Town Kilworth, wid	Monedrisane	KW	51
492 JONES	Patrick	60	B/L		Monedrisane	KW	51
493 McCRAITH	Margaret	45	head	Town Kilworth, wid	Monedrisane	KW	52
493 McCRAITH	John	28	son lab		Monedrisane	KW	52
493 McCRAITH	Maurice	26	son lab		Monedrisane	KW	51
494 RIORDAN	Maurice	na	husb	gone to America	Monedrisane	KW	52
494 RIORDAN	Mary	38	wife	Town Kilworth	Monedrisane	KW	52
494 RIORDAN	Margaret	9	dau		Monedrisane	KW	52
495 McLEAN	Hugh	32	head serv		Moorpark	KW	66
495 McLEAN	Catherine	30	wife		Moorpark	KW	66
495 McLEAN	Catherine	1	dau		Moorpark	KW	66
495 WHITE	Catherine	55	serv		Moorpark	KW	66
496 HOLEHAN	Thomas	50	head lab		Moorpark	KW	66
496 HOLEHAN	James	46	brot		Moorpark	KW	66
496 HOLEHAN	Mary	40	wife		Moorpark	KW	66
496 HOLEHAN	Honora	19	dau		Moorpark	KW	66
496 HOLEHAN	Martin	14	son		Moorpark	KW	66
496 HOLEHAN	James	11	son		Moorpark	KW	66
496 HOLEHAN	Hannah	8	dau		Moorpark	KW	66
496 HOLEHAN	Michael	6	son	(Michael? abbrev.)	Moorpark	KW	66
497 HUDSON	Henry	25	head gamekeeper	to America Jul 1 '51	Moorpark	KW	66
497 HUDSON	Jane	29	wife	to America May 1851	Moorpark	KW	66
498 SULLIVAN	Denis	44	head gatekeeper	fam. moved to Fermoy	Moorpark	KW	66
498 SULLIVAN	Bridget	47	wife		Moorpark	KW	66
498 GEAREY	Patrick	16	st/s		Moorpark	KW	66

755 HURST	George	42	head gardener	fam.moved to Macrony	Sharroclure	MA	71
755 HURST	Catherine	31	wife		Sharroclure	MA	71
755 HURST	Jane	9	dau		Sharroclure	MA	71
755 HURST	Catherine	7	dau		Sharroclure	MA	71
755 HURST	Ann	5	dau		Sharroclure	MA	71
755 HURST	George	2	son		Sharroclure	MA	71
755 HURST	Mary	4 m	dau		Sharroclure	MA	71
755 HURST	Mary	54	serv	(same surname)	Sharroclure	MA	71
499 DAWSON	James	52	head wood ranger		Toor	KW	71
499 DAWSON	Mary	50	wife		Toor	KW	71
499 DAWSON	Patrick	20	son		Toor	KW	71
500 AHERN	William	50	head wood ranger		Toor	KW	71
500 AHERN	Mary	40	wife		Toor	KW	71
500 AHERN	John	13	son		Toor	KW	71
500 AHERN	Thomas	7	son		Toor	KW	71
500 AHERN	Cornelius	5	son		Toor	KW	71
500 AHERN	Margaret	3	dau		Toor	KW	71
500 AHERN	David	11m	son		Toor	KW	71
500 AHERN	Catherine	70	moth		Toor	KW	71
500 AHERN	Thomas	52	brot	to America Oct 30'51	Toor	KW	71
500 DONOUGHUE	James	25	serv	to America Oct 30'51	Toor	KW	71
501 BOURKE	David	80	head farmer		Toor	KW	71
501 BOURKE	Honora	25	dau		Toor	KW	71
501 BOURKE	John	23	son	(BURKE on this record)	Toor	KW	71
501 CAREY	Michael	15	serv		Toor	KW	71
502 McCRAITH	Thomas	30	head farmer		Toor	KW	71
502 McCRAITH	Ellen	28	wife		Toor	KW	71
502 McCRAITH	Denis	2	son		Toor	KW	71
502 McCRAITH	Thomas	1	son		Toor	KW	71
502 ROCHE	Catherine	17	serv		Toor	KW	71
503 WALSH	Michael	69	head farmer		Toor	KW	71
503 WALSH	Mary	33	dau farmer		Toor	KW	71
503 WALSH	Elizabeth	30	dau farmer		Toor	KW	71
503 BURKE	Thomas	33	serv		Toor	KW	71
504 AHERN	Cornelius	44	head farmer		Toor	KW	72
504 AHERN	Catherine	30	wife		Toor	KW	72
504 AHERN	John	5	son		Toor	KW	72
504 AHERN	James	3	son		Toor	KW	72
504 AHERN	Catherine	7 m	dau		Toor	KW	72
505 CURTIN	Mary	48	head	widow	Toor	KW	72
505 CURTIN	Bridget	12	dau		Toor	KW	72
505 CURTIN	James	10	son		Toor	KW	72
506 CASEY	Bridget	40	head	widow	Toor	KW	72
506 CASEY	Honora	20	dau		Toor	KW	72
506 CASEY	Michael	13	son		Toor	KW	72

507 HALLORAN	James	57	head pensioner	(HALLARAN?)	Toor	KW	72
507 HALLORAN	Mary	47	wife		Toor	KW	72
508 CLANCY	William	50	head farmer		Toor	KW	72
508 CLANCY	Mary	40	wife		Toor	KW	72
508 CLANCY	Margaret	14	dau		Toor	KW	72
508 CLANCY	Mary	12	dau		Toor	KW	72
508 CLANCY	Patrick	10	son		Toor	KW	72
508 CLANCY	Bridget	8	dau		Toor	KW	72
508 CLANCY	Catherine	6	dau		Toor	KW	72
508 CLANCY	John	3	son		Toor	KW	72
509 QUINN	Daniel	40	head farmer		Toor	KW	72
509 QUINN	Mary	35	wife		Toor	KW	72
509 QUINN	Mary	10	dau		Toor	KW	72
509 QUINN	Patrick	8	son		Toor	KW	72
509 QUINN	Catherine	6	dau		Toor	KW	72
510 SHEEHAN	Maurice	50	head farmer		Whitebog	KW	72
510 SHEEHAN	Mary	43	wife		Whitebog	KW	72
510 SHEEHAN	Margaret	16	dau		Whitebog	KW	72
510 SHEEHAN	Patrick	14	son		Whitebog	KW	72
510 SHEEHAN	Elizabeth	10	dau		Whitebog	KW	72
510 SHEEHAN	Honora	8	dau		Whitebog	KW	72
510 SHEEHAN	Mary	6	dau		Whitebog	KW	72
510 SHEEHAN	Maurice	6	son		Whitebog	KW	72
510 SHEEHAN	Bridget	4	dau		Whitebog	KW	72
511 BULMAN	Michael	29	head farmer		Whitebog	KW	72
511 ENGLISH	Honora	26	sist		Whitebog	KW	72
511 ENGLISH	Andrew	5	neph		Whitebog	KW	72
512 SHERLOCK	Johanna	54	head farmer	widow	Whitebog	KW	72
512 SHERLOCK	Elizabeth	24	dau		Whitebog	KW	72
512 SHERLOCK	Thomas	17	son		Whitebog	KW	72
513 DONOUGHUE	Patrick	23	head farmer		Whitebog	KW	72
513 DONOUGHUE	Margaret	15	sist		Whitebog	KW	72
513 DONOUGHUE	Catherine	13	sist		Whitebog	KW	72
513 DONOUGHUE	Jeffry	16	cous		Whitebog	KW	72
514 SHEELY	James	40	head farmer		Whitebog	KW	72
514 SHEELY	Mary	33	wife		Whitebog	KW	72
514 SHEELY	Mary	7	dau		Whitebog	KW	72
514 SHEELY	Patrick	2	son		Whitebog	KW	72
514 CLIFFORD	Patrick	16	serv		Whitebog	KW	72

NAME	TOWNLAND	NUM

** Surname AHERN

Bridget	Kilmurry S	591
Catherine	Kilally W	237
Catherine	Kilclogh	681
Catherine	Monedrisane	468
Catherine	Toor	500
Catherine	Toor	504
Cornelius	Toor	500
Cornelius	Toor	504
David	Ballylackan	522
David	Toor	500
Elizabeth	Kilmurry N	576
Ellen	Ballinvoher	176
Ellen	Kilclogh	680
Ellen	Kilclogh	681
Ellen	Kilclogh	682
Honora	Kilclogh	681
James	Kilclogh	681
James	Kilmurry N	576
James	Kilmurry S	591
James	Monedrisane	468
James	Toor	504
Johanna	Ballylackan	522
Johanna	Kilclogh	681
Johanna	Monedrisane	468
John	Ballylackan	522
John	Downing N	088
John	Kilclogh	682
John	Kilmurry N	576
John	Kilmurry S	591
John	Monedrisane	468
John	Toor	500
John	Toor	504
Julia	Kilclogh	681
Margaret	Castlecooke	653
Margaret	Monedrisane	468
Margaret	Toor	500
Mary	Castlecooke	653
Mary	Kilclogh	681
Mary	Kilmurry N	576
Mary	Toor	500
Michael	Kilmurry N	579
Owen	Kilmurry N	581
Patrick	Ballinvoher	176
Patrick	Ballylackan	522
Patrick	Kilclogh	681
Thomas	Ballylackan	522
Thomas	Kilclogh	682
Thomas	Macroney Up	749

Thomas	Toor	500
Timothy	Kilmurry N	576
Timothy	Kilmurry S	591
William	Kilclogh	680
William	Toor	500

** SURNAME AMBROSE

Catherine	Castlecooke	648
David	Castlecooke	648
Ellen	Castlecooke	648
James	Castlecooke	648
Patrick	Castlecooke	648
Robert	Castlecooke	648

** SURNAME ANDREWS

Ellen	Monedrisane	471
Jane	Kilworth	335
John	Monedrisane	471
Margaret	Monedrisane	476

** SURNAME ARMOR

Arthur	Monedrisane	447
Elizabeth	Kilworth	332
Henry	Kilworth	332
Mary	Kilworth	332
Mary	Monedrisane	447

** SURNAME ASHBY

Ellen	Downing S	114
Mary	Downing S	114
Michael	Downing S	114
William	Downing S	114

** SURNAME ATKINS

John	Glanseskin	187
Mary	Glanseskin	187
Thomas	Glanseskin	187

** SURNAME BAKER

Ann	Ballydarown Glebe	048
John	Ballydarown Glebe	048
Margaret	Ballydarown Glebe	048
Michael	Ballydarown Glebe	048

** SURNAME BALDWIN

Cornelius	Ballinaparka N	540
Edmond	Ballinaparka N	540
Eliza	Ballinaparka N	540
Johanna	Ballinaparka N	540
Mary	Ballinaparka N	540

** SURNAME BANFIELD

| Mary | Glanseskin | 186 |
| Thomas | Glanseskin | 186 |

** SURNAME BARRETT

Cornelius	Kilworth	266
Edmond	Kilworth	266
Mary	Kilworth	266
Mary	Kilworth	315
Robert	Kilclogh	662

** SURNAME BARRY

Ann	Castlecooke	643
Ann	Monedrisane	462
Bridget	Kilmurry N	577
Catherine	Kilmurry N	577
David	Macroney Up	738
Edmond	Monedrisane	462
Ellen	Kilmurry N	577
Ellen	Monedrisane	462
Hannah	Monedrisane	462
James	Ballyderown	063
James	Coolalisheen	564
James	Loughnahilly	129
John	Coolalisheen	560
John	Coolalisheen	564
Julia	Kilmurry N	577
Margaret	Macroney Up	738
Mary	Coolalisheen	564
Mary	Kilmurry N	577
Mary	Loughnahilly	129
Richard	Kilmurry N	577
Richard	Macroney Up	754
Thomas	Ballyhenden	073
Thomas	Kilmurry N	577

** SURNAME BASSETT

| Catherine | Ballydarown Glebe | 046 |
| Maryann | Ballydarown Glebe | 046 |

** SURNAME BEARY

| Mary | Ballinvoher | 182 |

** SURNAME BEGLY

Bridget	Macroney Lr	699
Honora	Monedrisane	445
Thomas	Macroney Lr	699
Timothy	Ballylackan	536

** SURNAME BENNETT

| Sophia | Kilworth | 367 |

** SURNAME BERMINGHAM
John   Ballinrush Up   145
Mary   Kilmurry S   594
Walter   Kilmurry S   594
** SURNAME BIBLE
Ellen   Kilworth   313

** SURNAME BLAKE
Mary   Coolalisheen   559
Maurice   Ballylackan   527
William   Coolalisheen   559

** SURNAME BOLAND
Patrick   Kilworth   252
Thomas   Kilworth   252

** SURNAME BOLSTER
Angelina   Ballydarown Glebe 047
Richard   Ballydarown Glebe 047

** SURNAME BONYNGE
James   Kilworth   378

** SURNAME BOURKE
David   Toor   501
Honora   Toor   501
John   Toor   501

** SURNAME BOWEN
Anthony   Ballinacarriga   012
Bridget   Ballinacarriga   005
Bridget   Ballinacarriga   008
Catherine   Ballinacarriga   005
Elizabeth   Ballinacarriga   009
Ellen   Ballinacarriga   008
James   Ballinacarriga   008
Johanna   Ballinacarriga   009
John   Ballinacarriga   005
John   Ballinacarriga   009

** SURNAME BOWLER
John   Ballyhenden   075
Judith   Macroney Up   735
Thomas   Macroney Up   735

** SURNAME BOYCE
Mary   Kilworth   261

** SURNAME BRADY
Ann F.   Ballydarown Glebe 046
Charlotte E.   Ballydarown Glebe 046
Fanny S.   Ballydarown Glebe 046
Francis, Rev.   Ballydarown Glebe 046

Harriet   Ballydarown Glebe 046
Horace N.   Ballydarown Glebe 046
Letitia D. Ballydarown Glebe 046
Margaret   Ballinrush Lr   030
Susan T.   Ballydarown Glebe 046
T. T. H.   Ballydarown Glebe 046
** SURNAME BRIEN
Allice   Ballyderown   058
Anthony   Knockaskehane   632
Bridget   Ballyderown   058
Bridget   Kilally W   234
Bridget   Kilmurry S   584
Bridget   Knockaskehane   627
Bridget   Knockaskehane   628
Bridget   Knockaskehane   632
Catherine   Ballinvoher   164
Catherine   Ballinvoher   167
Catherine   Ballyderown   058
Catherine   Kilally W   234
Catherine   Kilally W   236
Catherine   Kilclogh   674
Catherine   Kilworth   284
Catherine   Knockaskehane   628
Catherine   Macroney Up   753
Daniel   Kilally W   232
Denis   Kilally W   234
Denis   Knockaskehane   628
Eliza   Kilmurry S   607
Elizabeth   Kilally W   236
Elizabeth   Kilworth   401
Elizabeth   Macroney Up   753
Ellen   Knockaskehane   628
Ellen   Leitrim   641
Ellen   Leitrim   642
Honora   Ballinvoher   167
Honora   Ballyderown   058
Honora   Kilclogh   674
James   Kilally W   236
James   Kilmurry S   608
Johanna   Ballinvoher   164
Johanna   Kilmurry S   607
Johanna   Kilworth   401
John   Ballinaparka N   543
John   Ballinaparka N   548
John   Ballinvoher   164
John   Ballyderown   058
John   Ballyhenden   075
John   Kilally W   234
John   Kilclogh   674
John   Kilmurry S   607
John   Kilworth   284
John   Kilworth   401
John   Knockaskehane   627

John   Knockaskehane   632
Judith   Ballinvoher   172
Julia   Glanseskin   203
Julia   Kilworth   401
Julia   Kilworth   415
Michael   Ballinvoher   172
Margaret   Ballyderown   058
Margaret   Kilally W   232
Margaret   Kilally W   233
Margaret   Kilally W   234
Margaret   Kilworth   401
Margaret   Knockaskehane   627
Margaret   Macroney Up   753
Mary   Ballinvoher   158
Mary   Ballinvoher   164
Mary   Ballyderown   058
Mary   Glanseskin   185
Mary   Glanseskin   203
Mary   Kilally W   232
Mary   Kilmurry S   588
Mary   Kilmurry S   607
Mary   Kilworth   284
Mary   Knockaskehane   632
Mary   Leitrim   642
Mary   Macroney Up   753
Mary   Monedrisane   442
Michael   Kilmurry S   607
Michael   Knockaskehane   627
Michael   Leitrim   642
Nicholas   Kilally W   234
Patrick   Ballinvoher   164
Patrick   Kilally W   232
Patrick   Kilmurry S   607
Patrick   Kilworth   401
Patrick   Knockaskehane   632
Patrick   Leitrim   641
Terence   Glanseskin   185
Terence   Glanseskin   203
Terence   Kilally W   233
Thomas   Ballinvoher   164
Thomas   Kilclogh   674
Thomas   Kilmurry S   607
Timothy   Kilmurry S   607
William   Ballinvoher   167
William   Ballinvoher   172
William   Kilally W   233
William   Kilally W   234
William   Kilmurry S   607
William   Kilworth   401

** SURNAME BRODERICK
Abby   Kilmurry N   583
Bridget   Kilmurry N   583
Denis   Kilmurry N   583

Ellen	Kilmurry N	583	** SURNAME BULMAN			Margaret	Ballylackan	528
John	Kilmurry N	583	Michael	Whitebog	511	Margaret	Graig	204
Margaret	Kilmurry N	583				Mary	Ballyderown	056
Mary	Kilmurry N	583	** SURNAME BURCHILL			Maurice	Macroney Up	736
			Thomas	Kilworth	364	Michael	Macroney Up	736
** SURNAME BRONIG						Patrick	Ballylackan	515
Johanna	Kilworth	388	** SURNAME BURKE			Richard	Graig	204
			Ann	Ballylackan	536	William	Ballyderown	056
** SURNAME BROUDER			Bridget	Kilworth	257	William	Ballylackan	525
Alice	Ballinaparka N	545	Catherine	Ballyvoskillikin	083	William	Macroney Up	736
Catherine	Ballinaparka N	545	David	Castlecooke	650			
Catherine	Leitrim	633	David	Monedrisane	446	** SURNAME CAHILL		
Daniel	Kilworth	395	Edmond	Kilworth	257	Catherine	Downing S	115
Eliza	Kilworth	395	Edmond	Monedrisane	446	Ellen	Ballydarown Glebe	053
Honora	Ballinaparka N	545	Eliza	Kilworth	257	John	Ballinrush Up	134
Honora	Leitrim	633	Ellen	Kilworth	257	John	Ballylackan	519
Johanna	Kilally W	239	Ellen	Monedrisane	446	Julia	Downing S	115
John	Ballinaparka N	545	George R.	Maryville	418	Michael	Ballydarown Glebe	053
Mary	Kilally W	239	Johanna	Ballylackan	521	Patrick	Downing S	115
Mary	Kilworth	395	Johanna	Kilworth	257			
Michael	Kilworth	395	John	Kilworth	257	** SURNAME CAINE		
Patrick	Ballinaparka N	545	Julia	Castlecooke	650	Michael	Ballylackan	517
Richard	Ballinrush Lr	030	Margaret	Ballylackan	518			
Thomas	Kilally W	239	Margaret	Kilworth	257	** SURNAME CALLAGHAN		
William	Kilally W	239	Margaret	Maryville	418	Bridget	Ballyhenden	071
William	Leitrim	633	Margaret	Monedrisane	446	Bridget	Ballyvoskillikin	079
			Mary	Ballylackan	536	Catherine	Ballyvoskillikin	079
** SURNAME BROWN			Mary	Ballyvoskillikin	083	Catherine	Maryville	420
Catherine	Glenwood	118	Mary	Kilworth	257	Daniel	Ballyvoskillikin	084
			Mary	Kilworth	332	Edmond	Ballyhenden	071
** SURNAME BROWNE			Mary	Macroney Up	750	Ellen	Coolalisheen	556
Bridget	Ballylackan	519	Richard	Kilworth	257	Ellen	Graig	204
Catherine	Ballylackan	519	Thomas	Ballyvoskillikin	083	George	Ballyvoskillikin	084
Edmond	Ballylackan	519	Thomas	Toor	503	Hannora	Graig	207
Ellen	Ballylackan	519				Honora	Graig	207
James	Ballylackan	519	** SURNAME BYRNES			Honora	Maryville	420
Margaret	Ballylackan	519	Bridget	Ballylackan	528	Johanna	Ballyvoskillikin	079
Mary	Ballylackan	519	Bridget	Graig	204	Johanna	Graig	204
Patrick	Ballylackan	519	Catherine	Ballyderown	056	John	Ballyhenden	071
			Catherine	Graig	204	John	Ballyvoskillikin	079
** SURNAME BRUNIG			Catherine	Kilclogh	661	John	Ballyvoskillikin	084
Honora	Kilworth	394	Catherine	Macroney Up	736	John	Kilworth	378
Mary	Kilworth	394	David	Graig	204	John	Loughnahilly	129
			David	Macroney Up	736	Julia	Graig	207
** SURNAME BRYAN			Eliza	Ballyderown	056	Margaret	Maryville	418
Ann	Kilworth	316	Eliza	Macroney Up	736	Mary	Ballinrush Lr	036
			Elizabeth	Coolalisheen	551	Mary	Ballyvoskillikin	079
** SURNAME BUCKLY			Ellen	Ballyderown	056	Mary	Ballyvoskillikin	084
James	Loughnahilly	129	Ellen	Ballylackan	528	Mary	Kilworth	348
Phillip	Loughnahilly	129	Ellen	Macroney Up	736	Maurice	Ballinrush Lr	036
			Eugene	Graig	204	Michael	Ballyhenden	071
** SURNAME BULL			Garrett	Ballylackan	528	Michael	Graig	207
Catherine	Kilworth	261	Hannah	Graig	204	Norry	Ballyhenden	071
			John	Graig	204	Norry	Ballyvoskillikin	084

Name	Place	No.
Thomas	Ballinrush Lr	036
Timothy	Ballinrush Lr	036
Timothy	Maryville	420
William	Graig	207

** SURNAME CAMPION

Name	Place	No.
Ann	Leitrim	633
Benjamin	Castlecooke	643
Thomas	Leitrim	633
William	Leitrim	633

** SURNAME CANE

Name	Place	No.
Ellen	Kielbeg	566
Mary	Kielbeg	566
Michael	Kielbeg	566

** SURNAME CAREY

Name	Place	No.
John	Macroney Up	727
Mary	Kilmurry S	592
Michael	Toor	501

** SURNAME CARROL

Name	Place	No.
Johanna	Downing N	087

** SURNAME CARROLL

Name	Place	No.
Anthony	Kilally W	235
Anthony	Kilally W	241
Catherine	Kilworth	253
Edmond	Kilally W	235
Eliza	Kilally W	235
Elizabeth	Kilally W	236
Ellen	Ballinrush Up	150
Hannah	Kilally W	241
Johanna	Ballinrush Up	150
John	Ballinrush Up	150
John	Kilally W	241
Julia	Kilally W	235
Julia	Kilally W	241
Mary	Ballinrush Up	150
Mary	Kilally W	241
Mary	Kilworth	253
Mary	Kilworth	347
Maurice	Ballinrush Up	150
Patrick	Ballinrush Up	150
Patrick	Kilally W	241
Thomas	Kilally W	235
Timothy	Ballinrush Up	150
William	Kilally W	235

** SURNAME CARTHY

Name	Place	No.
Catherine	Kilworth	301
Mary	Kilworth	301
Patrick	Kilworth	301
Richard	Kilworth	301

** SURNAME CASEY

Name	Place	No.
Ann	Ballinvoher	179
Bartholomew	Ballinvoher	179
Bridget	Ballinvoher	179
Bridget	Kilworth	258
Bridget	Kilworth	337
Bridget	Kilworth	407
Bridget	Macroney Lr	696
Bridget	Toor	506
Catherine	Ballinrush Lr	037
Catherine	Ballinvoher	179
Daniel	Macroney Lr	696
Denis	Kilworth	258
Edmond	Kilworth	338
Edward	Kilworth	338
Eliza	Kilworth	258
Eliza	Kilworth	311
Elizabeth	Ballinvoher	179
Elizabeth	Macroney Lr	696
Ellen	Ballinvoher	170
Ellen	Ballinvoher	179
Ellen	Downing S	113
Ellen	Kilworth	258
Ellen	Kilworth	412
Ellen	Macroney Lr	696
Eugene	Kilworth	311
Hanna	Kilworth	311
Honora	Toor	506
James	Kilclogh	688
Jane	Kilworth	268
Jeremiah	Kilworth	405
Jeremiah	Kilworth	407
Johanna	Ballinvoher	170
Johanna	Kilclogh	688
John	Ballinrush Lr	037
John	Ballinvoher	170
John	Ballydarown Glebe	048
John	Kilclogh	688
John	Kilworth	259
John	Kilworth	263
John	Kilworth	311
John	Kilworth	405
John	Macroney Lr	696
Judith	Glanseskin	190
Julia	Ballinvoher	170
Kate	Ballydarown Glebe	048
Margaret	Ballinrush Lr	037
Margaret	Kilmurry S	596
Margaret	Kilworth	311
Margaret	Kilworth	347
Mary	Ballinrush Lr	030
Mary	Ballinvoher	170
Mary	Ballyderown	062
Mary	Kilclogh	662
Mary	Kilmurry S	597
Mary	Kilworth	258
Mary	Kilworth	259
Mary	Kilworth	311
Mary	Kilworth	338
Mary	Macroney Lr	696
Maurice	Macroney Lr	696
Michael	Ballinvoher	170
Michael	Ballinvoher	179
Michael	Kilclogh	688
Michael	Kilworth	338
Michael	Toor	506
Nancy	Ballinvoher	170
Norry	Ballyderown	062
Norry	Kilworth	258
Norry	Kilworth	266
Patrick	Ballinrush Lr	037
Patrick	Ballinvoher	170
Patrick	Ballyderown	062
Patrick	Kilmurry S	597
Patrick	Kilworth	259
Patrick	Kilworth	279
Patrick	Kilworth	407
Redmond	Kilworth	311
Thomas	Ballinvoher	170
Thomas	Kilworth	258
Timothy	Macroney Lr	706
William	Ballinrush Lr	037
William	Ballinvoher	179
William	Kilworth	311
William	Kilworth	405
William	Macroney Lr	696

** SURNAME CASHEEN

Name	Place	No.
Ellen	Knockaskehane	613

** SURNAME CASHERAN

Name	Place	No.
Norry	Macroney Up	741
Patrick	Macroney Up	741

** SURNAME CAULEY

Name	Place	No.
Bridget	Downing N	088

** SURNAME CLANCY

Name	Place	No.
Bartholomew	Kilclogh	663
Bridget	Leitrim	637
Bridget	Leitrim	639
Bridget	Toor	508
Catherine	Kilclogh	663
Catherine	Knockaskehane	617
Catherine	Leitrim	640
Catherine	Toor	508
Daniel	Knockaskehane	615
Denis	Knockaskehane	612

Denis	Knockaskehane	618	Catherine	Kilworth	414	Bridget	Kilclogh	684
Ellen	Kilclogh	663	Daniel	Ballinrush Up	136	David	Ballinrush Up	153
Ellen	Knockaskehane	618	Denis	Ballinrush Up	136	Denis	Ballydarown Glebe	053
Honora	Leitrim	640	Ellen	Ballinvoher	172	Edmond	Ballinaparka N	546
James	Kilclogh	663	James	Ballinvoher	174	Edmond	Ballinrush Up	153
Jane	Knockaskehane	612	Johanna	Kilworth	306	Ellen	Ballinaparka N	546
Johanna	Knockaskehane	618	John	Ballinrush Up	136	Ellen	Ballinrush Up	153
Johanna	Leitrim	640	John	Ballinvoher	174	Ellen	Kilclogh	684
John	Kilclogh	663	John	Leitrim	633	John	Ballinrush Up	153
John	Knockaskehane	612	Margaret	Ballinrush Up	136	John	Kilclogh	684
John	Knockaskehane	618	Michael	Ballinvoher	174	Mary	Ballinrush Up	153
John	Leitrim	637	Thomas	Ballinvoher	168	Maurice	Ballydarown Glebe	053
John	Leitrim	641	Thomas	Ballinvoher	174	Maurice	Monedrisane	427
John	Toor	508	William	Ballinvoher	174	Michael	Ballinrush Up	153
Kate	Leitrim	637	William	Leitrim	633			
Margaret	Knockaskehane	615				** SURNAME COLEMAN		
Margaret	Leitrim	637	** SURNAME CLIFFORD			Alice	Knockaskehane	620
Margaret	Leitrim	640	Catherine	Kilally E	224	Catherine	Ballyhenden	068
Margaret	Leitrim	641	James	Ballinrush Up	155	Eliza	Kilworth	370
Margaret	Toor	508	John	Ballinrush Up	155	Ellen	Kilmurry S	608
Mary	Ballylackan	515	Margaret	Ballinrush Up	155	Ellen	Knockaskehane	620
Mary	Knockaskehane	615	Margaret	Kilally E	224	Ellen	Knockaskehane	621
Mary	Knockaskehane	618	Michael	Ballinrush Up	155	Johanna	Knockaskehane	620
Mary	Leitrim	637	Patrick	Ballinrush Up	155	John	Kielbeg	565
Mary	Toor	508	Patrick	Kilally E	224	John	Kilmurry S	608
Morgan	Leitrim	641	Patrick	Whitebog	514	Margaret	Kilmurry S	608
Patrick	Kilclogh	663	William	Ballinrush Up	155	Margaret	Knockaskehane	620
Patrick	Knockaskehane	612				Mary	Kilmurry S	586
Patrick	Knockaskehane	615	** SURNAME CODY			Mary	Knockaskehane	620
Patrick	Leitrim	637	David	Castlecooke	644	Michael	Kilmurry S	586
Patrick	Leitrim	640	Edmond	Castlecooke	644	Michael	Kilmurry S	608
Patrick	Toor	508	Edward	Kilmurry S	603	Michael	Knockaskehane	620
Thomas	Ballylackan	515	Ellen	Kilmurry S	603	William	Knockaskehane	620
Thomas	Glenwood	118	Hannah	Kilmurry S	603	William	Knockaskehane	621
Thomas	Knockaskehane	615	James	Kilmurry S	603			
Thomas	Knockaskehane	618	Jane	Castlecooke	644	** SURNAME COLLINS		
Thomas	Leitrim	639	Johanna	Castlecooke	644	James	Kilworth	376
William	Ballylackan	515	Margaret	Castlecooke	644			
William	Kilclogh	663	Margaret	Kilmurry S	603	** SURNAME COLLIS		
William	Leitrim	641	Mary	Castlecooke	644	Elizabeth	Castlecooke	643
William	Toor	508	Thomas	Castlecooke	644	John T.	Castlecooke	643
						Thomas	Knockaskehane	619
** SURNAME CLARKE			** SURNAME COFFEE			William Cooke	Castlecooke	643
Alexander	Kilworth	364	Catherine	Ballylackan	529			
Edward	Kilworth	364	Elizabeth	Ballylackan	529	** SURNAME CONDON		
Eliza	Kilworth	364	Ellen	Ballylackan	529	Ann	Kilworth	297
Hester	Kilworth	364	Jeremiah	Ballylackan	529	Arthur	Kilworth	263
Mary	Kilworth	364	John	Ballylackan	529	Bridget	Ballinglanna S	026
Richard	Kilworth	364	Mary	Ballylackan	529	Catherine	Ballinrush Up	134
Thomas	Kilworth	364	Thomas	Ballylackan	529	Catherine	Kilworth	347
						Catherine	Monedrisane	443
** SURNAME CLEARY			** SURNAME COLBERT			Catherine	Monedrisane	449
Bridget	Ballinvoher	174	Ann	Kilally W	232	David	Ballinrush Up	134
Catherine	Kilworth	306	Bridget	Ballinaparka N	546	David	Maryville	421

Name	Townland	No.	Name	Townland	No.	Name	Townland	No.
David	Monedrisane	464	William	Ballinrush Lr	034	Johanna	Kilworth	388
Edward	Monedrisane	464	William	Glanseskin	189	John	Kilworth	333
Eliza	Ballinrush Lr	034	William	Kilworth	347	John	Kilworth	388
Eliza	Kilworth	263	William	Monedrisane	442	John	Knockanabohelly	126
Eliza	Monedrisane	443	**** SURNAME CONNELL**			John	Macroney Lr	702
Elizabeth	Monedrisane	478	Honora	Kilworth	296	Julia	Kilworth	320
Ellen	Ballinglanna S	026	Honora	Kilworth	375	Margaret	Kilworth	353
Ellen	Ballinrush Up	146	Jeremiah	Kilworth	376	Maria	Kilworth	333
Ellen	Kilmurry N	581	John	Kilworth	375	Mary	Kilworth	379
Ellen	Kilworth	263	Kate	Kilworth	375	Mary	Kilworth	388
Ellen	Kilworth	267	Martin	Kilworth	296	Mary	Macroney Lr	702
Ellen	Kilworth	347	Mary	Kilworth	376	Michael	Kilworth	379
Ellen	Kilworth	352	William	Kilworth	375	Michael	Knockanabohelly	126
Ellen	Monedrisane	478	**** SURNAME CONNELLY**			Michael	Macroney Lr	702
Fanny	Kilworth	263	Denis	Kilmurry N	570	Patrick	Kilworth	320
Honora	Ballinrush Up	134	Johanna	Kilmurry N	570	Patrick	Kilworth	388
Jeremiah	Monedrisane	478	John	Kilmurry N	570	Patrick	Macroney Lr	702
Johanna	Glenwood	119	Michael	Kilmurry N	570	Patrick	Monedrisane	488
Johanna	Monedrisane	442	**** SURNAME CONNOLLY**			Thomas	Ballinvoher	178
John	Ballinrush Lr	034	Elizabeth	Kilmurry N	573	Thomas	Kilworth	388
John	Kilworth	297	Ellen	Kilmurry N	572	Thomas	Knockanabohelly	126
John	Monedrisane	449	Ellen	Kilmurry N	573	William	Kilworth	388
John	Monedrisane	464	Ellen	Kilmurry N	582	William	Macroney Lr	702
John	Monedrisane	484	James	Kilmurry N	572	**** SURNAME CONROY**		
Joseph	Monedrisane	449	Johanna	Kilmurry N	573	Bridget	Ballyhenden	073
Julia	Monedrisane	484	John	Kilmurry N	582	Bridget	Monedrisane	481
Margaret	Maryville	421	Judith	Kilmurry N	572	Catherine	Monedrisane	471
Margaret	Monedrisane	464	Mary	Kilmurry N	573	Elizabeth	Ballyhenden	073
Martin	Ballinrush Up	134	Michael	Kilmurry N	572	Ellen	Ballinrush Up	145
Mary	Ballinrush Lr	034	Patrick	Kilmurry N	573	Ellen	Monedrisane	481
Mary	Ballinrush Up	134	Patrick	Kilmurry N	582	Margaret	Ballyderown	057
Mary	Kilworth	280	William	Kilmurry N	572	**** SURNAME COONEY**		
Mary	Kilworth	347	William	Kilmurry N	573	Mary	Kilworth	369
Mary	Kilworth	411	William	Kilmurry N	582	**** SURNAME COPPINGER**		
Mary	Monedrisane	442	**** SURNAME CONNOLY**			Rebecca	Castlecooke	645
Mary	Monedrisane	449	Dennis	Glanseskin	192	**** SURNAME CORBAN**		
Maurice	Ballinrush Lr	034	**** SURNAME CONNORS**			Eliza	Maryville	418
Maurice	Kilworth	297	Ann	Kilworth	388	James	Graig	222
Michael	Ballinglanna S	026	Bartholomew	Knockanabohelly	126	John	Kilworth	277
Michael	Kilmurry N	581	Bridget	Macroney Lr	702	Laurence	Maryville	418
Patrick	Ballinglanna S	026	Bridget	Monedrisane	488	Mary	Maryville	418
Patrick	Ballinrush Up	146	Catherine	Kilworth	333	**** SURNAME CORBITT**		
Patrick	Glanseskin	189	Catherine	Kilworth	379	Catherine	Coolalisheen	563
Patrick	Glenwood	119	Catherine	Knockanabohelly	126	Catherine	Kilworth	386
Patrick	Kilworth	263	Daniel	Macroney Lr	702	Cornelius	Coolalisheen	563
Patrick	Kilworth	297	Edmond	Kilworth	353	Hannora	Coolalisheen	563
Patrick	Monedrisane	484	Ellen	Kilworth	388	Judith	Coolalisheen	563
Richard	Monedrisane	442	Felicia	Kilworth	333	Patrick	Kilworth	386
Richard	Monedrisane	449	James	Kilworth	335	Timothy	Coolalisheen	563
Thomas	Ballinrush Up	134						
Thomas	Ballinrush Up	146						
Thomas	Kilmurry N	581						
Thomas	Macroney Up	719						
Thomas	Monedrisane	449						

Timothy	Kilworth	386	William	Downing N	106	Catherine	Monedrisane	444
			William	Downing N	107	Ellen	Monedrisane	444
** SURNAME CORENCY						Patrick	Monedrisane	444
James	Kilworth	280	** SURNAME COURTNEY			Thomas	Kilworth	282
			Alexander	Monedrisane	429			
** SURNAME CORMACK			Bridget	Loughnahilly	130	** SURNAME CRONAN		
James	Kilworth	280	Catherine	Ballinrush Lr	035	Bridget	Monedrisane	439
			Catherine	Loughnahilly	130	Catherine	Monedrisane	439
** SURNAME CORMICK			David	Ballinrush Up	140	Daniel	Ballyhenden	073
James	Ballinrush Up	132	Edmond	Ballinrush Up	133	Edward	Ballyhenden	073
			Edmond	Ballinrush Up	140	Eliza	Ballyderown	063
** SURNAME COSGROVE			Edmond	Loughnahilly	130	Ellen	Ballyhenden	069
James	Graig	222	Edward	Ballinrush Lr	035	Johanna	Kilworth	358
John	Kilworth	408	Ellen	Ballinrush Up	135	Johanna	Ballyderown	063
Margaret	Graig	222	Ellen	Kilally W	227	John	Ballyhenden	073
Mary	Graig	222	Ellen	Kilally W	238	Judith	Ballyderown	063
Mary	Kilworth	408	George	Kilally W	238	Mary	Ballinrush Lr	030
Richard	Kilworth	408	Honora	Ballinrush Up	133	Michael	Ballyhenden	073
Terence	Kilworth	408	John	Ballinglanna N	017	Michael	Monedrisane	439
			John	Ballinrush Lr	035	Patrick	Ballyderown	063
** SURNAME COSKERAN			John	Ballinrush Up	135	Patrick	Ballyhenden	069
Edmond	Ballinvoher	162	John	Kilworth	343	Patrick	Ballyhenden	073
Margaret	Ballinvoher	162	Kate	Kilworth	343	Patrick	Monedrisane	439
			Margaret	Ballinrush Lr	035	Terence	Ballyhenden	073
** SURNAME COTTER			Margaret	Ballinrush Up	140	Thomas	Monedrisane	439
Bridget	Monedrisane	466	Margaret	Kilally W	238			
Catherine	Kilworth	288	Margaret	Monedrisane	429	** SURNAME CRONEEN		
Charles	Monedrisane	466	Mary	Ballinrush Lr	035	Mary	Kilworth	355
Ellen	Kilworth	288	Mary	Ballinrush Up	133			
Hanna	Kilworth	288	Mary	Ballinrush Up	135	** SURNAME CRONIN		
Honora	Monedrisane	434	Mary	Ballinrush Up	140	Elizabeth	Kilclogh	660
John	Kilworth	288	Mary	Kilally W	238			
John	Monedrisane	466	Mary	Kilworth	343	** SURNAME CROTTY		
Margaret	Kilworth	288	Michael	Ballinrush Up	132	Bridget	Ballinrush Up	148
Margaret	Monedrisane	434	Michael	Kilally W	238	Catherine	Downing N	093
Mary	Monedrisane	466	Patrick	Ballinrush Up	133	Eliza	Kilmurry S	590
Michael	Kilworth	288	Patrick	Kilally W	227	Honora	Gurtone	123
Patrick	Kilworth	288	Patrick	Kilworth	343	James	Ballinrush Up	148
			Patrick	Loughnahilly	130	James	Downing N	093
** SURNAME COUGHLAN			Susan	Ballinrush Up	132	Jeremiah	Ballinrush Up	148
Bartholomew	Downing N	106	Thomas	Ballinrush Up	133	Johanna	Ballinrush Up	148
Bridget	Downing N	107	Thomas	Ballinrush Up	140	John	Ballinrush Up	148
Catherine	Downing N	107	Thomas	Monedrisane	429	John	Downing N	093
Catherine	Kilclogh	665				John	Kilmurry S	590
Eliza	Kilworth	324	** SURNAME CRANWELL			Margaret	Downing N	093
James	Downing N	106	Ann	Kilworth	287	Mary	Ballinacarriga	008
Jeremiah	Downing N	106	James	Kilworth	287	Mary	Ballinrush Up	148
John	Downing N	107	Julia	Kilworth	287	Mary	Coolalisheen	560
John	Kilclogh	665	Margaret	Kilworth	287	Mary	Downing N	093
Judith	Downing N	106	Mary	Kilworth	287	Mary	Kilmurry S	590
Mary	Downing N	106	Thomas	Kilworth	287	Michael	Kilmurry S	590
Mary	Kilclogh	665				Rodger	Downing N	093
Thomas	Kilclogh	665	** SURNAME CREEDON					
Timothy	Ballylackan	519	Catherine	Kilworth	282	** SURNAME CROWE		

Ann	Ballyderown	065
Bridget	Kilworth	258
John	Kilworth	256
Mary	Ballyderown	065
Mary	Kilworth	256
Thomas	Kilworth	256
William	Graig	204
William	Kilworth	256

** SURNAME CROWLY

Anthony	Monedrisane	459
Charles	Monedrisane	459
Johanna	Monedrisane	459
Mary	Boherdeveroge	085
Mary	Monedrisane	459
Richard	Monedrisane	459

** SURNAME CUMMINS

Margaret	Kilmurry S	596

** SURNAME CUNNINGHAM

Ann	Kilworth	335
Charles	Ballydarown Glebe	050
Emelia	Kilworth	290
Frances	Kilworth	290
Honora	Ballydarown Glebe	050
John	Kilworth	290
Julia	Kilworth	290
Patrick	Castlecooke	654
Patty	Kilworth	290
Peter	Ballydarown Glebe	050
Thomas	Kilworth	290

** SURNAME CURTIN

Ann	Monedrisane	456
Bridget	Toor	505
Catherine	Glanseskin	193
Daniel	Ballinglanna N	024
Denis	Ballinglanna N	024
Hannora (sic)	Downing N	088
James	Downing N	088
James	Downing N	097
James	Toor	505
Jane	Glanseskin	193
Jane	Kilworth	380
Johanna	Downing N	097
John	Downing N	088
John	Kilworth	380
Margaret	Monedrisane	456
Mary	Kilworth	371
Mary	Toor	505
Michael	Glanseskin	193
Patrick	Glanseskin	193
Thomas	Downing N	097
Thomas	Glanseskin	193
Thomas	Kilworth	380
Timothy	Downing N	097

** SURNAME CURTIN

William	Downing N	088

** SURNAME DALTON

Denis	Macroney Up	734
Honora	Ballinglanna S	027
Margaret	Macroney Up	733
Margaret	Macroney Up	734
Mary	Macroney Up	734
William	Macroney Up	734

** SURNAME DALY

Ann	Downing N	099
Bridget	Monedrisane	457
Catherine	Downing N	108
Catherine	Kilworth	294
Catherine	Monedrisane	453
David	Ballinaparka N	542
David	Downing N	108
Denis	Ballylackan	516
Eliza	Downing N	108
Ellen	Monedrisane	427
Ellen	Monedrisane	453
Honora	Ballinaparka N	542
James	Ballinaparka N	542
James, Rev.	Ballyderown	054
James	Downing N	109
James	Monedrisane	457
James	Monedrisane	463
Jeremiah	Kilmurry N	581
Jeremiah	Kilworth	294
Johanna	Ballinrush Up	152
Johanna	Monedrisane	457
John	Ballinaparka N	542
John	Downing N	099
John	Monedrisane	427
John	Monedrisane	453
John	Monedrisane	457
Margaret	Ballinrush Up	152
Margaret	Ballylackan	516
Mary	Ballinrush Up	152
Mary	Ballylackan	516
Mary	Downing N	108
Mary	Kilworth	260
Mary	Monedrisane	453
Michael	Ballinrush Up	152
Michael	Monedrisane	453
Owen	Ballinrush Up	152
Patrick	Ballinrush Up	152
Patrick	Downing N	099
Patrick	Kilmurry S	597
Simon	Downing N	108
Thomas	Monedrisane	427
Thomas	Monedrisane	453
William	Castlecooke	659
William	Monedrisane	453
William	Monedrisane	457
William, Rev.	Monedrisane	445

** SURNAME DANIELS

Ann	Kilworth	367
Michael	Kilworth	378
Susan	Kilworth	378

** SURNAME DAWSON

Catherine	Ballinvoher	157
James	Toor	499
John	Ballinvoher	157
Mary	Toor	499
Michael	Ballinvoher	158
Patrick	Toor	499

** SURNAME DENNEHY

Bridget	Downing N	091
Catherine	Downing N	091
Ellen	Gurtone	123
Johanna	Downing N	091
Robert	Downing N	091
William	Downing N	091

** SURNAME DEVINE

William	Ballinacarriga	012

** SURNAME DIGEEN

Bridget	Knockaskehane	632
Daniel	Knockaskehane	632
William	Knockaskehane	632

** SURNAME DILLON

Eliza	Kilworth	329

** SURNAME DIVINE

Ann	Ballinrush Lr	040
Catherine	Ballinglanna N	023
Catherine	Ballinglanna N	024
Catherine	Ballinrush Lr	040
Daniel	Ballinglanna N	024
Edmond	Ballinglanna N	023
Ellen	Ballinglanna N	022
Ellen	Ballinrush Lr	040

(SURNAME DIVINE continued)				** SURNAME DONOVAN				Ann	Kilworth	272
James	Ballinglanna N	022		Bridget	Downing N	090		Catherine	Kilclogh	677
James	Ballinglanna N	023		Cornelius	Graig	213		Denis	Kilclogh	677
James	Ballinglanna N	024		Ellen	Downing N	090		Edmond	Kilclogh	677
James	Ballinrush Lr	040		Jeremiah	Downing N	090		Honora	Kilclogh	677
Johanna	Ballinrush Lr	040		Jeremiah	Graig	213		Jeremiah	Kilworth	272
John	Ballinglanna N	022		Johanna	Coolalisheen	558		Jeremiah	Kilworth	286
Mary	Ballinglanna N	023		Johanna	Graig	213		John	Kilclogh	677
Mary	Ballinglanna N	024		John	Coolalisheen	558		John	Kilworth	286
Mary	Ballinrush Up	132		John	Graig	213		Mary	Kilclogh	677
Michael	Ballinglanna N	023		Margaret	Graig	213		Mary	Kilworth	272
Michael	Ballinrush Lr	040		Michael	Downing N	090		Thomas	Kilworth	272
Thomas	Ballinglanna N	024		Michael	Kilworth	351				
William	Ballinglanna N	024		Norry	Graig	213		** SURNAME DOWNEY		
				Patrick	Coolalisheen	558		Catherine	Ballinvoher	182
** SURNAME DOHERTY				Patrick	Downing N	090		Catherine	Monedrisane	479
Denis	Kilworth	358		Simon	Coolalisheen	558		Cornelius	Ballinacarriga	002
Ellen	Kilworth	363		William	Downing N	090		Edmond	Ballinacarriga	002
								James	Ballinacarriga	002
** SURNAME DONEGAN				** SURNAME DOODY				Jeremiah	Ballinacarriga	002
Catherine	Macroney Up	727		Bridget	Glanseskin	185		Michael	Monedrisane	479
Catherine	Macroney Up	742						Samuel	Ballinvoher	182
Ellen	Castlecooke	657		** SURNAME DORAN				William	Ballinacarriga	002
Ellen	Macroney Up	727		Bridget	Ballinaparka S	550				
Jeremiah	Macroney Up	727		Bridget	Ballyderown	064		** SURNAME DOYLE		
Johanna	Castlecooke	657		Catherine	Ballinaparka N	548		Owen	Kilmurry S	587
John	Castlecooke	657		Catherine	Ballyderown	056				
Margaret	Castlecooke	657		Catherine	Ballyderown	064		** SURNAME DRAKE		
Margaret	Macroney Up	742		Catherine	Macroney Lr	697		Johanna	Ballinacarriga	014
Mary	Macroney Up	727		David	Coolalisheen	561		John	Ballinrush Lr	039
Maurice	Macroney Up	727		Edmond	Macroney Lr	697		Margaret	Ballinrush Lr	039
Maurice	Macroney Up	742		Edward	Ballinaparka S	550		Thomas	Ballinrush Lr	039
Thomas	Castlecooke	657		Elizabeth	Coolalisheen	561		William	Ballinrush Lr	039
Thomas	Macroney Up	727		Jane	Ballinaparka N	548				
				Jeremiah	Ballinaparka N	548		** SURNAME DRISCOLL		
** SURNAME DONOGHUE				Jeremiah	Ballyderown	056		Ann	Downing N	100
Ellen	Ballinacarriga	012		Jeremiah	Ballyderown	064		Cornelius	Downing N	100
				Judith	Coolalisheen	561		David	Ballylackan	525
** SURNAME DONOUGHUE				Margaret	Ballinaparka S	550		Ellen	Ballylackan	525
Bridget	Kilworth	260		Mary	Ballinaparka S	550		Mary	Ballylackan	525
Catherine	Whitebog	513		Mary	Coolalisheen	561		Patrick	Ballylackan	525
Edward	Kilmurry S	601		Mary	Macroney Lr	697				
James	Toor	500		Owen	Ballinaparka N	548		** SURNAME DUANE		
Jeffry	Whitebog	513		Patrick	Macroney Lr	697		Ann	Kilworth	336
Johanna	Castlecooke	645		Thomas	Coolalisheen	561		Elizabeth	Kilworth	336
John	Kilworth	305		Thomas	Macroney Lr	697		John	Kilworth	336
Margaret	Whitebog	513		William	Ballinaparka N	548		John	Monedrisane	487
Mary	Kilmurry S	601		William	Ballyderown	056		William	Kilworth	336
Maurice	Castlecooke	645		William	Ballyderown	064				
Patrick	Castlecooke	645						** SURNAME DUGGAN		
Patrick	Whitebog	513		** SURNAME DORLING				Edmond	Kilworth	273
Thomas	Castlecooke	645		Michael	Kilworth	298		James	Kilclogh	674
Thomas	Kilmurry S	601						James	Macroney Up	737
				** SURNAME DORNEY				John	Macroney Up	737

Martin	Macroney Up	737	** SURNAME ENGLISH			John	Boherdeveroge	086
			Andrew	Whitebog	511	Mary	Kilworth	303
** SURNAME DUNDAN			Honora	Whitebog	511	Michael	Kilworth	303
Edmond	Ballyderown	057	Phillip	Ballinvoher	170	Michael	Macroney Up	745

** SURNAME DUNN

** SURNAME ERLES

** SURNAME FENTON

Hannah	Ballyhenden	070	Maria	Monedrisane	447	Catherine	Graig	208
Jane	Ballyhenden	070				Daniel	Graig	208
Jeremiah	Ballyhenden	070				John	Graig	208
John	Ballyhenden	070				Mary	Graig	208
Mary	Ballyhenden	070	** SURNAME FANNESY			Rodger	Graig	208
Mary	Kilmurry N	574	Hanna	Kilworth	303	Simon	Graig	208
Michael	Ballyhenden	070				Thomas	Graig	208
			** SURNAME FANNING			Wiliam	Boherdeveroge	085

** SURNAME DWYER

			Catherine	Glanseskin	196			
John	Graig	204	Cornelius	Kilclogh	690	** SURNAME FEORE		
Mary	Ballinrush Lr	030	David	Kilally W	228	Michael	Kilmurry N	579
			Edmond	Kilworth	282			
			Eliza	Kilworth	282	** SURNAME FEY		
			James	Kilclogh	690	Henry	Kilworth	264
** SURNAME EGAN			Johanna	Kilally W	228	James	Kilworth	264
Eliza	Ballinacarriga	006	John	Kilclogh	690	Margaret	Kilworth	264
Eliza	Ballyderown	056	John	Kilworth	282			
Ellen	Ballinacarriga	006	Margaret	Kilally W	228	** SURNAME FING		
James	Ballinacarriga	006	Margaret	Kilworth	275	James	Ballinrush Up	139
John	Ballinacarriga	006	Margaret	Kilworth	282	Johanna	Ballinrush Up	139
Margaret	Kilworth	322	Mary	Kilclogh	690	Margaret	Ballinrush Up	139
Mary	Ballinacarriga	006	William	Kilclogh	690	Sib	Kilworth	341
Michael	Ballinacarriga	006				William	Ballinrush Up	139
Michael	Monedrisane	459	** SURNAME FARRELL					
			Ellen	Monedrisane	436	** SURNAME FINLEY		
** SURNAME ELLARD			Mary	Monedrisane	436	Ellen	Kilworth	342
Ellen	Kilworth	247	Michael	Monedrisane	436			
Ellen	Monedrisane	440	William	Monedrisane	436	** SURNAME FINN		
George	Kilworth	247				Bartholomew	Ballinacarriga	004
George	Monedrisane	440	** SURNAME FAWSITT			Bridget	Kilworth	334
Johanna	Kilworth	247	Ann	Kilworth	366	Catherine	Castlecooke	655
John	Kilworth	247	Arabella	Kilworth	366	David	Kilworth	360
John	Monedrisane	440	Edward	Kilworth	366	Ellen	Ballinacarriga	004
Joseph	Monedrisane	440	John	Kilworth	366	Ellen	Castlecooke	655
Margaret	Kilworth	247				Ellen	Kilworth	360
Margaret	Monedrisane	440	** SURNAME FENNELL			Hannah	Kilworth	334
Mary	Kilworth	247	Catherine	Macroney Lr	706	Jane	Kilworth	334
Mary	Monedrisane	440	Mary	Macroney Lr	706	Johanna	Kilally W	236
Patrick	Monedrisane	440	Thomas	Macroney Lr	706	John	Castlecooke	643
						John	Castlecooke	655
** SURNAME ELLAW			** SURNAME FENNESY			Margaret	Kilally W	236
Catherine	Glanseskin	198	Bridget	Kilworth	303	Margaret	Kilworth	360
George	Glanseskin	198	Catherine	Kilworth	303	Mary	Ballinacarriga	004
Nancy	Glanseskin	198	Ellen	Kilworth	303	Mary	Castlecooke	655
			Ellen	Macroney Up	745	Mary	Kilworth	360
** SURNAME ELSWORTH			Hanna	Kilworth	303	Michael	Kilworth	334
Thomas	Kilmurry S	597	Jeremiah	Kilworth	335	Nancy	Castlecooke	655
			Johanna	Macroney Up	745	Nancy	Kilworth	360

(SURNAME FINN continued)			Gerrard	Kilworth	295	John	Ballinaparka N	544
Patrick	Castlecooke	655				John	Ballylackan	520
Richard	Kilworth	334	** SURNAME FITZPATRICK			John	Kilmurry S	598
Thomas	Castlecooke	655	James C.	Monedrisane	445	John	Leitrim	640
William	Kilworth	334				Julia	Kilmurry S	597
			** SURNAME FLANAGAN			Julia	Kilmurry S	598
** SURNAME FITZGERALD			Arthur	Ballinvoher	169	Margaret	Ballylackan	535
Ann	Macroney Up	717	Bridget	Ballinvoher	168	Margaret	Kilworth	309
Bartholomew	Castlecooke	659	Catherine	Ballinvoher	168	Margaret	Kilworth	310
Bridget	Ballyvoskillikin	081	David	Ballinvoher	168	Martin	Kilworth	291
Bridget	Kilworth	356	James	Ballinvoher	168	Mary	Ballinaparka N	544
Bridget	Monedrisane	469	Jeremiah	Ballinvoher	168	Mary	Ballylackan	520
Catherine	Castlecooke	659	Margaret	Ballinvoher	169	Mary	Kilmurry N	575
Catherine	Kilworth	356	Thomas	Ballinvoher	169	Mary	Kilworth	291
Denis	Kielbeg	565	Thomas	Kilclogh	669	Mary	Kilworth	310
Edward	Macroney Lr	702				Maurice	Ballylackan	534
Ellen	Kilmurry N	571	** SURNAME FLEMMING			Thomas	Ballinaparka N	544
Ellen	Kilworth	356	Mary	Kilclogh	686	Thomas	Ballylackan	520
Ellen	Monedrisane	469	Michael	Ballyhenden	075	Thomas	Kilworth	291
Garret	Kilworth	250	Michael	Kilclogh	686	Timothy	Ballylackan	535
Garrett	Castlecooke	659				William	Kilmurry N	575
Hannah	Kilally E	225	** SURNAME FLYNN			William	Kilworth	309
Honora	Castlecooke	659	Ann	Ballylackan	520			
James	Kilally E	225	Anne	Ballinaparka N	544	** SURNAME FOLEY		
James	Kilworth	250	Catherine	Ballinaparka N	544	Ann	Kilclogh	675
James	Kilworth	356	Catherine	Ballylackan	520	Catherine	Kilclogh	675
James	Macroney Up	717	Catherine	Ballylackan	534	Daniel	Macroney Up	737
James	Monedrisane	469	Catherine	Kilmurry N	575	Eliza	Glenwood	119
Jane	Graig	214	Catherine	Kilmurry S	598	Eliza	Macroney Up	737
Johanna	Graig	214	Catherine	Kilworth	310	Johanna	Macroney Up	737
John	Castlecooke	659	Edmond	Ballinaparka N	539	Margaret	Macroney Up	737
John	Kilworth	356	Edward	Kilmurry S	597	Mary	Macroney Up	737
Julia	Kilally E	225	Edward	Kilmurry S	598	Nanne	Monedrisane	446
Margaret	Kilworth	356	Elen	Ballinaparka N	544	Patrick	Kilclogh	675
Marks	Monedrisane	469	Eliza	Kilmurry S	597			
Mary	Castlecooke	658	Eliza	Kilmurry S	598	** SURNAME FOUHY		
Mary	Graig	214	Ellen	Ballylackan	515	Catherine	Monedrisane	428
Mary	Kilworth	250	Ellen	Ballylackan	520	David	Monedrisane	428
Mary	Kilworth	313	Ellen	Ballylackan	534	Johanna	Monedrisane	428
Mary	Kilworth	356	Ellen	Ballylackan	535	John	Monedrisane	428
Mary	Macroney Up	717	Ellen	Kilmurry S	602	Richard	Monedrisane	428
Maryanne	Leitrim	633	Ellen	Kilworth	309	Thomas	Monedrisane	428
Michael	Kilmurry N	571	Emilia	Kilmurry S	597			
Patrick	Kilally E	225	Hanna	Kilworth	291	** SURNAME FRAZIER		
Patrick	Kilworth	250	James	Ballinaparka N	544	Thomas	Boherdeveroge	086
Patrick	Kilworth	356	James	Ballylackan	520			
Patrick	Knockaskehane	613	James	Kilmurry N	575			
Robert	Kilally E	225	James	Kilmurry S	591			
William	Graig	214	James	Kilmurry S	598	** SURNAME GALAVAN		
William	Kilally E	225	James	Kilworth	291	David	Glanseskin	202
William	Monedrisane	469	Johanna	Ballinaparka N	544	Mary	Glanseskin	202
			Johanna	Ballylackan	520			
** SURNAME FITZGIBBON			Johanna	Coolalisheen	561			
Elizabeth	Kilworth	295	John	Ballinaparka N	539	** SURNAME GALLIGAN		

Ellen	Kilworth	373	Ellen	Kilworth	328	Grizalda	Kilworth	335
Honora	Kilmurry S	584	John	Kilworth	328			
			Mary	Kilworth	328	** SURNAME HAGARTY		
** SURNAME GARRETT			William	Kilworth	328	Catherine	Kilworth	415
Mary	Kilworth	349				Edmond	Kilworth	415
			** SURNAME GRANT			Mary	Kilworth	415
** SURNAME GEAREY			Mrs.	Kilmurry S	584	Michael	Kilworth	415
Patrick	Moorpark	498	Thomas H. J.	Kilmurry S	584	Richard	Kilworth	415
** SURNAME GEARY			** SURNAME GREEHY			** SURNAME HALES		
Catherine	Ballinglanna S	026	Abina	Macroney Up	721	Eliza	Kilworth	248
Catherine	Kilworth	339	Catherine	Ballylackan	527	James	Kilworth	248
Daniel	Kilworth	313	Ellen	Kilworth	281	Mary	Kilworth	248
Daniel	Kilworth	374	John	Ballylackan	527	Patty	Kilworth	248
Ellen	Kilworth	339	John	Kilworth	281			
Honora	Kilworth	374	Julia	Ballylackan	527	** SURNAME HALLORAN		
James	Kilworth	339	Patrick	Ballylackan	527	James	Toor	507
Johanna	Kilworth	374	Thomas	Macroney Up	721	John	Glanseskin	194
John	Kilworth	339				John	Kilmurry S	584
John	Macroney Up	732	** SURNAME GREEN			Mary	Glanseskin	194
Margaret	Kilworth	374	William	Castlecooke	652	Mary	Toor	507
Margaret	Macroney Up	732				Patrick	Glanseskin	194
Mary	Macroney Up	732	** SURNAME GRIFFIN			William	Glanseskin	194
Michael	Macroney Up	732	Daniel	Macroney Up	730			
Patrick	Kilworth	258	David	Kilclogh	670	** SURNAME HALY		
			David	Kilclogh	671	Elizabeth	Leitrim	634
** SURNAME GEELEHER			David	Kilclogh	673	Jane	Leitrim	634
Elizabeth	Macroney Up	726	Edmond	Kilclogh	671	John	Leitrim	634
Honora	Macroney Up	726	Ellen	Kilclogh	670	Maurice	Leitrim	634
James	Macroney Up	726	Ellen	Kilclogh	673	Thomas	Leitrim	634
John	Macroney Up	726	George	Kilclogh	673			
Mary	Macroney Up	726	Honora	Monedrisane	473	** SURNAME HANDLEY		
Maurice	Macroney Up	726	James	Macroney Up	730	Bridget	Kilally W	240
			Judith	Macroney Up	730	Catherine	Kilally W	240
** SURNAME GERAN			Margaret	Kilclogh	671	John	Kilally W	240
Allice	Ballinrush Lr	030	Margaret	Macroney Up	730	Margaret	Kilally W	240
Anthony	Ballinrush Lr	030	Mary	Kilclogh	673	Mary	Kilally W	240
Catherine	Kilclogh	662	Mary	Macroney Up	730	Patrick	Kilally W	240
Daniel	Ballinrush Lr	030	Matthew	Monedrisane	473	William	Kilally W	240
Edward	Ballinrush Lr	030	Michael	Kilclogh	673			
Ellen	Maryville	418	Patrick	Ballyderown	056	** SURNAME HANLON		
John	Graig	205	Patrick	Kilclogh	671	Ann	Kilworth	289
Julia	Graig	205	Patrick	Macroney Up	730	Catherine	Ballinrush Lr	043
Mary	Ballinrush Lr	030	Thomas	Macroney Up	730	Catherine	Kilworth	278
Maryann	Ballinrush Lr	030	William	Kilclogh	673	Catherine	Kilworth	381
						Catherine	Macroney Up	740
** SURNAME GOVLD			** SURNAME GUINEVAN			Edmond	Kilworth	352
Bridget	Kilworth	399	John	Kilworth	349	Edward	Kilworth	381
Catherine	Kilworth	399	Pat	Kilworth	349	Ellen	Kilworth	278
Henry	Kilworth	399				Ellen	Kilworth	381
Honora	Kilworth	399				Ellen	Macroney Up	740
John	Kilworth	399				Honora	Kilworth	352
						James	Graig	206
** SURNAME GOVLDE			** SURNAME HACKETT			James	Kilworth	278

-100-

James	Kilworth	354	Catherine	Macroney Lr	708	Andrew	Kilmurry S	585
Johanna	Ballinrush Lr	043	Daniel	Macroney Lr	708	Ann	Kilworth	324
Johanna	Kilworth	352	Ellen	Macroney Lr	704	Anne	Monedrisane	485
John	Ballinrush Lr	043	Ellen	Macroney Lr	707	Bridget	Graig	220
John	Kilworth	278	Ellen	Macroney Lr	708	Bridget	Kilmurry S	593
John	Kilworth	352	Hannah	Ballylackan	524	Bridget	Monedrisane	489
John	Kilworth	354	Johanna	Macroney Lr	707	Catherine	Ballinacarriga	014
John	Kilworth	381	Julia	Ballylackan	524	Catherine	Kilmurry S	585
John	Macroney Up	740	Julia	Macroney Lr	704	Catherine	Monedrisane	460
Margaret	Kilworth	354	Julia	Macroney Lr	708	David	Downing S	113
Mary	Graig	206	Michael	Macroney Lr	707	Eliza	Monedrisane	460
Mary	Kilworth	278	Margaret	Macroney Lr	707	Ellen	Ballinacarriga	014
Mary	Kilworth	354	Mary	Macroney Lr	704	Ellen	Ballylackan	523
Mary	Kilworth	381	Mary	Macroney Lr	708	Ellen	Kilmurry S	585
Mary	Macroney Up	740	Maurice	Macroney Lr	708	Henry	Monedrisane	485
Maurice	Ballinrush Lr	043	Patrick	Macroney Lr	704	James	Ballinacarriga	014
Maurice	Kilworth	354	Patrick	Macroney Lr	707	James	Downing N	104
Michael	Kilworth	354	Patrick	Macroney Lr	708	James	Kilmurry S	593
Patrick	Ballinrush Lr	043	Thomas	Ballylackan	524	James	Monedrisane	459
Patrick	Kilworth	354	Timothy	Macroney Lr	708	James	Monedrisane	489
Richard	Graig	206				John	Kilworth	277
Thomas	Kilworth	354	**** SURNAME HEALY**			John	Monedrisane	489
			Catherine	Ballylackan	537	Margaret	Downing N	104
** SURNAME HANRAHAN			Ellen	Ballylackan	537	Mary	Ballinacarriga	014
John	Kilally W	239	Ellen	Coolalisheen	557	Mary	Ballylackan	523
			Johanna	Ballylackan	537	Mary	Downing N	104
** SURNAME HARDING			John	Ballinacarriga	012	Mary	Graig	220
Ellen	Kilworth	253	John	Ballylackan	537	Mary	Monedrisane	485
			Mary	Ballylackan	537	Maurice	Monedrisane	485
** SURNAME HARRINGTON			Mary	Coolalisheen	557	Maurice	Monedrisane	489
Ellen	Glenwood	120	Thomas	Coolalisheen	557	Michael	Kilmurry S	593
James	Glenwood	120				Pat	Kilmurry S	593
Johanna	Glenwood	120	**** SURNAME HEFFERNAN**			Patrick	Graig	220
John	Glenwood	120	Michael	Downing S	113	Patrick	Kilmurry S	585
John	Loughnahilly	129				Patrick	Monedrisane	460
Mary	Glenwood	120	**** SURNAME HEFFERNON**			Patrick	Monedrisane	485
Michael	Glenwood	120	Bridget	Ballinacarriga	002	Richard	Graig	220
			Edward H.	Ballydarown Glebe	046	Robert	Ballylackan	523
** SURNAME HARRIS						Thomas	Downing N	104
Catherine	Ballylackan	521	**** SURNAME HEGARTY**			Timothy	Kilmurry S	585
			Anne	Ballinaparka S	549	Timothy	Kilmurry S	593
** SURNAME HARTNETTY						William	Ballylackan	523
Catherine	Kilworth	345	**** SURNAME HENDLEY**			William	Monedrisane	460
John	Kilworth	345	Arthur	Downing S	112			
Thomas	Kilworth	345	Arthur	Kilworth	398	**** SURNAME HENRY**		
			Eliza	Downing S	112	Mary	Maryville	419
** SURNAME HAYES			Francis	Downing S	112			
David	Downing N	102	James	Kilworth	398	**** SURNAME HESKIN**		
Eliza	Downing N	102	Mary	Downing S	112	Alexander	Kilally W	227
James	Downing N	102	Mary	Downing S	117	Catherine	Kilally W	230
John	Downing N	102	Phebe	Downing S	112	Edmond	Kilally W	227
						Edmond	Kilally W	230
** SURNAME HEAFY			**** SURNAME HENNESY**			Eliza	Kilally W	227
Amelia	Macroney Lr	707	Allice	Ballylackan	523	Margaret	Kilally W	227

-101-

Mary	Kilally W	227	** SURNAME HOLMES			Ellen	Ballyderown	054
Patrick	Kilally W	227	William	Kilworth	378	John	Ballinrush Lr	032
William	Kilally W	230				Mary	Ballinrush Lr	032
			** SURNAME HORGAN			Maurice	Ballinrush Lr	032
** SURNAME HICKEY			Eliza	Monedrisane	432	Norry	Ballinrush Lr	032
Bridget	Gurtone	121	Ellen	Monedrisane	432	Patrick	Ballinrush Lr	032
Jane	Gurtone	121	John	Monedrisane	432	Timothy	Ballinrush Lr	032
Johanna	Kilmurry N	578	John	Monedrisane	488			
Mary	Gurtone	121	Michael	Monedrisane	432	** SURNAME HURST		
Maurice	Kilmurry N	583				Ann	Sharroclure	755
Michael	Gurtone	121	** SURNAME HOSKIN			Catherine	Sharroclure	755
Peter	Gurtone	121	George	Ballinacarriga	012	George	Sharroclure	755
Simon	Gurtone	121				Jane	Sharroclure	755
			** SURNAME HOWARD			Mary	Sharroclure	755
** SURNAME HIGGINS			Bridget	Graig	216			
Anne	Ballyderown	057	Catherine	Ballinrush Up	137	** SURNAME HUTCHINSON		
Chessy	Ballyderown	057	George	Ballinrush Up	137	James	Kilclogh	660
Elizabeth	Ballyderown	057	James	Graig	216	Jane	Kilclogh	660
Jane	Ballyderown	057	John	Graig	216	John	Kilclogh	660
Martha	Ballyderown	057	Martin	Graig	216	William	Kilclogh	660
Susan	Ballyderown	057	Mary	Graig	216			
			Michael	Ballinrush Up	137	** SURNAME HYDE		
** SURNAME HOGAN			Michael	Graig	216	Anne	Monedrisane	482
Catherine	Kilworth	396	William	Ballinrush Up	137	Mary	Monedrisane	482
David	Kilclogh	668	William	Graig	216	Nancy	Monedrisane	482
Ellen	Kilclogh	664						
Ellen	Kilclogh	668	** SURNAME HOWE					
Honora	Kilclogh	668	Catherine	Kilworth	276			
Johanna	Kilclogh	668	Catherine	Kilworth	285			
John	Kilclogh	664	Edmond	Kilworth	276	** SURNAME ILARD		
Mary	Kilworth	396	Ellen	Kilworth	276	Ellen	Kilworth	413
Michael	Kilclogh	668	Joseph	Kilworth	276	George	Kilworth	413
			Julia	Kilworth	285	John	Kilworth	413
** SURNAME HOLEHAN			Martin	Ballinvoher	161	Margaret	Kilworth	268
Catherine	Kilworth	355	Martin	Kilworth	285	Michael	Kilworth	413
Denis	Kilworth	355	Mary	Kilworth	285	Nicholas	Kilworth	413
Hannah	Moorpark	496				William	Kilworth	413
Honora	Moorpark	496	** SURNAME HUDSON					
James	Moorpark	496	Hannah	Kilworth	317			
John	Kilworth	362	Henry	Moorpark	497			
Julia	Kilworth	355	Jane	Moorpark	497			
Julia	Kilworth	362	John	Kilworth	317			
Martin	Moorpark	496						
Mary	Kilworth	355	** SURNAME HUGHES			** SURNAME JOHNSON		
Mary	Moorpark	496	Edward	Kilworth	378	Mary	Monedrisane	448
Michael	Kilworth	355				Thomas	Monedrisane	448
Michael	Kilworth	362	** SURNAME HURLEY					
Michael	Moorpark	496	Bridget	Macroney Up	723	** SURNAME JONES		
Norry	Kilworth	355	John	Macroney Up	723	Ellen	Monedrisane	492
Owen	Kilworth	362	Patrick	Macroney Up	723	Patrick	Monedrisane	492
Patrick	Kilworth	355						
Peter	Kilworth	362	** SURNAME HURLY			** SURNAME JOYCE		
Thomas	Moorpark	496	Bridget	Ballinrush Lr	032	Ann	Macroney Up	751
			Eliza	Ballinrush Lr	032	Bridget	Ballylackan	517

(SURNAME JOYCE continued)

Carey	Ballylackan	517
Catherine	Ballylackan	521
Catherine	Ballyvoskillikin	077
Edmond	Ballylackan	521
Elizabeth	Macroney Up	751
Ellen	Ballinvoher	163
Ellen	Ballylackan	517
Ellen	Kilworth	357
Ellen	Macroney Up	751
Honora	Ballyvoskillikin	080
James	Ballylackan	521
James	Macroney Up	751
John	Ballylackan	521
John	Ballyvoskillikin	077
Julia	Ballylackan	521
Kate	Ballylackan	517
Margaret	Ballyvoskillikin	077
Mary	Ballinrush Up	138
Mary	Ballylackan	521
Mary	Ballyvoskillikin	077
Mary	Macroney Up	751
Michael	Ballinrush Up	138
Michael	Ballylackan	517
Michael	Ballylackan	521
Michael	Ballyvoskillikin	077
Michael	Macroney Up	751
Patrick	Kilworth	357
Sarah	Ballylackan	517
Terence	Ballyvoskillikin	080
Thomas	Kilworth	357

** SURNAME KANE

Dennis	Macroney Up	744
Ellen	Macroney Up	744
Johanna	Macroney Up	744
Michael	Macroney Up	744
Thomas	Macroney Up	744

** SURNAME KEANE

Ellen	Kilmurry S	599

** SURNAME KEARNEY

John	Maryville	418

** SURNAME KEATING

Bridget	Ballyhenden	075
Catherine	Macroney Up	730
Catherine	Monedrisane	460
Eliza	Ballyhenden	075

Ellen	Kilmurry S	599
James	Ballyhenden	075
John	Ballyhenden	075
John	Monedrisane	460
Patrick	Monedrisane	460
Richard	Monedrisane	460
Thomas	Kilmurry S	599

** SURNAME KEEFFE

Bridget	Leitrim	636
Catherine	Kilclogh	686
Catherine	Leitrim	636
Cornelius	Downing N	101
Daniel	Ballinvoher	166
Daniel	Kilclogh	689
Daniel	Leitrim	636
Eliza	Monedrisane	423
Ellen	Ballinrush Up	132
Ellen	Ballinvoher	166
Ellen	Macroney Up	718
Jeremiah	Ballinvoher	166
Jeremiah	Macroney Up	718
Johanna	Ballinvoher	166
Johanna	Kilclogh	689
Johanna	Monedrisane	436
John	Ballinvoher	166
John	Macroney Lr	712
Margaret	Ballyhenden	076
Margaret	Downing N	101
Margaret	Macroney Lr	712
Margaret	Macroney Up	718
Margaret	Macroney Up	719
Mary	Downing N	101
Mary	Kilmurry N	574
Mary	Macroney Up	718
Michael	Ballinvoher	166
Michael	Kilmurry N	574
Pat	Monedrisane	436
Patrick	Ballinvoher	166
Patrick	Macroney Up	719
Thomas	Kilclogh	689
Thomas	Macroney Up	718

** SURNAME KELEHER

Bridget	Ballyhenden	074
Cornelius	Graig	209
Eliza	Ballylackan	518
Eliza	Graig	209
Hannah	Graig	209
Johanna	Ballylackan	518
John	Ballylackan	518
John	Graig	209
Margaret	Ballinvoher	163
Margaret	Graig	209

Mary	Ballyhenden	076
Mary	Ballylackan	518
Mary	Graig	209
Mary	Kilmurry N	581
Michael	Ballylackan	518
Patrick	Boherdeveroge	086
Timothy	Ballylackan	518

** SURNAME KELLY

Catherine	Downing N	096
John	Kilmurry N	580
John	Kilmurry S	606
Margaret	Macroney Up	737
Mary	Kilmurry N	580
Michael	Kilmurry N	580

** SURNAME KENNEDY

Ann	Kilworth	293
Bridget	Ballinrush Up	156
Catherine	Ballinrush Up	156
Cornelius	Kilworth	382
Eliza	Graig	204
Eliza	Kilworth	293
John	Ballinrush Up	156
Margaret	Ballinrush Up	156
Mary	Ballinrush Up	156
Mary	Kilworth	293
Michael	Ballinrush Up	156
Michael	Kilally W	229

** SURNAME KENNY

Ansty	Monedrisane	477
Bridget	Kilworth	322
Catherine	Kilworth	329
Cornelius	Kilworth	364
Edmond	Monedrisane	477
Edward	Monedrisane	477
Ellen	Kilworth	329
Honora	Monedrisane	467
James	Monedrisane	467
John	Monedrisane	467
Margaret	Monedrisane	477
Mary	Monedrisane	467
Patrick	Monedrisane	477
Thomas	Monedrisane	467
Thomas	Monedrisane	477

** SURNAME KENRICK

Catherine	Ballinglanna N	010
Hannah	Ballinglanna N	010
Mary	Ballinglanna N	010
Michael	Ballinglanna N	010
Thomas	Ballinglanna N	010
William	Ballinglanna N	010

** SURNAME KENT		
David	Ballyhenden	076
Elizabeth	Ballyhenden	076
Ellen	Ballyhenden	076
John	Ballyhenden	076
** SURNAME KERESY		
Margaret	Kilmurry N	579
Mary	Kilmurry N	579
Michael	Kilmurry N	579
** SURNAME KINNEALY		
Ellen	Monedrisane	441
Johanna	Monedrisane	441
Mary	Monedrisane	441
Patrick	Monedrisane	441
William	Monedrisane	441
** SURNAME KNOWLES		
Amelia	Monedrisane	423
Catherine	Monedrisane	423
Henry	Monedrisane	423
Thomas	Monedrisane	423
** SURNAME LANDE		
Edmond	Kilworth	373
Edward	Kilmurry N	568
Hannah	Kilmurry N	568
James	Kilmurry N	568
Kate	Kilworth	373
Mary	Kilmurry N	568
Mary	Kilworth	373
Patrick	Kilmurry N	568
William	Kilmurry N	568
William	Kilworth	373
** SURNAME LANE		
Alice	Macroney Up	715
Catherine	Castlecooke	654
Catherine	Kilworth	344
Elizabeth	Macroney Up	715
Ellen	Castlecooke	646
Ellen	Castlecooke	654
George	Macroney Up	715
Goen	Castlecooke	646
Henry	Castlecooke	646
James	Macroney Up	715
Jane	Kilworth	344
John	Castlecooke	646
John	Kielbeg	565

John	Macroney Up	715
Maria	Kilworth	268
Mary	Castlecooke	654
Mary	Kilworth	344
Mary	Macroney Up	715
Richard	Castlecooke	654
William	Kilworth	344
** SURNAME LEAHY		
Catherine	Ballinrush Up	147
Catherine	Kilmurry S	586
Jeremiah	Ballinrush Up	147
Johanna	Coolalisheen	556
Julia	Kilmurry S	586
Mary	Ballinrush Up	147
Mary	Downing S	112
** SURNAME LEAMY		
Elizabeth	Ballyderown	055
John	Ballyderown	055
** SURNAME LEARY		
Patrick	Ballyvoskillikin	080
** SURNAME LEE		
John	Kilworth	307
** SURNAME LEHANE		
Cornelius	Ballinrush Lr	033
Daniel	Ballinrush Lr	033
Denis	Ballinrush Lr	033
Johanna	Ballinrush Lr	033
** SURNAME LENARD		
William	Kilmurry N	579
** SURNAME LENEHAN		
Patrick	Ballylackan	517
** SURNAME LEONARD		
Johanna	Monedrisane	435
Mary	Monedrisane	435
** SURNAME LINEHAN		
Bridget	Downing N	105
Catherine	Ballinaparka N	547
Edmond	Kilworth	387
Ellen	Downing N	105
Ellen	Kilworth	387
Jeremiah	Downing N	105
Mary	Downing N	105
Mary	Kilworth	387
Michael	Downing N	105
Timothy	Downing N	105

** SURNAME LODGE		
Ann	Monedrisane	454
George	Monedrisane	454
** SURNAME LOMASNEY		
Daniel	Kilworth	269
Edmond	Monedrisane	452
Ellen	Monedrisane	452
James	Kilworth	269
John	Kilworth	269
John	Monedrisane	452
Judith	Coolalisheen	562
Mary	Kilworth	269
Mary	Monedrisane	452
Matthew	Monedrisane	452
Michael	Kilworth	269
** SURNAME LONDREGAN		
Michael	Macroney Lr	702
** SURNAME LONDRIGAN		
Ann	Castlecooke	658
Daniel	Castlecooke	658
Margaret	Castlecooke	658
Mary	Castlecooke	658
Thomas	Castlecooke	658
** SURNAME LONERGAN		
Bridget	Kilworth	320
Mary	Kilworth	339
** SURNAME LOONEY		
David	Kilworth	312
Hanna	Kilworth	312
James	Kilworth	312
Mary	Kilworth	312
** SURNAME LUBY		
Ellen	Ballinacarriga	012
** SURNAME LUKEY		
Eliza	Kilworth	335
** SURNAME LYNCE		
Elizabeth	Kilclogh	667
Honora	Kilclogh	667
James	Kilclogh	667
Jane	Kilclogh	667
John	Kilclogh	667
Mary	Kilclogh	667
Thomas	Kilclogh	667
** SURNAME LYONS		
Alice	Macroney Lr	711

(SURNAME LYONS continued)		
Alice	Macroney Up	729
Bridget	Castlecooke	655
Catherine	Kilworth	304
Catherine	Macroney Lr	705
Catherine	Macroney Lr	711
Denis	Macroney Lr	705
Eliza	Kilworth	304
Ellen	Ballyvoskillikin	078
Ellen	Macroney Lr	705
Ellen	Macroney Lr	711
Ellen	Macroney Up	729
Honora	Ballyvoskillikin	078
James	Kilworth	304
James	Macroney Lr	711
Jane	Macroney Lr	705
Johanna	Kilworth	304
John	Macroney Lr	705
John	Macroney Lr	711
John	Macroney Up	729
Margaret	Kilworth	304
Margaret	Macroney Lr	711
Martin	Macroney Up	729
Mary	Ballyvoskillikin	078
Mary	Macroney Lr	705
Michael	Ballyderown	066
Michael	Macroney Lr	705
Patrick	Kilworth	304
Patrick	Macroney Lr	705
William	Macroney Lr	711

** SURNAME MACKESY

Elizabeth	Kilmurry N	569
James	Kilmurry N	569
James	Kilworth	277
Johanna	Kilmurry N	569
Mary	Kilmurry N	569
Patrick	Kilmurry N	569
Thomas	Kilmurry N	569

** SURNAME MADDEN

Bridget	Monedrisane	481
Julia	Monedrisane	481
Maurice	Monedrisane	481
Michael	Kilworth	407
Thomas	Monedrisane	481

** SURNAME MAGNER

Bridget	Glanseskin	189

David	Glanseskin	189
Edward	Kilally W	226
Eliza	Maryville	421
John	Glanseskin	189
Mary	Glanseskin	189
Mary	Kilworth	273

** SURNAME MAHONEY

Ellen	Macroney Up	727

** SURNAME MAHONY

Bridget	Coolalisheen	556
Catherine	Ballinrush Up	131
Catherine	Kilworth	398
Catherine	Kilworth	402
Catherine	Knockaskehane	614
Daniel	Coolalisheen	556
Daniel	Kilworth	244
Daniel	Kilworth	384
David	Coolalisheen	556
David	Kilworth	244
David	Kilworth	402
David	Macroney Up	741
Denis	Kilworth	402
Denis	Macroney Up	741
Edward	Ballinrush Up	131
Eliza	Kilmurry S	590
Eliza	Kilmurry S	595
Elizabeth	Kilworth	244
Ellen	Kilworth	327
Ellen	Macroney Up	741
Honora	Ballinrush Up	131
James	Macroney Up	741
Jane	Ballyderown	061
Jane	Kilworth	384
Jane	Macroney Up	741
John	Ballinrush Up	131
John	Kilmurry S	595
John	Kilworth	388
John	Kilworth	402
John	Knockaskehane	614
John	Macroney Up	741
Kate	Kilworth	244
Margaret	Coolalisheen	556
Mary	Ballinrush Up	131
Mary	Kilworth	384
Mary	Kilworth	402
Michael	Kilworth	384
Patrick	Knockaskehane	614
Patrick	Macroney Lr	706
Thomas	Ballinrush Up	131
William	Kilmurry S	595
William	Leitrim	637

** SURNAME MALONE

James	Kilally W	239
Margaret	Kilmurry S	611
Mary	Kilmurry S	611
Mary	Kilworth	393
Michael	Kilworth	393
Patrick	Kilmurry S	611

** SURNAME MANGAN

James	Coolalisheen	563
Patrick	Coolalisheen	556

** SURNAME MANSERGT

Michael	Macroney Lr	696

** SURNAME MEADE

Honora	Downing S	114

** SURNAME MEAGHER

Honora	Ballinglanna N	021
John	Ballinglanna N	021
Margaret	Ballinglanna N	021
Terence	Ballinglanna N	021

** SURNAME MEANY

Mary	Kilworth	310

** SURNAME MEARA

Mary	Ballinrush Lr	034

** SURNAME MILLER

Denis	Ballylackan	531
Elizabeth	Ballylackan	531
James	Ballylackan	517
James	Leitrim	641
Margaret	Ballylackan	531
Margaret	Kilmurry S	585
Richard	Ballylackan	531
Thomas	Ballylackan	531

** SURNAME MILLS

Ellen	Kilworth	270
Hannah	Kilworth	270
John	Kilworth	270
Margaret	Kilworth	270
Mary	Kilworth	270
Peter	Kilworth	270
Stephen	Kilworth	270

** SURNAME MILTON

Maria	Ballydarown Glebe	046

** SURNAME MOAKLEY

Andrew	Knockanabohelly	124

Catherine	Knockanabohelly	124	** SURNAME MOLOWPY			Margaret	Kilworth	400
Eliza	Knockanabohelly	124	Bridget	Ballinvoher	183	Norry	Kilworth	400
John	Knockanabohelly	124	Edward	Ballinvoher	184	Richard	Kilworth	391
Margaret	Knockanabohelly	124	Elizabeth	Ballinvoher	183	Richard	Kilworth	400
			Ellen	Ballinvoher	184	William	Kilworth	400
** SURNAME MOHER			John	Ballinvoher	183			
Andrew	Macroney Up	743	John	Kilclogh	687	** SURNAME MORRISON		
Bridget	Castlecooke	656	Mary	Ballinvoher	183	James	Boherdeveroge	085
Bridget	Macroney Up	746	Mary	Kilclogh	687			
Catherine	Castlecooke	656	Mary	Loughnahilly	129	** SURNAME MORROGH		
David	Ballinvoher	175	Maurice	Ballinvoher	183	Catherine	Kilworth	268
David	Macroney Up	743	Patrick	Gurtone	123	Edmond	Kilworth	268
David	Macroney Up	746	Thomas	Ballinvoher	184	George	Kilworth	268
Edmond	Castlecooke	656				Henry	Kilworth	268
Eliza	Kilworth	342	** SURNAME MONTGOMERY			James	Kilworth	268
Ellen	Ballinvoher	173	Arabella	Graig	212	Michael	Kilworth	268
Ellen	Castlecooke	656	Catherine	Graig	212			
Ellen	Kilworth	342	Frances	Graig	212	** SURNAME MULCAHY		
Ellen	Macroney Up	743	Honnora	Kilclogh	666	Catherine	Kilworth	265
Honora	Castlecooke	656	Howard	Graig	212	Daniel	Ballyvoskillikin	081
James	Ballinvoher	171	Johanna	Graig	212	Denis	Ballyvoskillikin	081
James	Castlecooke	656	John	Graig	212	Elizabeth	Monedrisane	426
Jane	Macroney Up	746	Margaret	Graig	212	Ellen	Ballyvoskillikin	081
Jeremiah	Macroney Up	743	Marta (sic)	Graig	212	Ellen	Coolalisheen	559
Johanna	Castlecooke	656	Mary	Kilclogh	666	Garrett	Ballyvoskillikin	081
Mary	Ballinvoher	178	Susan	Graig	212	Johanna	Ballyvoskillikin	081
Mary	Castlecooke	656	Thomas	Kilclogh	666	John	Ballyvoskillikin	081
Mary	Kilworth	342				John	Coolalisheen	559
Mary	Macroney Up	746	** SURNAME MOORE			Mary	Ballyvoskillikin	081
Michael	Macroney Up	743	Stephen	Ballyderown	066	Mary	Coolalisheen	559
Norry	Kilworth	369				Michael	Ballyvoskillikin	081
Patrick	Ballinvoher	173	** SURNAME MORAN			Michael	Coolalisheen	559
Patrick	Kilworth	342	Eliza	Kilworth	368	Owen	Ballyvoskillikin	081
Richard	Macroney Up	746				Polly	Kilworth	261
Thomas	Ballinvoher	173	** SURNAME MORIARTY					
Thomas	Ballinvoher	178	Catherine	Monedrisane	470	** SURNAME MULLINS		
William	Castlecooke	656	Ellen	Kilworth	321	Michael	Kilworth	278
			John	Monedrisane	470			
** SURNAME MOLAN			Marks	Monedrisane	470	** SURNAME MURPHY		
Bridget	Kilworth	280	Patrick	Monedrisane	470	Bridget	Boherdeveroge	086
						Bridget	Macroney Up	731
** SURNAME MOLONE			** SURNAME MORONEY			Catherine	Ballinrush Up	142
Ann	Downing S	117	David	Glanseskin	188	Catherine	Kilmurry S	600
			James	Ballyhenden	076	Catherine	Kilworth	299
** SURNAME MOLONY			Margaret	Glanseskin	188	Catherine	Macroney Up	731
Ellen	Kilworth	414	William	Glanseskin	188	Daniel	Ballinglanna N	011
Mary	Kilworth	414				Daniel	Macroney Up	731
			** SURNAME MORONY			David	Boherdeveroge	086
** SURNAME MOLOWPHY			Daniel	Kilworth	400	David	Knockaskehane	631
Bridget	Ballinvoher	163	Edward	Kilclogh	684	Edward	Kilmurry S	600
Catherine	Ballinvoher	163	Ellen	Kilclogh	684	Elizabeth	Knockaskehane	631
James	Ballinvoher	163	Honora	Kilworth	391	Ellen	Ballinglanna N	011
Maurice	Ballinvoher	159	Jeremiah	Kilworth	391	Ellen	Macroney Up	731
			John	Kilworth	400	Ellen	Macroney Up	739

(SURNAME MURPHY continued)

Hannora	Ballinglanna N	011	James	Ballinaparka N	541	Jeremiah	Ballylackan	532
Honora	Macroney Up	731	Jane	Knockaskehane	629	Jeremiah	Kilworth	329
Honora	Macroney Up	739	Jeremiah	Glanseskin	195	Johanna	Kilworth	346
James	Kilworth	299	Jeremiah	Knockaskehane	629	John	Ballylackan	532
Jeremiah	Kilworth	299	Johanna	Kilworth	285	John	Kilworth	351
Johanna	Boherdeveroge	086	Johanna	Knockaskehane	629	Kate	Kilworth	385
Johanna	Kilworth	406	John	Glanseskin	195	Margaret	Kilworth	346
John	Boherdeveroge	086	John	Kilworth	285	Michael	Ballylackan	532
John	Kilmurry S	600	John	Kilworth	412	Michael	Graig	204
John	Kilworth	299	John	Knockaskehane	629	Timothy	Ballyvoskillikin	081
John	Kilworth	406	Margaret	Kilworth	397			
John	Macroney Up	731	Mary	Glanseskin	195	** SURNAME McCAULEY		
Margaret	Ballinrush Up	142	Mary	Kilmurry N	579	James	Gurtone	122
Margaret	Boherdeveroge	086	Mary	Kilworth	285			
Mary	Ballinglanna N	011	Michael	Knockaskehane	629	** SURNAME McCOY		
Mary	Boherdeveroge	086	Patrick	Ballinaparka N	541	John	Macroney Up	749
Mary	Kilmurry S	600	Patrick	Ballylackan	538			
Mary	Kilworth	299	Patrick	Kilworth	397	** SURNAME McCRAITH		
Mary	Kilworth	406	Sarah	Knockaskehane	629	Ann	Kilclogh	679
Mary	Knockaskehane	629	Thomas	Kilmurry S	589	Ann	Macroney Up	752
Maurice	Ballinglanna N	011	Thomas	Kilmurry S	597	Bridget	Ballinrush Lr	038
Michael	Boherdeveroge	086	Thomas	Kilworth	397	Bridget	Knockanabohelly	127
Norry	Macroney Up	737	William	Glanseskin	195	Catherine	Ballinrush Lr	041
Patrick	Ballinglanna N	011	William	Knockaskehane	629	Catherine	Kilworth	412
Patrick	Boherdeveroge	086				Catherine	Knockanabohelly	127
Richard	Kilworth	406				Daniel	Ballinrush Lr	038
Thomas	Ballinglanna N	011				Daniell	Kilworth	314
William	Ballinglanna N	011	** SURNAME McAULIFFE			David	Ballinrush Lr	041
			Ann	Monedrisane	463	Denis	Kilworth	326
** SURNAME MURRAY			Catherine	Ballyvoskillikin	079	Denis	Kilworth	348
John	Kilclogh	685	Catherine	Macroney Up	747	Denis	Toor	502
Margaret	Ballydarown Glebe	052	Catherine	Monedrisane	463	Edmond	Knockanabohelly	127
Margaret	Kilclogh	685	Daniel	Monedrisane	463	Eliza	Monedrisane	483
Mary	Ballydarown Glebe	052	Ellen	Monedrisane	463	Ellen	Kilclogh	679
Mary	Kilclogh	685	Jeremiah	Ballyvoskillikin	079	Ellen	Knockanabohelly	127
Mary	Kilmurry S	608	Margaret	Macroney Up	747	Ellen	Toor	502
Patrick	Kilclogh	685	Mary	Ballyvoskillikin	079	Eugene	Kilworth	314
Richard	Ballydarown Glebe	052	Mary	Kilworth	242	Hannah	Castlecooke	646
			Mary	Kilworth	409	James	Downing S	113
** SURNAME MURRY			Mary	Monedrisane	463	Jeremiah	Ballinrush Lr	034
Daniel	Knockaskehane	632	Patrick	Monedrisane	463	Jeremiah	Kilworth	292
James	Knockaskehane	632	Timothy	Ballyvoskillikin	077	Johanna	Kilworth	348
						John	Kilally W	226
** SURNAME MYLES			** SURNAME McCARTHY			John	Kilclogh	672
Bartholomew	Knockaskehane	629	Bridget	Ballylackan	532	John	Kilclogh	679
Catherine	Ballinaparka N	541	Bridget	Kilworth	385	John	Kilworth	314
Daniel	Ballinaparka N	541	Catherine	Kilworth	346	John	Kilworth	326
Edmond	Ballinaparka N	541	Charles	Kilworth	385	John	Kilworth	348
Eliza	Kilmurry S	589	Ellen	Ballylackan	532	John	Macroney Lr	702
Ellen	Kilworth	397	Honora	Ballydarown Glebe	052	John	Monedrisane	493
Ellen	Knockaskehane	629	James	Ballylackan	532	Julia	Glanseskin	194
Honor	Kilmurry S	589	James	Kilworth	385	Margaret	Kilclogh	679
Honora	Kilmurry S	589				Margaret	Kilworth	292
						Margaret	Kilworth	314

Margaret	Kilworth	326	Mary	Kilworth	337	Thomas	Ballinrush Up	142
Margaret	Monedrisane	493						
Mary	Ballylackan	538	** SURNAME McNAMARA			** SURNAME NOLAN		
Mary	Kilworth	292	Bridget	Downing N	099	Andrew	Kilworth	331
Mary	Kilworth	293	Catherine	Ballinglanna S	025	Jeremiah	Kilworth	251
Mary	Kilworth	314	Cornelius	Ballinglanna S	025	John	Kilworth	331
Mary	Kilworth	348	Daniel	Ballinglanna S	025	Margaret	Monedrisane	455
Mary	Monedrisane	483	Daniel	Downing N	099	Mary	Kilworth	251
Maurice	Kilworth	326	Edmond	Graig	205	Mary	Monedrisane	455
Maurice	Monedrisane	483	Edward	Ballinglanna S	025	Patrick	Monedrisane	455
Maurice	Monedrisane	493	Eliza	Graig	205	Thomas	Monedrisane	455
Michael	Kilclogh	679	Elizabeth	Ballinglanna S	025			
Michael	Kilworth	292	Ellen	Ballinaparka N	547	** SURNAME NOONAN		
Michael	Kilworth	314	Ellen	Ballinglanna S	025	Catherine	Kilworth	273
Michael	Kilworth	326	Ellen	Downing N	099			
Michael	Kilworth	332	J. W.	Downing N	099	** SURNAME NORCOTT		
Michael	Kilworth	348	James	Ballinglanna S	025	Catherine	Kilworth	363
Norry	Kilworth	326	John	Ballinglanna S	025	Edward	Downing S	112
Norry	Kilworth	348	John	Graig	205	Helen	Kilworth	363
Patrick	Kilworth	314	Margaret	Graig	205	Mary	Kilworth	363
Redmond	Ballinrush Lr	038	Margaret	Kilworth	412	Richard P.	Downing S	112
Redmond	Monedrisane	483	Mary	Ballinglanna S	025	William	Kilworth	363
Redmond	Monedrisane	486	Mary	Downing N	099			
Rodger	Knockanabohelly	127	Mary	Kilworth	412	** SURNAME NORMAN		
Sarah	Kilworth	326	Maurice	Ballinglanna S	025	John	Ballydarown Glebe	046
Thomas	Kilclogh	679	Michael	Ballinglanna S	025	Susan M.	Ballydarown Glebe	046
Thomas	Kilworth	292	William	Downing N	099			
Thomas	Kilworth	326				** SURNAME NORRIS		
Thomas	Toor	502	** SURNAME McNAMARRA			Bridget	Gurtone	122
			Andrew	Macroney Up	722	Bridget	Macroney Lr	700
** SURNAME McDONALD			Catherine	Macroney Up	722	Catherine	Gurtone	122
Mary	Ballinrush Up	146	Margaret	Macroney Up	722	David	Kilworth	262
Michael	Ballinrush Up	146	Stephen	Macroney Up	722	Ellen	Gurtone	122
Thomas	Ballinrush Up	146				Ellen	Kilworth	262
						Ellen	Macroney Lr	700
** SURNAME McDONNELL						Johanna	Ballyderown	066
Johanna	Ballinrush Lr	038				John	Gurtone	122
						John	Knockanohill	416
** SURNAME McENERNAY			** SURNAME NAGLE			John	Monedrisane	438
Bridget	Macroney Lr	703	John	Macroney Lr	692	Julia	Gurtone	122
Catherine	Macroney Lr	703				Julia	Kilworth	262
Jeremiah	Macroney Lr	703	** SURNAME NEIL			Margaret	Gurtone	122
Margaret	Macroney Lr	703	Catherine	Ballinrush Up	141	Margaret	Monedrisane	438
Mary	Macroney Lr	703	Ellen	Ballinrush Up	141	Mary	Gurtone	122
Patrick	Macroney Lr	703	Ellen	Ballinrush Up	141	Mary	Kilworth	262
			John	Ballinrush Up	141	Mary	Kilworth	306
** SURNAME McGRATH			John	Ballinrush Up	142	Mary	Knockanohill	416
Margaret	Monedrisane	435	Margaret	Ballinrush Up	141	Maurice	Gurtone	122
			Margaret	Ballinrush Up	142	Michael	Kilworth	262
** SURNAME McLEAN			Mary	Ballinrush Up	142	Michael	Knockanohill	416
Catherine	Moorpark	495	Mary	Monedrisane	482	Michael	Macroney Lr	700
Hugh	Moorpark	495	Michael	Ballinrush Up	142	Patrick	Knockanohill	416
			Myles	Ballinrush Up	142	Thomas	Gurtone	122
** SURNAME McMAHON			Stephen	Ballinrush Up	141	Thomas	Kilworth	262

Thomas	Macroney Lr	700
William	Ballyderown	066
William	Monedrisane	438

** SURNAME NUGENT

Catherine	Kilclogh	678
Mary	Kilclogh	678
Mary	Monedrisane	425
Michael	Kilclogh	678
Patrick	Kilclogh	678

** SURNAME NUNAN

Catherine	Ballinglanna S	028
Catherine	Knockaskehane	619
David	Ballinrush Lr	039
Deborah	Monedrisane	424
Edmond	Ballinglanna S	028
Ellen	Ballinglanna S	027
Ellen	Ballinglanna S	028
Ellen	Knockaskehane	619
Honora	Ballinglanna S	027
Honora	Ballinglanna S	028
Johanna	Ballinglanna S	027
John	Ballinglanna S	027
John	Ballinglanna S	028
John	Knockaskehane	619
John	Monedrisane	424
Margaret	Maryville	422
Mary	Ballinglanna S	028
Mary	Kilworth	271
Mary	Knockaskehane	619
Maurice	Ballinglanna S	028
Michael	Ballinglanna S	028
Patrick	Ballinglanna S	027
Patrick	Ballinglanna S	028
Patrick	Knockaskehane	619
Patrick	Maryville	422
Richard	Knockaskehane	619
Thomas	Maryville	422
William	Ballinglanna S	027
William	Knockaskehane	619

** SURNAME O'BRIEN

Catherine	Knockaskehane	630
Cornelius	Downing S	111
Denis	Kilworth	266
Denis	Kilworth	267
Eliza	Ballinrush Lr	037
Eliza	Kilworth	246
Elizabeth	Ballylackan	530

Hannah	Ballylackan	530
James	Leitrim	637
Jeremiah	Kilworth	246
Margaret	Ballylackan	530
Margaret	Downing S	111
Mary	Kilworth	267
Michael	Ballylackan	521
Michael	Downing S	111
Michael	Kilworth	246
Thomas	Ballylackan	519
Thomas	Kilworth	267
William	Ballylackan	530

** SURNAME O'CONNOR

Mary	Glanseskin	188

** SURNAME O'DONNELL

Ann	Downing N	094
Bridget	Ballinrush Up	151
Catherine	Ballinrush Up	151
Cornelius	Downing N	094
Edmond	Ballylackan	515
Eliza	Ballinrush Up	151
Eliza	Downing N	094
Elizabeth	Ballinrush Up	151
Honora	Downing N	095
Honora	Downing N	096
James	Downing N	094
James	Downing N	095
Johanna	Ballinrush Up	151
John	Ballylackan	515
John	Downing N	094
John	Monedrisane	425
Julia	Downing N	094
Mary	Ballylackan	515
Mary	Downing N	095
Michael	Ballinrush Up	151
Owen	Ballylackan	515
Patrick	Ballylackan	515
Rodger	Ballinrush Up	151
Timothy	Downing N	095

** SURNAME O'FLANAGAN

Ellen	Downing S	116

** SURNAME O'HARA

Elizabeth	Kilworth	369
Michael	Kilworth	369
Patrick	Kilworth	369

** SURNAME O'LEARY

Ellen	Downing N	110
Hannah	Downing N	110
James	Downing N	087

Jeremiah	Downing N	087
Margaret	Downing S	116
Peter	Downing S	116
William	Downing N	087

** SURNAME O'NEIL

Bridget	Ballyvoskillikin	082
Bridget	Downing N	098
Cornelius	Ballinglanna N	020
Ellen	Knockanabohelly	124
James	Ballyvoskillikin	082
James	Downing N	098
Margaret	Ballyvoskillikin	082
Mary	Ballinglanna N	020
Mary	Ballyvoskillikin	082
Michael	Ballinglanna N	020
Patrick	Ballinglanna N	020
Richard	Downing N	098

** SURNAME O'NEILL (sic)

James	Ballyvoskillikin	082

SURNAME PARKER

Eliza	Ballylackan	517

** SURNAME PAYNE

Thomas	Kilworth	327

** SURNAME PENDERGAST

Catherine	Macroney Lr	698
Edward	Macroney Lr	698
Mary	Macroney Lr	698
Thomas	Macroney Lr	698
Thomas	Macroney Lr	701

** SURNAME PIERCE

Ann	Glanseskin	185
John	Glanseskin	185
John P.	Glanseskin	185
Mary	Glanseskin	185
William	Glanseskin	185

** SURNAME PIGOTT

Catherine	Graig	221
Catherine	Kilally W	233
Catherine	Kilworth	363
Cornelius	Graig	221
Denis	Graig	221
Edmond	Ballinvoher	180
Edmond	Kilally W	231
Ellen	Ballinvoher	180

Johanna	Graig	221
Johanna	Kilworth	302
John	Graig	221
John	Kilally W	231
Margaret	Ballinvoher	180
Margaret	Graig	221
Margaret	Kilally W	231
Margaret	Kilworth	302
Mary	Monedrisane	437
Maurice	Kilally W	231
Michael	Ballinvoher	180
Thomas	Graig	221
Thomas	Kilally W	233
William	Graig	221
William	Kilworth	266

** SURNAME PILLON

Mary	Ballinacarriga	012

** SURNAME PINCHON

Elizabeth	Ballinrush Up	155
Michael	Ballinrush Up	155

** SURNAME PINE

Catherine	Ballinrush Lr	031
David	Ballinrush Lr	031
Edward	Ballinrush Lr	031
Johanna	Ballinrush Lr	031
John	Ballinrush Lr	031
John	Monedrisane	445
Patrick	Ballinrush Lr	031
Walter	Ballinrush Lr	031

** SURNAME POWER

Ann	Macroney Up	720
Bridget	Coolalisheen	553
Catherine	Coolalisheen	553
Charles	Coolalisheen	553
Ellen	Ballyvoskillikin	080
Ellen	Coolalisheen	554
Ellen	Macroney Up	720
George	Macroney Up	720
Johanna	Macroney Up	743
John	Macroney Up	752
Margaret	Coolalisheen	554
Margaret	Monedrisane	451
Mary	Coolalisheen	553
Mary	Coolalisheen	554
Mary	Kilworth	300
Mary	Macroney Up	720
Mary	Monedrisane	465
Michael	Coolalisheen	553
Michael	Coolalisheen	554
Nicholas	Kilworth	300

Richard	Coolalisheen	553
Richard	Coolalisheen	554
Thomas	Coolalisheen	554
Thomas	Macroney Up	720

** SURNAME PRICE

Kate	Downing S	112
Mary	Ballyderown	058
Mary	Downing S	112
Michael	Downing S	112

** SURNAME PRIOR

Julia	Kilworth	414

** SURNAME QUINLAN

Ann	Downing S	117
Catherine	Glanseskin	198
Denis	Glanseskin	198
Johanna	Downing S	117
John	Downing S	117
Margaret	Glanseskin	198
Richard	Downing S	112

** SURNAME QUINN

Ann	Kilworth	365
Arthur	Kilworth	330
Bartholomew	Kilworth	325
Bridget	Kilworth	262
Catherine	Kilworth	325
Catherine	Kilworth	330
Catherine	Toor	509
Daniel	Toor	509
David	Kilworth	330
David	Kilworth	331
David	Kilworth	365
David	Kilworth	372
Edmond	Kilworth	325
Eliza	Kilworth	330
Ellen	Kilworth	318
Ellen	Kilworth	331
Ellen	Kilworth	372
Fanny	Kilworth	318
George	Kilworth	365
Hannah	Kilworth	319
James	Kilworth	319
James	Kilworth	330
James	Kilworth	372
Jane	Kilworth	365
Johanna	Kilworth	331
John	Kilworth	318

John	Kilworth	319
John	Kilworth	331
John	Kilworth	365
Margaret	Kilworth	365
Margaret	Kilworth	372
Maria	Kilworth	365
Mary	Kilworth	318
Mary	Kilworth	325
Mary	Kilworth	372
Mary	Toor	509
Michael	Kilworth	403
Nanne	Kilworth	319
Norry	Kilworth	325
Patrick	Toor	509
Richard	Kilworth	365
Richard	Kilworth	372
Robert	Kilworth	318
Terence	Kilworth	318

** SURNAME QUIRK

Abigail	Ballydarown Glebe	053
Bridget	Ballydarown Glebe	053
Denis	Coolalisheen	555
Honora	Coolalisheen	555
James	Ballydarown Glebe	053
James	Coolalisheen	555
Margaret	Ballydarown Glebe	053
Mary	Ballydarown Glebe	053
Mary	Ballylackan	517
Mary	Coolalisheen	555
Mary	Kilmurry S	598
Mary	Kilworth	274
Norry	Ballydarown Glebe	053
Thomas	Ballydarown Glebe	053
Thomas	Coolalisheen	555

** SURNAME QUIRKE

Mary	Macroney Up	724
Michael	Macroney Up	724

** SURNAME RANKIN

Mary	Kilworth	329
Thomas	Kilworth	329

** SURNAME REA

Mary	Boherdeveroge	086

** SURNAME READEY

James	Monedrisane	472
Margaret	Monedrisane	472

Michael	Monedrisane	472
Nancy	Monedrisane	472
Peter	Monedrisane	472
** SURNAME REALLY		
Catherine	Knockaskehane	622
Eliza	Knockaskehane	622
James	Knockaskehane	622
Mary	Knockaskehane	622
** SURNAME REDDING		
Mary	Kilworth	309
Norry	Kilworth	309
William	Kilworth	309
** SURNAME REGAN		
Edmond	Ballinglanna N	021
Margaret	Ballinglanna N	021
** SURNAME RIAL		
Edward	Knockanohill	417
** SURNAME RICE		
Bridget	Ballinglanna S	028
Catherine	Kilworth	313
Catherine	Ballinaparka N	543
Catherine	Kilclogh	661
Edmond	Ballinacarriga	012
Edmond	Downing S	113
Edward	Ballinacarriga	012
Edward	Kilclogh	661
Edward	Kilworth	313
Eliza	Ballinacarriga	012
Eliza	Kilclogh	661
Ellen	Ballinacarriga	012
Ellen	Ballinaparka N	543
Ellen	Kilally W	229
Ellen	Kilclogh	661
Ellen	Kilworth	313
Hannah	Kilally W	229
James	Ballinacarriga	012
Jane	Ballinacarriga	012
John	Ballinaparka N	543
John	Kilclogh	661
John	Kilworth	313
Julia	Kilworth	313
Margaret	Kilclogh	661
Margaret	Leitrim	635
Mary	Ballinacarriga	012
Peter	Kilworth	313
Richard	Ballinacarriga	012
Richard	Ballinaparka N	543
Richard	Kilclogh	661
Richard	Kilworth	313
Thomas	Ballinaparka N	543
Thomas	Downing S	113
Thomas	Kilworth	313
Thomas	Leitrim	635
William	Ballinacarriga	012
** SURNAME RILEY		
Elizabeth	Macroney Lr	692
Joseph	Macroney Lr	692
Mary	Macroney Lr	692
Michael	Macroney Lr	692
** SURNAME RIORDAN		
Bridget	Ballinrush Lr	044
Bridget	Kilally W	237
Bridget	Kilworth	377
Bridget	Monedrisane	433
Catherine	Ballyderown	060
Catherine	Kilally W	240
Edward	Kilally W	237
Eliza	Monedrisane	433
Ellen	Ballyderown	060
Hanna	Ballyderown	060
John	Ballinrush Lr	042
John	Ballyderown	060
John	Monedrisane	433
Judith	Ballyderown	060
Margaret	Ballinrush Lr	042
Margaret	Monedrisane	494
Mary	Ballinrush Lr	042
Mary	Ballyderown	060
Mary	Monedrisane	494
Maurice	Monedrisane	494
Michael	Ballinrush Lr	044
Michael	Ballyderown	060
Patrick	Ballyvoskillikin	080
Thomas	Ballyderown	060
Timothy	Kilally W	237
William	Ballinrush Lr	044
William	Ballyderown	060
William	Macroney Up	727
William	Monedrisane	433
** SURNAME ROCHE		
Allice	Ballyderown	059
Andrew	Kilworth	249
Bridget	Ballinrush Up	154
Bridget	Monedrisane	458
Catherine	Ballinrush Up	154
Catherine	Castlecooke	649
Catherine	Kilworth	280
Catherine	Monedrisane	458
Catherine	Toor	502
David	Ballinrush Up	154
David	Kilally E	223
Ellen	Castlecooke	649
Ellen	Kilworth	249
Ellen	Knockaskehane	616
Ellen	Knockaskehane	630
Ellen	Monedrisane	426
Garrett	Monedrisane	458
Honora	Ballinvoher	157
James	Ballyhenden	068
James	Castlecooke	649
James	Downing N	089
James	Knockaskehane	616
James	Knockaskehane	626
James	Monedrisane	458
Jane	Ballylackan	522
Johanna	Ballinrush Up	154
Johanna	Castlecooke	649
Johanna	Knockaskehane	626
Johanna	Monedrisane	426
John	Ballinrush Up	144
John	Downing N	089
John	Graig	219
John	Kilally E	223
John	Kilmurry S	587
John	Kilworth	249
John	Knockanabohelly	124
John	Knockaskehane	630
John	Leitrim	637
John	Leitrim	638
John	Macroney Lr	693
John	Monedrisane	426
Julia	Glanseskin	201
Julia	Kilworth	249
Margaret	Ballinrush Lr	030
Margaret	Castlecooke	649
Margaret	Kilally E	223
Margaret	Monedrisane	458
Martin	Downing N	089
Mary	Ballinrush Lr	030
Mary	Ballinrush Up	154
Mary	Kilally E	223
Mary	Kilclogh	666
Mary	Kilworth	249
Mary	Knockaskehane	626
Mary	Leitrim	638
Mary	Monedrisane	458
Maurice	Castlecooke	649
Maurice	Knockaskehane	616
Norry	Kilworth	350
Patrick	Downing N	089
Patrick	Kilworth	258
Richard	Glanseskin	201
Thomas	Ballyhenden	068
Thomas	Castlecooke	649

Thomas	Kilworth	249
Thomas	Kilworth	253
Thomas	Knockaskehane	630
William	Ballyderown	059
William	Kilworth	249
William	Leitrim	638

** SURNAME RONAN

Catherine	Downing N	092

** SURNAME RUSSELL

Ann	Ballinvoher	159
Bridget	Ballinvoher	159
Catherine	Ballinvoher	159
Eliza	Ballinvoher	159
Ellen	Ballinvoher	159
Honnora	Ballinvoher	159
Johnanna	Ballinvoher	159
Margaret	Ballinvoher	159
Mary	Ballinvoher	159
Michael	Ballinvoher	159

** SURNAME RYALL

Bartholomew	Ballinrush Up	150
Bartholomew	Ballinvoher	160
Catherine	Ballinvoher	160
James	Ballinvoher	160

** SURNAME RYAN

Amelia	Kilworth	283
Amelia	Kilworth	321
Ann	Graig	211
Bridget	Ballinrush Up	149
Bridget	Monedrisane	431
Catherine	Ballinrush Up	145
Catherine	Monedrisane	425
Catherine	Monedrisane	431
Cornelius	Boherdeveroge	086
David	Kilworth	283
David	Kilworth	361
Edmond	Kilworth	378
Edmond	Monedrisane	431
Elizabeth	Kilmurry N	582
Elizabeth	Kilworth	361
Ellen	Ballinrush Up	144
Ellen	Kilmurry N	582
Emmy	Monedrisane	431
Honora	Ballinrush Up	145
Honora	Ballyhenden	072
Ignatius	Kilworth	321
James	Kilmurry N	583
Jane	Graig	211
Jeremiah	Monedrisane	431
John	Ballinrush Up	145

John	Ballinrush Up	149
John	Glanseskin	190
John	Graig	211
John	Kilmurry N	582
John	Kilworth	283
John	Monedrisane	431
Julia	Monedrisane	425
Margaret	Ballinrush Up	144
Margaret	Ballinrush Up	145
Margaret	Ballinrush Up	149
Mary	Ballinrush Up	145
Mary	Ballinrush Up	149
Mary	Downing N	103
Mary	Glanseskin	190
Mary	Kilmurry N	582
Mary	Kilworth	316
Mary	Kilworth	321
Mary	Monedrisane	425
Michael	Ballinrush Up	144
Michael	Ballinrush Up	145
Michael	Ballinrush Up	149
Michael	Monedrisane	425
Patrick	Ballinrush Up	144
Patrick	Ballinrush Up	149
Patrick	Ballyhenden	072
Patrick	Gurtone	123
Patrick	Kilworth	283
Phillip	Kilmurry N	582
Rodger	Ballinrush Up	145
Thomas	Graig	211
Thomas	Kilworth	321
William	Ballyhenden	072
William	Downing N	103
William	Graig	211
William	Kilmurry N	582
William	Kilworth	283
William	Kilworth	321

** SURNAME SAUL

Henry	Boherdeveroge	085

** SURNAME SAVAGE

Edward	Kilmurry S	606
Ellen	Macroney Up	728
Jane	Macroney Lr	710
Johanna	Macroney Lr	713
Johanna	Macroney Up	728
John	Macroney Up	728
Maurice	Macroney Up	728
Michael	Macroney Up	728
Patrick	Macroney Lr	710

** SURNAME SCANLON

Ellen	Kilworth	255
Honora	Kilworth	255
James	Ballinvoher	171
James	Kilworth	409
John	Ballinvoher	165
Margaret	Kilworth	409
Mary	Ballinvoher	165
Mary	Ballinvoher	171
William	Kilworth	255

** SURNAME SCULLY

Alice	Monedrisane	476
Alice	Monedrisane	490
Ann	Monedrisane	490
Catherine	Monedrisane	490
Daniel	Kilworth	289
Daniel	Monedrisane	475
Daniel	Monedrisane	490
Edward	Kilworth	289
Eliza	Monedrisane	475
Ellen	Monedrisane	475
Ellon (sic)	Monedrisane	475
Hannah	Monedrisane	475
Honora	Kilworth	289
James	Monedrisane	490
John	Monedrisane	476
Margaret	Kilworth	289
Margaret	Monedrisane	475
Martin	Monedrisane	475
Mary	Kilworth	289
Mary	Monedrisane	475
Maurice	Kilworth	289
Michael	Monedrisane	490
Patrick	Monedrisane	490
Timothy	Monedrisane	475

** SURNAME SENNOTT

Ansty	Kilworth	279
Bridget	Kilworth	279
Edmond	Kilworth	279
Margaret	Glanseskin	185
Mary	Kilworth	279
Patrick	Kilworth	279

** SURNAME SEXTON

Ann	Kilworth	245
Eliza	Kilworth	245
Eliza	Kilworth	350
Eliza	Monedrisane	465
John	Kilworth	350
Margaret	Kilworth	245
Mary	Kilworth	350
William	Kilworth	350

Patrick	Kilworth	245	Mary	Whitebog	510	** SURNAME SPALANE		
William	Kilworth	245	Maurice	Whitebog	510	Johanna	Monedrisane	491
			Michael	Ballinvoher	178	John	Monedrisane	491
** SURNAME SHANAHAN			Michael	Kilworth	370	Patrick	Monedrisane	491
Bridget	Monedrisane	430	Patrick	Ballydarown Glebe	051			
Catherine	Kilmurry S	606	Patrick	Kilmurry S	602	** SURNAME STACK		
Catherine	Kilworth	308	Patrick	Whitebog	510	Thomas	Ballyhenden	068
Daniel	Kilworth	308	Thomas	Kilworth	370			
Edmond	Kilworth	308	Thomas	Knockaskehane	613	** SURNAME STANTON		
Edmond	Kilworth	392	William	Knockaskehane	613	Bridget	Castlecooke	647
Edward	Kilworth	308				Catherine	Castlecooke	647
Eliza	Kilworth	305	** SURNAME SHEELY			Edmond	Macroney Lr	714
Eliza	Kilworth	308	Ellen	Ballinaparka N	542	Jane	Macroney Lr	714
Ellen	Kilworth	305	James	Whitebog	514	Johanna	Kilworth	404
Hannah	Kilworth	392	Mary	Whitebog	514	John	Macroney Lr	714
James	Kilworth	308	Patrick	Whitebog	514	Mary	Ballinaparka N	543
Johanna	Kilmurry S	606				Mary	Kilworth	404
John	Kilmurry S	606	** SURNAME SHERLOCK			Mary	Macroney Lr	714
Margaret	Kilmurry S	606	Catherine	Kilworth	275	Michael	Leitrim	641
Margaret	Kilworth	392	Edmond	Graig	218	Richard	Macroney Lr	714
Martin	Kilworth	305	Elizabeth	Whitebog	512	Thomas	Macroney Lr	714
Mary	Kilworth	392	Ellen	Graig	218			
Mary	Knockaskehane	631	James	Kilworth	275	** SURNAME STARKIE		
Nancy	Kilworth	308	Johanna	Whitebog	512	Thomas	Downing S	112
Patrick	Kilmurry S	606	John	Graig	215			
Patrick	Kilworth	308	Margaret	Graig	215	** SURNAME STEELE		
Patrick	Kilworth	392	Patrick	Graig	215	Ellen	Ballinacarriga	003
Thomas	Kilmurry S	606	Thomas	Whitebog	512	John	Ballinacarriga	003
** SURNAME SHEEDY			** SURNAME SIMMONS			** SURNAME STRAPP		
John	Kilworth	410	Helena	Kilworth	242	Catherine	Kilworth	243
Judith	Kilworth	372	Mary	Kilworth	242			
Mary	Kilworth	398				** SURNAME SULLIVAN		
Mary	Kilworth	410	** SURNAME SINNOTT			Alice	Ballylackan	533
			Michael	Kilworth	340	Andrew	Ballyhenden	074
** SURNAME SHEEHAN			Norry	Kilworth	340	Ann	Ballinacarriga	006
Bridget	Castlecooke	651				Ann	Kilworth	310
Bridget	Kilmurry N	567	** SURNAME SLATTERY			Arthur	Kilclogh	674
Bridget	Whitebog	510	Honora	Macroney Up	754	Arthur	Kilclogh	676
Cornelius	Macroney Lr	696	Johanna	Ballylackan	526	Bridget	Ballinrush Up	143
Daniel	Ballylackan	518	John	Ballylackan	529	Bridget	Downing N	107
David	Ballinrush Lr	030	John	Macroney Up	754	Bridget	Moorpark	498
David	Ballydarown Glebe	051	Julia	Macroney Up	754	Catherine	Ballinglanna N	016
Denis	Kilmurry N	567	Mary	Ballylackan	526	Catherine	Ballinrush Lr	045
Elizabeth	Whitebog	510	Mary	Macroney Up	754	Catherine	Monedrisane	471
Ellen	Kilmurry S	602	Michael	Macroney Up	754	Daniel	Monedrisane	476
Ellen	Knockaskehane	613	Patrick	Macroney Up	754	David	Ballinacarriga	001
Francis	Kilmurry S	602	Thomas	Graig	216	Denis	Ballinrush Up	143
Honora	Whitebog	510	Timothy	Macroney Up	754	Denis	Knockanabohelly	124
James	Castlecooke	651				Denis	Moorpark	498
Jane	Castlecooke	651	** SURNAME SMYTH			Edmond	Downing N	107
John	Kilworth	370	Alicia	Kilworth	268	Edward	Kilworth	335
Margaret	Whitebog	510	Edmond	Kilworth	268	Elizabeth	Ballinvoher	161
Mary	Kilmurry N	567				Eliza	Glenwood	118

(SURNAME SULLIVAN continued)									
Elizabeth	Kilmurry S	587	** SURNAME SWAYN			John	Ballyhenden	067
Ellen	Ballinacarriga	001	Catherine	Kilworth	263	John	Downing N	109
Ellen	Ballinglanna N	016				John	Kilmurry S	609
Ellen	Ballinrush Lr	045	** SURNAME SWEENY			John	Monedrisane	451
Ellen	Ballinvoher	161	Catherine	Kilclogh	676	John	Monedrisane	461
Ellen	Ballylackan	533	Catherine	Kilmurry S	610	Julia	Ballyhenden	067
Ellen	Graig	210	Daniel	Kilclogh	676	Margaret	Downing N	109
Ellen	Kilworth	254	Daniel	Macroney Lr	701	Mary	Ballinvoher	181
Ellen	Monedrisane	430	Edward	Kilworth	280	Mary	Ballyhenden	067
Florence	Ballinvoher	161	Francis	Kilclogh	676	Mary	Downing N	109
Hannora	Ballinglanna N	016	Honora	Kilclogh	676	Mary	Glanseskin	191
Honora	Ballinglanna S	029	Honora	Macroney Lr	701	Mary	Knockanabohelly	128
Honora	Kilworth	346	John	Graig	217	Mary	Monedrisane	461
James	Ballinglanna N	016	John	Graig	219	Maurice	Glanseskin	191
James	Gurtone	123	John	Kilclogh	676	Michael	Ballyhenden	067
James	Kilworth	359	John	Knockaskehane	625	Michael	Kilmurry S	609
Jeremiah	Kilworth	351	John	Macroney Lr	701	Patrick	Ballinvoher	181
Johanna	Ballinacarriga	001	Julia	Graig	217	Patrick	Downing N	109
Johanna	Ballyhenden	074	Margaret	Graig	217	Patrick	Monedrisane	461
John	Ballinglanna N	016	Margaret	Graig	219	Richard	Glanseskin	191
John	Ballinglanna S	029	Mary	Graig	217	Thomas	Ballyhenden	067
John	Ballinrush Lr	045	Mary	Graig	219	Thomas	Glanseskin	191
John	Ballinrush Up	143	Mary	Kilclogh	676	Thomas	Kilmurry S	609
John	Ballylackan	522	Mary	Knockaskehane	624	Thomas	Monedrisane	461
Margaret	Ballinacarriga	001	Mary	Knockaskehane	625			
Margaret	Graig	210	Michael	Graig	219	** SURNAME TOOHILL		
Margaret	Kilworth	351	Michael	Knockaskehane	625	Bridget	Ballinglanna N	018
Martin	Downing N	107	Patrick	Graig	217	Catherine	Ballinglanna N	017
Mary	Ballinglanna N	016	Patrick	Knockaskehane	625	David	Ballinglanna N	016
Mary	Ballinrush Up	143	Thomas	Kilclogh	676	David	Ballinglanna N	017
Mary	Ballinvoher	161	Thomas	Macroney Lr	701	David	Ballinglanna N	019
Mary	Ballylackan	517				Edmond	Ballinglanna N	017
Mary	Kilworth	318				Edmond	Ballinglanna N	019
Michael	Ballinvoher	161				Edward	Ballinglanna N	018
Michael	Kilmurry S	587	** SURNAME TEULON			Elenor	Ballinglanna N	017
Michael	Kilworth	254	Peter	Glenwood	118	Eliza	Ballinglanna N	019
Patrick	Ballinglanna S	029				Ellen	Ballinglanna N	017
Patrick	Ballinrush Up	143	** SURNAME THOMPSON			Hannah	Ballinglanna N	017
Patrick	Kilworth	254	William	Kilworth	368	James	Ballinglanna N	017
Stephen	Ballinacarriga	001				James	Ballinglanna N	019
Stephen	Kilmurry S	587	** SURNAME TOBIN			Johanna	Ballinglanna N	019
Timothy	Graig	210	Bridget	Ballinvoher	181	John	Ballinglanna N	017
William	Ballinrush Lr	045	Catherine	Knockanabohelly	128	John	Ballinglanna N	019
William	Ballylackan	533	Catherine	Monedrisane	461	Julia	Ballinglanna N	018
			Edmond	Ballyhenden	067	Maurice	Ballinglanna N	019
** SURNAME SWAIN			Edmond	Knockanabohelly	128	Patrick	Ballinglanna N	017
Catherine	Kilworth	313	Ellen	Ballinvoher	181	Patrick	Ballinglanna N	019
			Ellen	Downing N	109	Susan	Ballinglanna N	019
** SURNAME SWAINE			Honora	Kilmurry S	609			
Bridget	Kilworth	246	James	Downing N	109	** SURNAME TORBETT		
Charles	Monedrisane	450	James	Kilmurry S	609	John	Kilworth	378
Francis	Monedrisane	450	James	Monedrisane	461			
Honora	Monedrisane	450	Johanna	Ballinvoher	181	** SURNAME TORHILL		
						Alice	Macroney Up	725

Bridget	Macroney Up	725	Abigail	Glanseskin	192	Jeffery	Macroney Up	748
Catherine	Macroney Up	725	Thomas	Glanseskin	192	Jeremiah	Kilmurry S	605
David	Macroney Up	725				Johanna	Ballinvoher	177
Johanna	Macroney Up	725	** SURNAME VERLIN			Johanna	Kilclogh	691
Mary	Macroney Up	725	Ellen	Knockaskehane	623	Johanna	Macroney Up	748
Timothy	Macroney Up	725	Patrick	Knockaskehane	623	John	Ballinvoher	177
			Richard	Kilmurry S	598	John	Kilclogh	691
** SURNAME TOUEL						John	Kilmurry S	604
Denis	Ballyhenden	072	** SURNAME VERLING			John	Kilmurry S	605
			Hannah	Ballyhenden	075	John	Knockanohill	417
** SURNAME TREHY						Julia	Kilworth	371
Bridget	Kilmurry N	578				Julia	Macroney Lr	692
Edward	Kilmurry N	578				Margaret	Kilally W	226
James	Kilmurry N	578				Margaret	Kilmurry S	604
Mary	Kilmurry N	578	** SURNAME WADE			Margaret	Kilmurry S	605
Patrick	Kilmurry N	578	Mary	Kilworth	287	Margaret	Kilworth	371
						Margaret	Macroney Up	748
** SURNAME TROY			** SURNAME WALL			Margaret	Monedrisane	487
Hannah	Kilworth	403	Alexander	Kilworth	323	Mary	Ballinvoher	177
James	Macroney Up	716	Honora	Kilworth	323	Mary	Ballydarown Glebe	046
John	Kilmurry S	584	Margaret	Kilworth	323	Mary	Ballyhenden	072
John	Macroney Up	716	Mary	Kilmurry S	608	Mary	Coolalisheen	560
Julia	Castlecooke	644	Mary	Kilworth	323	Mary	Glanseskin	200
Margaret	Macroney Up	716	Michael	Kilworth	323	Mary	Glanseskin	201
Mary	Kilworth	403	Patrick	Ballylackan	517	Mary	Kilclogh	691
Mary	Macroney Up	716	Patrick	Kilworth	323	Mary	Kilmurry S	604
Maurice	Macroney Up	716				Mary	Kilmurry S	605
Patrick	Kilworth	403	** SURNAME WALSH			Mary	Knockanohill	417
Thomas	Kilworth	403	Abigail	Kilworth	335	Mary	Macroney Up	748
			Ann	Kilworth	371	Mary	Toor	503
** SURNAME TWOMY			Bridget	Kilmurry S	604	Michael	Glanseskin	200
Ann	Coolalisheen	552	Bridget	Knockanohill	417	Michael	Kilmurry S	604
Edmond	Glanseskin	199	Bridget	Macroney Up	748	Michael	Kilworth	268
Ellen	Monedrisane	480	Catherine	Kilally W	226	Michael	Kilworth	371
Hannah	Downing S	113	Catherine	Kilclogh	691	Michael	Monedrisane	487
Honora	Monedrisane	480	Catherine	Kilmurry S	604	Michael	Toor	503
Johanna	Coolalisheen	551	Catherine	Knockanohill	417	Nancy	Monedrisane	487
Margaret	Kilmurry S	587	Catherine	Macroney Up	748	Patrick	Kilally W	226
Margaret	Monedrisane	480	David	Kilmurry S	604	Patrick	Kilmurry S	604
Mary	Ballinrush Lr	030	David	Kilmurry S	605	Patrick	Kilmurry S	605
Mary	Coolalisheen	551	Denis	Monedrisane	487	Terence	Kilally W	226
Mary	Glanseskin	199	Edmond	Kilworth	383	Thomas	Kilmurry S	604
Mary	Monedrisane	480	Eliza	Kilally W	226			
Maurice	Coolalisheen	551	Elizabeth	Toor	503	** SURNAME WARNER		
Michael	Coolalisheen	552	Ellen	Kilally W	226	Henry	Ballydarown Glebe	046
Patrick	Coolalisheen	551	Ellen	Kilmurry N	574			
Patrick	Coolalisheen	552	Ellen	Kilmurry S	605	** SURNAME WATERS		
Thomas	Coolalisheen	551	Ellen	Knockanohill	417	James	Kilworth	305
Thomas	Coolalisheen	552	Honora	Kilclogh	691			
			Honora	Kilmurry S	605	** SURNAME WATSON		
			James	Ballylackan	522	Ann	Ballydarown Glebe	049
			James	Glanseskin	197	Jane	Ballydarown Glebe	049
			James	Kilally W	226	John	Ballydarown Glebe	049
** SURNAME VEALE			James	Kilmurry S	604	Mary	Ballydarown Glebe	049

| Rebecca | Ballydarown Glebe | 049 |
| William | Ballydarown Glebe | 049 |

** SURNAME WATTS

Margaret	Monedrisane	474
Richard	Monedrisane	474
William	Monedrisane	474

** SURNAME WHELAN

Ann	Kilmurry S	588
Bridget	Castlecooke	643
Bridget	Macroney Lr	694
Catherine	Castlecooke	643
Eliza	Macroney Lr	709
Ellen	Macroney Lr	709
Ellen	Monedrisane	482
Francis	Kilmurry S	588
Honora	Kilmurry S	592
Isabella	Kilworth	390
James	Kilmurry S	588
Jane	Kilworth	390
Johanna	Macroney Lr	694
John	Kilmurry S	588
John	Macroney Lr	709
Judith	Macroney Up	749
Margaret	Kilworth	390
Mary	Kilworth	390
Mary	Monedrisane	482
Maurice	Macroney Lr	709
Michael	Macroney Lr	694
Nancy	Kilmurry S	592
Patrick	Kilmurry S	592
Pierce	Macroney Up	749
Thomas	Kilmurry S	588
Thomas	Macroney Lr	694
Thomas	Macroney Up	749
William	Macroney Lr	694

** SURNAME WHIBBS

Catherine	Kilworth	389
John	Kilworth	389
Michael	Kilworth	389

** SURNAME WHITE

Catherine	Ballinglanna N	022
Catherine	Moorpark	495
Honora	Kilclogh	683
Thomas	Kilclogh	683

** SURNAME WILKINSON

Bridget	Ballinacarriga	007
Catherine	Ballinacarriga	007
Edmond	Ballinacarriga	007
Mary	Ballinacarriga	007
Michael	Ballinacarriga	007
William	Ballinacarriga	007
William	Downing S	112

** SURNAME WILLIAMS

| Charlotte | Kilworth | 243 |
| John | Kilworth | 243 |

** SURNAME WOODS

Ann	Ballinacarriga	013
Bartholomew	Knockanabohelly	125
Catherine	Knockanabohelly	125
Ellen	Knockanabohelly	125
Johanna	Ballinacarriga	013
Judith	Leitrim	637
Margaret	Ballinacarriga	013
Margaret	Leitrim	637
Mary	Ballinacarriga	013
Mary	Knockanabohelly	125
Maurice	Ballinacarriga	013

Maurice	Knockanabohelly	125
Patrick	Ballinacarriga	013
Timothy	Knockanabohelly	125
William	Ballinacarriga	013

** SURNAME WORRELL

Eliza	Kilworth	327
Ellen	Kilworth	327
Gertrude	Kilworth	327
Joseph	Kilworth	327

** SURNAME WRIGHT

Alexander	Kilworth	377
Eliza	Maryville	419
George	Maryville	419
Jane	Kilworth	377
Mary	Kilworth	377
Nathaniel	Kilworth	377
Richard	Kilworth	377
William	Kilworth	377
William	Maryville	419

** SURNAME YOUNG

Ann	Kilworth	324
Eliza	Kilworth	324
Hannah	Kilworth	271
John	Kilworth	271
Mary	Kilworth	324
Matthias	Kilworth	271
Pierce	Kilworth	324
Sarah	Kilworth	324
William	Kilworth	324

APPENDIX

The following list of persons found in the 1851 Census for the Union of Kilworth, County Cork, Ireland, was obtained from Manuscript 999/643, a transcript of the original transcript held at the National Archives, Dublin, Ireland, which was obtained by the National Archives separately from Manuscript M4685 and at a different date. This appears to be a transcription done by another person. Record numbers 78 - 107 are reported as missing from Manuscript M4685 in the preceding pages. They belong between computer numbers 102 and 103 for the Townland of Downing North, Kilcrumper Parish. No. 44 refers to the page number in Manuscript 999/643, a duplicate of M4685.

102 continued

HAYES	John	2	son	Downing N	KC	44
HAYES	Julia	30	sister	Downing N	KC	44
HAYES	Honora	25	sister	Downing N	KC	44
MURPHY	Mary	19	niece	Downing N	KC	44
BRIEN	John	25	serv lab	Downing N	KC	44
CASEY	James	25	serv	Downing N	KC	44
SHEMERLING	Patrick	18	serv	Downing N	KC	44
HAYES	John	11	nephew	Downing N	KC	44

102a

CONNORS	Robert	60	farmer	Downing N	KC	44
CONNORS	Eliza	50	wife	Downing N	KC	44
CONNORS	Mary	17	dau	Downing N	KC	44
CONNORS	Thomas	17	son	Downing N	KC	44
CONNORS	Michael	16	son	Downing N	KC	44
CONNORS	Catherine	13	dau	Downing N	KC	44

102b

HENDLEY	Henry	30	farmer	Downing N	KC	44
HENDLEY	Naomi	32	wife	Downing N	KC	44
HENDLEY	Dorcas	5	dau	Downing N	KC	44
HENDLEY	Thomas	3	son	Downing N	KC	44
HENDLEY	Robert	5m	son	Downing N	KC	44
COUGHLAN	Catherine	11	serv	Downing N	KC	44

102c

FITZGERALD	James	32	lab	Downing N	KC	44
FITZGERALD	Ann	25	wife	Downing N	KC	44
FITZGERALD	James	12	son	Downing N	KC	44
FITZGERALD	Mary	9	dau	Downing N	KC	44
FITZGERALD	William	5	son	Downing N	KC	44

102d

AHERN	John	40	farmer	Downing N	KC	44
QUINN	Catherine	20	serv	Downing N	KC	44
KELEHER	Cornelius	26	serv	Downing N	KC	44

103a

RYAN	John	30	carpenter & cattle dealer	Downing N	KC	44
RYAN	Catherine	26	wife	Downing N	KC	44

(Children of John and Catherine RYAN, William 6 and Mary 2, are shown as 103 in Manuscript M4685.)